Supply Chain 4.0

From Stocking Shelves
To
Running the World

Fuelled by
Industry 4.0

Table of Contents

Chapter 1 - The Legacy Supply Chain

Introduction to the Supply Chain

Today's competitive edge is tomorrow's price of entry

Look at any struggling company and with diligent analysis it is often found that their supply chain is the root cause of all their ills. Many companies only think about their supply chain when dark clouds loom when profits fall and inventory levels are too high, customers are complaining about poor service, or a supplier is late with a critical shipment. It is perhaps only then that they will look to a benchmarking analysis, which shows that their supply chain performance is suboptimal relative to competitors in their industry.

This reactive response which only addresses the supply chain when there's a dire problem, suggests that managers don't see it as a valuable asset. If this is the case, then companies that do use their supply chain as a strategic tool will have the advantage.

Supply chain is no longer a boring administrators task as companies such as Dell, Amazon, Shell, and Airbus are clearly demonstrating by rewriting the rules of competition in their industries.

Market leaders in their own sectors such as Amazon, Wal-Mart and Dell realised early that the supply chain can be a strategic differentiator. They constantly search for new ways to add value and push the boundaries of supply chain performance. Furthermore, these leaders keep refining their supply chains so they stay one step ahead of the competition.

Michael Dell is widely viewed as a pioneer in the personal computer (PC) business. He transformed Dell from a highly successful but financially struggling PC maker to the market leader. This might sound contradictory but Dell's problem was they had too many orders and subsequent cash flow issues. However, by introducing supply chain innovations such as direct-to-consumer sales and build-to-order manufacturing to the computer industry Michael Dell turned the business around through supply chain management. Michael Dell managed this transformation by implementing an optimized supply chain: Sell direct, build to order, and ship direct.

Another supply chain visionary was Sam Walton. He is credited with being the instigator of Wal-Mart's innovative partnership with Procter & Gamble to replenish inventory automatically. This strategy demonstrated the efficiency of sharing data and the policy of tactically integrating with key suppliers. Building on this success, Wal-Mart were to further reduce inefficiencies and costs through buying directly from manufacturers for a broad range of merchandise thereby cutting out the middle-man and streamlining the supply chain. It was this type of strategic thinking regards supply chain management that enabled Wal-Mart to deliver on the promise of "always low prices"—the strategy that has helped Wal-Mart come one of the world's largest retailers.

Defining the Supply Chain

The concept of a supply chain is often presented as a linear process of independent organisations connected together through the products and services that they produce or consume. Each entity in the line will either separately and/or jointly add value to the product or service before delivery to the end consumer.

It can be thought of as an external but extended concept of an organisation's internal value chain where individual functional departments adds their own value to the products or services and delivers them to its customers.

 The term 'supply chain' or as it is sometimes referred to as a demand-chain persists due to the conceptual visualization of the flow of a product from raw materials through to a finished product delivered to the end-customer.

This representation persists despite the common recognition that supply chains are not simply linear processes indeed they are typically complex networks of a myriad of independent or autonomous relationships between suppliers and their consumers. For now though we will persist in the interest of clarity with the simplified 'chain' representation but later we will address networks and their context within Industry 4.0, Demand Supply Networks (DSN) and beyond. Therefore as there is no commonly agreed definition of 'supply chain' we will consider two that emerged in the late 1990s.

'a network of connected and interdependent organizations, mutually and co-operatively working together to control, manage and improve the flow of material and information from suppliers to end users'. Aitken (1998)

Around the same time emerged a definition with a more value-based variation on the 'supply' theme, which defined a supply chain as -

'the network of organisations that are linked through upstream and downstream relationships in the different processes and activities that produce value in the form of products and services in the hands of the ultimate customer'. Christopher (1998)

Thus we have two separate definitions which in combo provide us with the modern definition of the concept of a supply chain in so much as it comprises:

` flows of materials, goods and information (including money), which pass within and between organizations, linked by a range of tangible and intangible facilitators, including relationships, processes, activities, and integrated information systems. They are also linked by physical distribution networks, and the national / international communications and transport infrastructures. In their totality, supply chains link organizations, industries and economies.'

Logistics Vs Supply Chain

"Logistics typically refers to activities that occur within the boundaries of a single organization and Supply Chain refers to networks of companies that work together and coordinate their actions to deliver a product to market. Also, traditional logistics focuses its attention on activities such as procurement, distribution, maintenance, and inventory management. Supply Chain Management (SCM) acknowledges all of traditional logistics and also includes activities such as marketing, new product development, finance, and customer service" - Michael Hugos

Thus, we can determine that a supply chain differs from logistics as it is formed and can only be formed through relationships with more than one company.

Additionally, the participating companies within a supply chain will typically be legally independent entities and not the same company. Moreover and very importantly, those independent companies relate to one another on a common commitment to add value to the stream of material flow that runs through the supply chain. Therefore the material flow, which is specific to each company, comes in as the transformed inputs and goes out as the value added outputs.

Modeling the Supply Chain

Intuitively, we can visualize this material flow as a "chain", in which the "links" are the participating companies that are inter-connected in the value adding process (see figure 1.1).

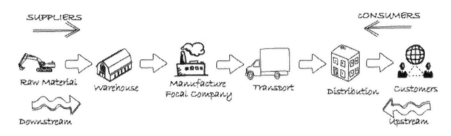

Figure 1.1- The basic Supply Chain model

As we can see in figure 1.1, the supply-chain consists of links on the upstream side of the material flow, which is the supplier's supplier; and on the downstream side of the material flow is the supplier's consumer.

 A supply chain is therefore typically presented relative to a core company as it will be the focal point of the flow of materials. This company is usually represented as being the OEM – Original Equipment Manufacturer or the OBM – Original Brand Manufacturer, or simply the "focal company."

As can be seen in figure 1.1 at the end of a supply chain is the product and/or service that were created by the supply chain for the end consumer. Consequently, the fundamental reason of a supply chain's existence is to serve the end-consumer. Hence, the effectiveness of a supply chain can be judged by how well it serves their consumer, which ultimately defines its competitive edge in the market place.

 In practice a supply chain is much more complex than the one depicted in Figure 1.1 as it is typically not really a "chain", rather it is more like a "network".

This becomes clear when you consider that there are usually multiple suppliers and multiple customers for each participating companies, which are acting autonomously within the chain. These are in reality nested chains within the overall concept of the supply chain. For example in car manufacturing the engine or chassis supply chains may be autonomous nested supply chains within the overall automobile supply chain.

Furthermore, the actual term supply-chain in itself may be ambiguous as depending on the perspective - from any entity in the chain - the supply chain may have its emphasis on material, value or demand. Although these are similar concepts and constructs they have different names which define their purpose. For example, from the perspective of a participating company they may envisage the purpose of the supply chain as a construct for procuring supply of materials and hence refer to it as a 'Supply-Chain'. However, another participant in the overall chain may from their perspective consider it a mechanism for value adding activities, and so call it a "Value Chain". Further, another participating company may take the view that the supply chain exists to serve the continuous demands originated from their consumer, so may call the supply chain the "Demand Chain". In the interests of clarity in this book we will use the generic term supply chain except where Value or Demand are seen as being the primary and specific functions that determine the nature of the inter-connected relationships from the perspective of the OEM.

Nonetheless, supply-chains in the real world consist of networks of interconnected businesses with a web of relationships of varying strengths of allegiances and by their nature are typically pervasive, perfidious, and promiscuous as each company perceives benefit from their own point of view.

Therefore to understand the dynamics within a supply chain - and they will all be different - it is important to understand the four intrinsic flows and their direction within the supply chain.

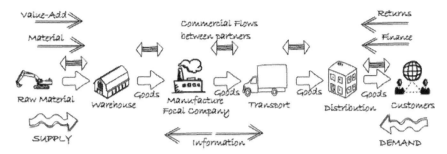

Figure 1.2 –Supply Chain Flows

Material Flow: If we consider manufacturing as an example we can see that the supply chains purpose is to aid the material flow from the raw materials at the beginning of the supply chain to the finished products at the end of the supply chain.

For example, a furniture company such as Ikea will have the Pine wood cut down from forests at the beginning of its supply chain as the raw material. There will be saw mills to cut the wood to size and a manufacturing process. In addition to these supply functions there will be a transportation requirement and a distribution network of retail outlets before it becomes home furniture for the customer at the end of the supply chain.

This continuous flow of material, in this case wood, has transformed the raw material through the process of the supply chain and it ends up as furniture. This flow of material is determined by the supply-chain, which ties the whole process together and defines its clear boundary. Furthermore, it is industry specific in so much as a furniture supply chain will be notably different from a automobile manufacturing supply chain because the material flows in between are clearly different.

Information Flow: It is not just about material flows as all supply chains have and make use of information flows. Consequently, a supply chain is constructed with the purpose to facilitate the communication of the multitude of information flows between participating companies.

For example there are requirements to exchange information on, amongst others, demand information flow, forecasting information flow, production and scheduling information flows, and design and NPI information flows.

Furthermore, unlike the material flow, the process of communicating the information flow is fully duplex in so much as the information can run both directions, towards upstream and downstream simultaneously.

Again the constructs that enable Information Flows are mostly unique to an industry's specific supply chain. For example, the information flow from a cosmetics or pharmaceutical supply chain has no intrinsic value to an automobile supply chain.

Moreover, with information flows there will be no generic industry type supply-chain as each OEM will have its own set of information flows that are vital to protecting its Intellectual Property (IP) its product's differentiators and its innovation which are all pivotal to the company's existence. Consequently the design and protection of these information flows will be jealously protected from other supply chains.

Finance Flow: Another important function of the supply chain is to facilitate the finance flow.

All supply chains will handle the flow of money as it is the blood stream of a supply chain. Without the financial flow, a supply chain cannot function as it is the mechanism to move the single-source of the money – the end-customer upstream to the material suppliers. The perspective of there being a single source of finance is the basis for the concept of "single entity", which is considered the foundation for supply chain integration and collaboration. This is because, when done fairly on a basis of contribution and reward, the distribution and sharing of this single financial resource across a supply chain will allow for better alignment between the participating companies within the supply-chain.

Commercial flow: An inherent feature of a supply-chain is that it embodies and represents a transactional commercial flow.

What this means is that with respect to the material flow that runs downstream the material (product) changes ownership from one company to another, from supplier to buyer.

The transactional process of buying and selling shifts the material flow's ownership from the supplier to the buyer repeatedly until the end of the supply chain – the end-consumer. The transactional commercial flow requires there to be more than one companies involved in the supply chain. As a result, the presence of a commercial flow distinguishes a supply-chain from a logistics materials flow within an individual organisation. This is because within an organisation there will be material flow, but no ownership change, and hence no commercial flow.

Determining Supply Chain Boundaries

The four flows inherent to any supply-chain enable us to not only explain the function of the supply chain, but also to help us determine its boundaries. For as we have determined supply-chains in the real world are not simple linear representations but a pervasive, living network constantly growing through building new relationships or breaking old ones.

After all a manufacturer will typically have several products each with its own unique supply chain. Indeed the manufacturer will almost certainly have more than one supplier for a given product or service. Similarly the suppliers will have several customers downstream as well as other upstream suppliers to provide their material input. As a result the supply chain's boundaries are often difficult to determine.

What Starts a Supply Chain?

The best way to demonstrate the boundaries constraining a supply-chain is to take a look at a simplified example.

In the supply chain diagram in Figure 1.2 we can see the 4 major flows within a simple supply chain.

The flow of materials is depicted as sourcing from the left of the diagram and in this example the flow of the raw materials, flows to and through works in progress (functional silos), all the way to the customers as the finished goods. This goods flow between each entity or participating company represents the passage of the product from the supplier's supplier through to the end consumer.

Additionally, in the diagram there is a representation of the flow of information, e.g. order confirmation or dispatch advice.

Furthermore, there are also depicted reverse flows and these manifest themselves in the form of:

- Goods, e.g. quality defect products or obsolete products
- Information, e.g. customer feedback
- Packaging material, e.g. outer cartons
- Transportation equipment, e.g. cages, pallets or containers

However, the most conspicuous reverse flow is that of money in the form of the reverse flow of funds. This is the money that flows back into the supply chain from the single-source of funds, the end-customer.

Figure 1.2 also depicts two additional forces in this supply-chain,

1. Product supply

2. Customer demand

These additional forces are catalysts for the entire supply-chain indeed they are the purpose that create the supply chains and they are triggered by product supply (commodities) or by customer demand (products).

The customer demand which is driven by the degree of customization of the product creates its own issues. This is because the range of product choice will dictate how much and in which format the supplying company holds inventory: no stock at all, raw or basic materials only, or sub-assemblies of their products. Therefore the product supply is not necessarily related to customer demand except in the case of commodity products. For example, a car may come in six basic colour options but demand is unlikely to be spread equally across each. In the case of customized products the OEM needs to derive strategies that take into account the decoupling of product supply from customer demand and this exercise is the bases of supply chain management

Chapter 2 - Supply Chain Management (SCM)

A basic model for SCM is the Plan, Source, Make, Deliver, Return model which covers every building block process within the supply chain. The supply chain planning and construction will typically involve several processes that span all levels of the company from the highest strategic planning in the C-suite down to the operational level on the factory floor. The three essential tasks that are required are Supply Chain Configuration (strategic level), Supply Chain Relationship (strategic, tactical and operations), and Supply Chain Coordination (operational), and we will discuss these later.

However, before we get too emerged into the executive and management side of Supply Chain Management, it will be helpful to have a simplified example of how a SCM function can be constructed. We can demonstrate this following the functional components of the Supply Chain Operations Reference depicted in figure 2.1.

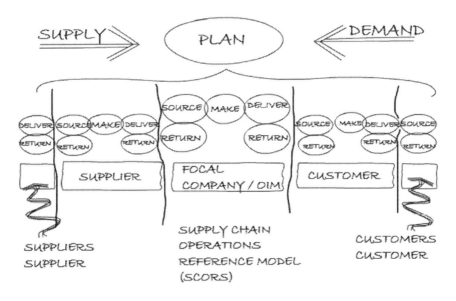

Plan

During the initial planning stage it is likely that planners will be confronted with some of these typical operational questions:

- How many individual products are we going to sell?
- Where are we going to sell them and when?
- How much production do we need to schedule in your factory?
- What are our raw and packaging materials we will need in order to fulfil the production plan?

All of these elementary questions belong to the functional plan process, where the task is to balance the demand and supply in order to develop a course of action to meet sourcing, production and delivery requirements.

Source

The next step in the development of the SCM will be to find suppliers of the raw material, packaging, cartons, etc, in order to source what is needed for production. The emphasis at this stage of the planning process is on selecting suppliers, establishing policies and assessing performance.

At this point in the planning process a decision may be made to out-source services such as transport and warehousing. This source function is procurement, and it describes the process of buying goods or services to meet planned or actual demand.

Make

Now that the procurement process is completed the materials are sourced and the demand and supply are planned, the next step will be to plan the actual manufacturing of the product. Thus, the Make process within this model describes all processes that transform the raw materials or sub-assemblies into the finished product with the aim to meet customer demand. This process within the supply chain operations reference model looks at questions such as:

- How to set up manufacturing?
- How to make sure the production runs efficiently?
- How to improve the making process?

After manufacturing, the completed products are ready for distribution or delivery.

Deliver

Under the deliver function, all supply chain processes are included that provide finished goods to customers. Thus, the order management, warehousing and transport management of the product all form part of this process.

Return

The last process in the chain concerns reverse logistics or product return. This functional process comprises all tasks that are associated with the return of product. Returns can occur for quality reasons, for recycling or for post-sales customer support.

The supply chain operations reference model furthermore shows that these functional processes of plan, source, make, deliver and return take place within every stage of the supply chain.

Supply Chain Dynamics

Despite their set-up often appearing static, supply chains in reality are dynamic in nature. Typically, supply chains react to changes in their environment. For example, supply chains are susceptible to external influences, which will affect the equilibrium. This can be best demonstrated through a change in an external factor such as the weather where in this case the demand for ice cream will fluctuate. Ice cream sales are dependent on weather so sales are related to how hot it is during the summer. Another scenario is that price cuts and promotional activities will influence the sale of commodity goods but there are other macroeconomic factors which can affect sales such as fluctuations in exchange rates, which will affect world transportation costs and foreign consumption.

In supply chains, managers are constantly monitoring the level of inventory against the risk of being out of stock. They may decide to increase the level of inventory and therefore reduce the level of stock outs. However there is a downside to that as unsold inventory may be wasted. This is especially important when managing inventory for high value fashionable goods such as smart phones where sales can be extremely volatile with high sales one week followed by a sudden collapse. The challenge in supply chain management is to balance the level of inventory while maintaining a high level of availability. Managing inventory therefore is essentially about balancing supply and demand. The task would be very easy in a situation where end customers inform us to exactly how much they require and give us time to order from suppliers. Also it would be ideal if suppliers were to deliver exactly when we need stock and in full. If these three conditions were true, we wouldn't need a buffer but could order from a supplier and ship it on to customers in time to satisfy their needs. However that is rarely if ever the case and this is why we need diligent supply chain management.

Defining Supply Chain Management

Supply Chain Management (SCM) has come to the fore in recent decades as the business environment has undergone rapid evolution driven by factors such as globalization and disruptive technological impacts, which in turn have introduced severe competition, heightened customer expectation, as well as geopolitical factors and so on.
 Under such a rigorous business environment, it is no longer sufficient to deliver the required competitiveness if an organisation is focused internally.
 As a result it is necessary for managers to understand that their businesses are only part of the supply chain and it is now not the company but the supply chain that wins or loses the competition.

Thus, the popular business mantra today is that competition is no longer about 'organisation against organisation' for there has been a shift towards 'supply chain against supply chain'.

Furthermore, with this realization of the changes to the competitive arena managers are looking to more assured ways of better managing the supply chain.

They are achieving this through appropriate strategic positioning, collaboration, integration and leadership. The managers of today are seeing the tangible benefits and success that comes from nurturing and managing the supply-chain.

Of course this holistic approach to management should not come as a surprise as supply chain management is by nature pervasive. Indeed it is hard to find any aspect of business that has nothing to do with supply chain management. If we take for example the area of quality management, which is a fundamental part of enterprise business management. It should become clear that it will be difficult to manage and improve the quality standard of the product or service, if measured by the end-consumer, without managing the suppliers and buyers in the supply chain. Hence, it has become the accepted principle that business value creation only comes about through a collective contribution from the entire supply chain.

However, despite the general acceptance of the principles of SCM there has been no general consensus on the methods of practice within even industry verticals. Furthermore, supply chain management is practiced in diverse ways across industry. However, what is common across the field of SCM is that any supply chain management practice and the associated activities are driven by three conceptual components: Supply Chain Configuration; Supply Chain Relationship; and Supply Chain Coordination.

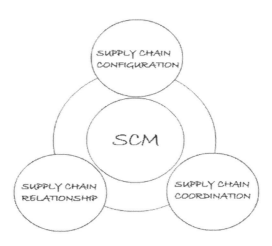

Figure 2.2 - Supply Chain Management Conceptual Model

• **Supply Chain Configuration** relates to how a supply chain is constructed from all its participating companies. This function includes evaluating the size of the supply base of the OEM (original equipment manufacturer); for example, how wide or narrow is the extent of vertical integration; how much of the OEM's operations are outsourced; how the downstream distribution channel is designed; and so on. In this context vertical integration relates to consecutive activities being undertaken by a single company within the supply chain.

Supply Chain Configuration is also known as supply chain architecture and as it is strategic in nature it operates at the highest executive level.

• **Supply Chain Relationship** relates to the inter-company relationships and connections across the supply chain. However as the supply chain is often viewed from the perspective of the OEM as the focal point the key focus of relationship is often limited to the OEM and its first tier suppliers and first tier customers and the relationship in between. Relationships are distinguished via the type and level of the relationship, which is determined by the strengths of inter-company exchanges. As an example, relationships are likely to be considered to be "arm's length" if they only exchange the volume and price of the transaction; on the other hand, the relationship would be regarded as close partnership if the parties exchanged their vision, investment planning, NPI process and detailed financial information. Therefore, supply chain relationship operates at the strategic and operational level.

• **Supply Chain Coordination** refers to the inter-company operational coordination within a supply chain. It involves the coordination of continuous material flows from the suppliers to the buyers and through to the end-consumer in a preferably 'Just In Time' (JIT) manner.

Typically it is the need for robust Inventory Management throughout the supply chain that could well be the driver and a key focal point for the coordination of the supply chain.

However, coordination covers many other disciplines such as production capacity, forecasting, manufacturing scheduling, even customer services as these will all required to be coordinated within the supply chain. As these functions constitute the main contents of the coordination activities in the supply chain then supply chain coordination tends to be at the operational level.

A common feature across the three key supply chain management functions is that they all work by considering the external organisation to be an extension of their own processes within the same supply chain. This is conceptually supply chain thinking rather than being inward looking 'Within the 4 Walls' focused. These SCM concepts also demonstrate the pervasiveness of supply chain management as it involves managerial decision making across not just strategic, tactical and operational levels but also across organisational boundaries.

Developing Trends in SCM

A difficulty in understanding and defining supply chain and supply chain management is that it is volatile, dynamic and the subject has been evolving since its inception in the early 1980s. The continuous development is partly driven by the changes of the overall business environment and heightened competitions in the global market place. However that is only partly true as it is also influenced by the new understanding of supply chain management. There are a number of early development trends that have changed the perception of SCM.

1) **Functional to process perspective**. Business management used to see and take action on the functional silos in the business. It was natural as the function is the delivery part of the business.

   But, today with supply chain management, managers tend to view their problems more from the process perspective, by understanding that functions only make sense from the perspective of the entire supply chain process.

2) **From operational to strategic viewpoint.** In the early years of SCM the managers tended to see it as another suite of operational tactics that helped to reduce operational cost, such as through purchasing function improvement and via optimizing the logistics operations as a whole. Gradually, the trend changed and managers realised that effective change can only come about if the operational issues are addressed tactically from the supply chain perspective. Such as, operational excellence can only be manifested through its *strategic fit*.

3) **Single enterprise to extended enterprise.** Enterprise management is now arguably usurped by SCM, for now the supply chain is by definition the extended enterprise. The long established enterprise focused thinking was based on the premise that competition was waged between organisations. Evolved management thinking rendered that strategy obsolete as the competition is now predominantly between the supply chains. Moreover an added bonus was that SCM released management thinking over the extended enterprise, which produces greater scope of ideas than single enterprise thinking can do alone.

4) **From transactional to relationship based engagement.** Business engagement between suppliers and buyers in the past was predominantly transaction based and cost driven.
The KPIs related to any purchasing and procurement of externally sourced materials and services was judged by the transactional measures such as price, volume and delivery terms. But those traditional metrics have been usurped by new metrics that measure so called relationship based engagement. This relationship approach does not abandon the transactional activities altogether but bases its decisions on much wider consideration of knowledge exchange, long-term commitment, incentives and reward.

5) **From local to regional, from regional to global**. The connections of supply chain networks over the last two decades have grown from local based to regional and now extended to even global preference. Hardly any major enterprise and their supply chains do not have connections that span the globe. This global trend was spurred by the lower cost of labour and materials in many parts of the world, as well as first mover advantages in setting up global market presence.

Chapter 3 - Global Supply Chain Operations

Global Business Environment

Global market convergence, which is the tendency that indigenous markets start to converge on a set of similar products or services across the world

Presently, the global market is dominated mostly by many well established global brands. This has come about over the last three decades, as there has been a steady trend towards global market convergence, which is the tendency that indigenous markets start to converge on a set of similar products or services across the world. The end-result of the global market convergence is that companies which have succeeded with their products or services in their regional markets now have the whole wide world to embrace for marketing, selling as well as material sourcing.

The strength of globalization is that now everybody knows what everybody else is doing, and everyone wants the same thing if it is perceived as being any good. Globalization is also evident in the rise of emerging economic powers led by BRICs (Brazil, Russia, India and China), which have significantly improved their populations living standards and the spending-power of millions if not billions of people. For organizations the logic of going global with their supply chains is also beneficial from an economic perspective.

Inter-organizational collaborations in technology and market presence in the predominantly non-homogeneous markets can also be the strong drivers behind the scene. In such a global stage there are a number of key characteristics that global supply chains must recognize before they can establish a firm base, through:

- **Borderless**: National borders are no longer the limits for supply chain development in terms of sourcing, marketing, manufacturing and delivering. Evidently, the national borders are far less constrictive than they used to be. Arguable this is perhaps the result of technology development, regional and bilateral trade agreements, and the facilitation or world organizations such as WTO, WB, GATT, OECD, OPEC and so on.
- **Cyber-connected**: The global business environment is no longer a cluster of many indigenous independent local markets, but rather it has evolved into a single market through predominantly inter-connected cyber relationships.
- **Deregulated**: Economic and free-trade zones around the world have promoted open and fair competition and reduced trade barriers around the world creating a level playing field on the global stage.
- **Environmental Consciousness**: Growing concerns on the negative impact of business and economic development on the natural environment have escalated over the last decade. Organizations and their supply chains cannot ignore the global movement towards green and more eco sustainable business strategies. This growing awareness by organisations of their environmental accountabilities provides a major constraint in today's global supply chain development.
- **Social Responsibility**: Along with awareness for ecological sustainability there is also a wider socio-economic impact. Fair trade and business ethics have become key factors for business decision making and strong metrics for an organisation's social responsibility. As a result, organisations can no longer ignore the social-economical and ethical issues as a failure of duty strikes at the heart of a company's brand in the mind of the consumer.

Strategic Challenges

There are at least five key strategic challenges that we will have to overcome when contemplating the supply chain architecture as these will have long term impact on the management of the global supply chains. Those five strategic challenges will vary in ratio and magnitude within specific industry but across all industry they will have the shared characteristics of being inherent, interrelated and intricately and dynamically entwined with one another. These strategic challenges are:

Market dimension

Demand fluctuation poses a serious challenge to supply chains with regards to asset configuration, capacity synchronization, and lead-time management. Demand volatility if left unchecked can trigger the 'bullwhip effect' throughout the supply chain, which results in higher operating cost and unsatisfactory delivery of products and services.

This issue is even more problematic in the global market for the root causes of the demand volatility are usually unpredictable and even less controllable.

The first significant challenge is in addressing the development lead-time challenge. The lead-time from innovative ideas to testing, prototyping, manufacturing, and marketing has been significantly shortened. The second challenge comes from its disruptive power. The third challenge lies in the supply chain network.

The innovative ideas and new technologies usually emerge from a supplier or a contractor in the supply chain network. To convince the whole supply chain of the value adding or cost reduction is not guaranteed. Each supplier and contractor will have its own value stream and will make technology adoption decisions based on the needs of its own customers.

Innovative ideas that surface from subcontractors may be stifled due to the supply chain's inability to coordinate value contribution between individual members and the whole supply chain. The cost and profit structures in the value network can also limit the attractiveness of an innovation.

Resource dimension

When we use the term resource in this context it is taken to mean any strategically important resources, including financial resource, labour resource, intellectual property resource, natural material resources, transportation, infrastructure and asset related resources, and so forth. Globalization has the effect of flexibility or elasticizing the supply chains' downstream operations from a local/regional reach to a world-wide scope. It allows organisations to trade around the globe and optimizes the use of internal resources, i.e. the same level of local resources can now be used to satisfy a much wider and larger market in terms of product volume, variety, quality and functionality.

Time dimension

Time is always a major factor in SCM and so it is with key global supply chain factors. Global supply chains challenges are intensely time related, as given that everything else is equal; the differences on time could make or break a supply chain.

How are Global Supply Chains Responding

Knowing the challenges is one thing but learning and mitigating their effects is another. This issue is exacerbated by the fact that all supply chains – even within a narrow vertical industry scope – are different. Consequently, despite the huge academic interest behind SCM theory and the challenges of globalization on supply chains, there are still no industry specific 'Best Practices' or a consensus of a "one size fits all" prescribed solution to address and mitigate the challenges.

However, there has been a plethora of academic and empirical studies that reveal that supply chains have implemented some common approaches which have proved relatively successful in addressing their own specific global challenges.

- **Collaboration**

A common technique used by supply chains that have mitigated many of their global supply chain challenges is partner collaboration. Successful supply chains have a common feature in so much as they realise that supply chain management activities are not about competing against one another, rather it is more about collaboration and partnering. Inter-Company collaboration is essential in supply chain management context and it is simply defined as working together to achieve a common goal.

- **Sharing resources**: An additional bonus that collaboration between two companies delivers is that it enables them to share the complementary resources, thus avoiding unnecessary duplication of work and resources such as expensive assets such as, manufacturing equipment, service and maintenance facilities, transportation and distribution networks and so on. Furthermore, collaboration between supplier and buyer makes sense as suppliers tend to have expert knowledge on their product. The buyer can engage this expertise to improve their own product and hence derive more value that they would from a basic sales transaction. Thus, the sharing of information, knowledge and intellectual resources can raise supply chain performance through increased product innovation, differentiation and quality.

- **Innovation**: collaboration in technology development and R&D is a particularly effective way to improve the supply chain's competitive advantage. Supply chains that actively encourage and participate in collaboration at this level have made notable advances in innovation. These technological advances are derived through people from different companies blending their expertise and experience and brain-storming to create new innovative ideas.

• **Achieve synergy**: The benefits of collaboration and particularly the sharing of knowledge and expertise will often outweigh the risks. This is because collaboration at this level when undertaken between two or more partnering firms where resources and intellectual property are shared will usually result in what is called 'synergy.'

Synergy, in general, may be defined as two or more things functioning together to produce a result not independently obtainable i.e. they are stronger together. In the context of supply chain collaboration, synergy is about creating additional business value that neither can achieve individually.

• **Risk sharing**: collaboration can help to mitigate the company's market and supply risk significantly for all participating parties. By collaborating on shared resources, design and innovation, investment and marketing, the negative impact of the supply chain risk can be borne proportionately by all parties and thus shared.

Supply chain integration

A supply chain is typically a network which consists of a number of participating companies as its members. For a global supply chain the network and the participating member companies can be independent entities in any country around the world.

Traditionally, and still to this day many supply chains where loosely constructed based on a transactional bases typically price. As a consequence the supply chain consisted of 'organisations' that were promiscuous and fickle in their loyalties. Often, there were antagonistic relations in between the member companies as sometimes they would be natural competitors.

The result of such a poorly planned and constructed supply chain was that cooperation, communication and visibility along the supply chain were usually poor. In other words, the supply chains were simply not integrated.

Divergent product portfolio

Another common technique used to address the challenges that arise in supply chains is to develop a divergent product portfolio. This strategy introduced by leading multinational organisations aims to make the supply chain more capable of satisfying the divergent demand of the world market. These market leaders - For example, Virgin Group, General Electric, British Aerospace - have developed a wide range of products within their business-sector portfolio to cater for the market needs.

The logic behind developing a divergent product portfolio strategy is that it will significantly mitigate the market risks that surface through global market volatility. If one product is not doing well, the supply chain can still be stabilized by others that do well.

Pursuing world class excellence

Business consensus is that to be a world class supply chain it must excel in four dimensions. The first dimension is demonstratable operational excellence. All world class supply chains must have optimized operations, which are measured in productivity, efficiency, cost effectiveness, quality, customer service and satisfaction.

The second dimension is what is referred to as the strategic fit. All world class supply chains are optimized and tightly coupled with the company's business model, strategic objectives and stakeholder's interests; and that the internal resources are compatible with the external market needs.

The third dimension is the capability to adapt. World class supply chains must be dynamic and be able to adapt to changes and volatility in the market, economy, and the environment in order to sustain a quality operation.

The fourth dimension is the supply chain will have a unique voice.

Chapter 4 - Supply Chain Design and Planning

The fundamental issue in supply chain management is to design and plan the overall architecture of the supply chain network. The construction should be planned to include all of the factors above with regards to operational excellence, strategic fit, adaptability and voice. The fundamental design criteria should also include key architecture factors such as the extent of vertical integration, strategic outsourcing, location decisions, capacity planning, and dealing with the bullwhip effect.

Supply Chain Configuration

When undertaking the planning of a supply chain, we have to consider the network configuration. The network represents how the participating company members of the chain are inter-connected. The importance here is to understand that connections within the network are business relationships between the connected parties.

 The companies will be expected to form a working bond with each other to deliver the product or service. Of course we cannot expect companies that are natural competitors to suddenly work in harmony. Similarly as an Original Equipment Manufacturer, we cannot realistically expect our suppliers to supply only us, or for that matter our downstream customers to buy from only us.

 Therefore, an important part of supply chain configuration for an OEM is determining how many upstream suppliers it uses, how the suppliers are grouped, categorised or tiered as this forges their relations with other companies.

Hence the OEM must be clear on a potential supplier's business relations with other suppliers, their allegiances to potential OEM competitors, the ownership and independence of the suppliers, and the choice of distribution channels are all major configuration factors for the supply chain.

When an OEM constructs its supply network through a hierarchy of tiered suppliers and distributor with medium and long term stability in mind, it is called a 'Stable Network.' On the other hand, when the OEM constructs their supply chain using dynamic and mostly short term connections with suppliers and distributors to achieve a high level of operational flexibility and strategic agility, it can be called the 'Dynamic Network.'

In comparison, the tiered stable network has more control over its suppliers and distributors' operations than the dynamic network.

Extent of Vertical Integration

Much of the supply chain design will be determined by the extent of vertical integration within the OEM itself. Vertical integration is defined as the single ownership of consecutive activities, on the other hand horizontal activities relate to those undertaken along the supply chain. Vertical integration must not be confused with the concept of supply chain integration as vertical integration consists of activities performed within an organisations own four walls. Hence vertical integration of activities is not part of the supply chain it is internal logistics. For example, a well integrated supply chain may not have extensive vertical integration. For example, an OEM that does not have direct control of its suppliers and customers is regarded as having a narrow span of vertical integration. On the other hand if it owns a number of tiers of suppliers and customers, it is regarded as having a large extent of vertical integration. Obviously it could also be a forward integrated one or backward integrated one as shown in figure 4.1

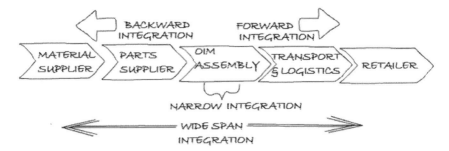

Figure 4.1 - The extent of vertical integration

To a large extent a company's strategy, operation and performance will depend on the right design of the supply chain configuration. Generally speaking, process based industry such as oil industry and chemical industry tends to be more vertically integrated; and the technology intensive electronics industry tends to be less vertically integrated.

Outsourcing and Offshoring

A common term in supply chain and logistics is the "make-or-buy" decision and this relates to strategic outsourcing.

Organisations may decide that it is easier or more cost efficient to outsource much of the production of a product or service.

For example, many commodity goods are manufactured as unbranded 'white boxes' that manufacturers can rebrand and improve through additional software or technology. Therefore it is common for OEMs to contract some of its in-house operations such as design, manufacturing and marketing to its external suppliers.

Most often such decisions to 'buy' the operation instead of 'make' is purely to reduce cost and time to market.

For example, a manufacturer will have to evaluate whether it is cheaper to buy or to make the product. For the manufacturer reimagining the production facility will be expensive and time consuming so buying in may be the best solution. Indeed most technology startups have no option as they have no manufacturing facilities. Hence, many OEM (Other Equipment Manufacturers) are based in China and these organisations can produce and assemble the same technology components into sub-assemblies or 'white box' products at lower costs than those based in the US or the EU. Therefore, it will make sense for OEMs to outsource the production of the components to these third parties. However, it may not just be about price as it is also possible, that it makes sense to outsource a highly specialised function, for example the software development operations to a dedicated software house in order to gain the supply chain value add. The decision and processes of moving any strategically significant operations out to the external suppliers is called outsourcing.

The most common reasons for outsourcing are driven by either maximizing the consumer value add and/or minimizing the total cost but outsourcing has many other potential benefits which could form the prime motive for the decision makers:

• Focus on and further developing the core competences
• Further differentiated competitive edge
• Increasing business flexibility, thus supply chain flexibility
• Improved supply chain responsiveness
• Raise the entry barrier through focused investment
• Enhanced ROI or ROE through downsizing the fixed asset

Case examples of outsourcing are all around us. Dell is a computer manufacture. In order to develop its strategic competitiveness in customized product configuration, assemble to order, and distribution channel transformation, it decided to put its strategic emphasis on product design and downstream services. To this end they decided to outsource most of its manufacturing operations to Taiwan but retain the design and also vertically integrated downstream channels. Another example is the Benetton Group which is a leading edge garment supply chain in the world. It has the presence in over 120 countries. Its core business is fashion apparel. But, 80% of its manufacturing operation is outsourced to thousands of independent small manufactures. This helped the Benetton group to reduce its manufacturing cost, synchronize the supply chain capacity with the fluctuated market demand, and alleviate the bullwhip effects.

An industry wide survey by Supply Chain Management Review revealed that 84% of manufacturers outsource at least some of their production processes. At those levels, outsourcing has become pervasive and we need to start seeing this as the norm, rather than an exception to the rule.

When the public thinks about outsourcing, it brings to mind a manufacturer sending work to another country to take advantage of lower labor costs. That is often the primary driver as labour cost plays a significant part in the overall production costs. However, it is only one of the reasons why manufacturers choose to outsource. Indeed, many manufacturers base their decision upon adding capacity or taking advantage of unique skills. Furthermore, the supply chain partner with which they choose to outsource isn't always out of the country.

Moreover, even should the manufacturer keeps the entire process in-house, it is still likely that the final product will pass through one or more facilities before it gets shipped to the customer.

For example, another company might supply additional components or be responsible for the final assembly. In all probability it will be another company that provides the regional or national distribution centers responsible for routing the finished goods to the appropriate channel.

Hence, although outsourcing has a reputation for being all about saving on labour cost it can be unavoidable as what happens inside the four walls of the factory is only one factor when it comes to profitably providing the products your customers want to buy. True continuous improvement needs to be made at the supply chain level and that includes every aspect, from planning to schedule to execution. Another closely related concept in supply chain architecture design is called 'offshoring'. However, offshoring is not synonymous with outsourcing as it is defined as moving the on-shore operations to offshore locations i.e. moving manufacturing from the UK to China. Off-shoring is undertaken in order to take the advantages of abundant cheaper local resources, and to reduce operating cost or create market presence. Initially practically all offshoring was driven by cheaper labour and resources which offset the higher costs of transportation and logistics.

Today though as a result of globalization offshoring has become attractive to manufacturers mainly as a means to get product production, distribution and marketing closer to the customer. However, an important distinction is that offshoring does not necessarily mean outsourcing, especially when the ownership of the off-shored operation remains unchanged for in that case no outsourcing has taken place. Nevertheless, outsourcing may be cheaper and certainly more convenient but like many management decisions it does not come without risk. Indeed outsourcing is extremely high risk activity on so many levels. However, the biggest concern of outsourcing is perhaps the variety of risk vectors that it enables:

• Negative impact on company's personnel moral

• Loss control over key strategic design task, sub-system or component, resulting in negative impact on the company's competitiveness.

• Could well be creating tomorrow's competition

• Risk of severe business disruption due to failed supply from single sourced suppliers

• Tactical, short term approach to outsourcing may inhibits continuous improvement and long term investment

• Intellectual property right risks

• Foreign currency exchange risk if involves overseas suppliers

Therefore, with due consideration to a cost/benefit assessment, a resulting strategic outsourcing decision must be regularly reviewed and assessed against risk. The review is essential because the changing business environment could easily make the originally right decision no longer justifiable. When the capital or financial circumstance changes like the one in the economic downturn, the outsourcing decision may have to be revised accordingly. Internal development of technologies and technical competences could also affect the outsourcing decisions.

Capacity Planning

With respect to the linear chain representation of a supply chain then capacity planning is rather intuitive. It can be readily determined that the total capacity of the supply chain, depends on the capacity of the smallest supplier.

For example, if we imagine the supply chain as a piece of water pipe with different diameters at different sections. The overall flow of the pipe, which represents supply chain capacity, is determined by the minimum diameter – a bottleneck - of the pipe at any one stage.

In the situation of networked tiered supply chain structure, the overall capacity of the supply chain becomes the double layered minimum. For each tier i the overall capacity is; and the whole supply chain's capacity becomes.

Bottlenecks are common in supply chains as each company in the chain will have varying capacity of resources. These bottlenecks have come under considerable academic scrutiny and as a result there is actually a well established theory on the bottleneck problem, called 'the theory of constraint'.

The Theory of Constraint

The Theory of Constraint in the context of supply chain management does not only apply to capacity planning. Indeed the Theory of Constraint has its uses in quality, technology, and lead-time management, because every part of a supply chain has bottlenecks. To perform a capacity planning exercise in real-world supply chain requires investigation at three levels. The first level is at the company's internal capacity planning and management, which is the companies own internal 'Logistics' capacity management. The second level is concerned with the company's external capacity coordination, at the supply chain. At this level synchronization with the other members within the same supply chain with regards capacity is the focus. Hence at this level the supply chain synchronizes with the requirements of the focal company. The third level is the supply chain's capacity responsiveness to changes in the market demand, which can be understood as the capacity synchronization between the supply chain and the customer demand. The effect of capacity synchronization has another major benefit as it helps to alleviate the *Bullwhip Effects* in the supply chain.

The bullwhip effect is a very common and undesirable phenomenon which has many negative impacts on the supply chain performances. Understanding the bullwhip effect is therefore essential to the supply chain design and planning.

The Bullwhip Effect

The Bullwhip effect manifests when the small demand ripple in the market place is felt by the retailer at the end of the supply chain, the retailer will then start adjusting their orders to the wholesalers, and the wholesaler in turn will adjust its orders to the distributer, and the distributer to the factory. We would expect that when the factory receives the orders, it will have received orders that equate to those equally small changes. Unfortunately, this is not so, instead those small ripples of fluctuating demand in the market have been significantly amplified stage by stage towards the upstream of the supply chain. When it reaches the factory or components manufacture the magnitude of fluctuation becomes vastly exaggerated.

How to we alleviate the bullwhip effect?

There is no single panacea but there are some commonly used countermeasures to the bullwhip effect:

• Improve information sharing through EDI (electronic data interchange), POS (point of sale systems), and web-based IS (information systems).

• Reducing batch ordering

• Coordinating capacity and production planning

• Apply appropriate safety stocks to insulate the oscillation

• Reducing inventory level through JIT (just in time), VMI (vendor managed inventory), QR (quick response).

All the proposed approaches to mitigating the effects of the Bullwhip effect must be executed cohesively in an integrated manor.

Moreover the only effective strategy in achieving a supply chain that is resistant to the Bullwhip effects calls for a very high degree of inter-organisational collaboration within the supply chain.

It is only through collaboration throughout the supply chain that the required coordination in capacity planning, inventory management, cost-to-serve, lead-time reduction and responsiveness can be effectively achieved.

Chapter 5 - The Lean Supply Chain

Focusing on Cost-to-Serve

The fundamental concept of lean is in identifying and eliminating waste in the material, processes, time, information, and adding value perceived from the eyes of consumer. Thus waste is to be cut across the management spectrum, but importantly not necessarily the cost. When a function or process which has a cost is identified as being waste, as it does not seem to have added any value, it should be culled. The key issue here, therefore, is to hone in on costs that add no value. If a cost does add value to the supply chain and it is culled, then value has been removed and that is counter-productive.

Wasteful activities are therefore defined as non-value adding activities. This is where the concept of 'serve' kicks in. If the activity adds value and the value is perceived by the customer, the activity 'serves' the customer. Therefore an appropriate translation of the lean principles in terms of attitude towards the cost should be that to identify and eliminating the non-value adding or non- 'serving' activities. Thus, a measure for how wasteful is a cost or a cost incurring activity can be defined by what's known as 'cost-to-serve'.

Drivers for Lean Supply Chain

What makes a supply chain lean? Academic research and industry literature have pointed to six key drivers that will lead to a lean supply chain.

Figure 5.1 Lean Concepts

Driver 1: Waste Reduction

Elimination of waste is one of the key tenets of lean manufacturing. In the broadest sense, waste can be found from all aspect of business activities. It can take the form of time, inventory, redundant process and defects.

Driver 2: Demand Management

Demand management is an important activity in supply chain optimization as it is a major factor in how supply chains are judged and a major point of competition in the market place. It is also an area that is ripe for early improvements and success – 'picking the low hanging fruit' - as there is always significant room for improvement. Realistically, the performance of the supply chain in the eyes of the end-consumer is solely determined by how the consumer demand is managed, fulfilled and satisfied. How well companies manage the consumer demand and their own demand related intelligence such as forecasting and market signals is also indicative in how they view and manage their collaboration with buyers and suppliers.

Driver 3: Process Standardization

The concept of process standardization is a key principle of Lean as it enables the continuous 'flow' - the uninterrupted movement of a product or service through the system to the customer - through the company and the supply chain. Major inhibitors of flow are work in queue, batch processing, and transportation. These are bottlenecks that slow the flow and consume time from product or service initiation to delivery. Furthermore by wasting time these inhibitors increase the material and work in process carrying cost.

Flow is best enabled when bottlenecks are minimized and material and processes are standardized across the supply chain to reduce resistance. But the standardization of processes can only be achieved through a culture of close collaboration within members of the supply chain.

An initial first steps approach would be to standardize the planning and production processes.

Having a shared and thorough understanding of the process involved across the supply chain both up and downstream will lead to products and material standardization. This will lead to volume advantages, consistency and operational cost savings.

Driver 4: Engaging People

The Lean manufacturing principles differs significantly from production systems in its people engagement. It was radical from a western perspective back in the 80's as it is essentially driven by empowering the shop floor workers.

To understand this it helps to see how companies can implement a lean process and develop a lean supply chain. To execute a Lean implementation the managers must start with engaging people.

This means the lean campaign is not just a strategic vision from the CEO it is a task that everyone in the organisation must get involved in, especially the operators and engineers on the shop floor.

This is because despite popular belief ideas for process improvements and innovative changes often come directly from the people who do the job and not managers and data scientists. This also requires that ownership of the lean campaign is in the hands of every employee not just a small group of senior managers. Engaging people is essential for successful lean transformation and this can be achieved:

• First, by engaging the intellectual assets of the employees and harvest their knowledge and expertise. Then they will be committed to contribute to the value adding activities.

• Second, engaging people is the best way to motivate them. People are the only active force in the business. How powerful this force is depends almost entirely how well they are motivated for the common courses of the supply chain.

• Third, change the organisational culture; a culture can only be carried and displayed by people. A lean supply chain can be built to last if and only if it is created with the embedded culture of engagement.

Driver 5: Collaboration

Lean philosophy promotes working together and collaboration. Lean supply chain thrives on collaboration, which can take place between organisations within the supply chain or across different supply chains. Collaboration often results in shared resources leading to a high level of economy of scale and scope; it also significantly reduces the business risks for the partners by sharing it and jointly averting it; it promotes technological advancement and innovative product and service development.

The power of collaboration has undoubtedly been recognized in all lean enterprises.

Driver 6: Continuous improvement

Lean philosophy believes the journey to improve will never end. If better is possible then good is not enough.

It does not need to be a quantum leap; any small steps of change toward better operations will be encouraged. Indeed most impressive improvements come about through tiny incremental steps.

Some successful implementations of the continuous improvement have been known as 'Kaizen', which is basically the Japanese word for continuous improvement. The key features of Kaizen are:

• Improvements are based on many, small changes rather than one radical change

• Ideas of changes are often come from the workers at the operational front

• Small improvements do not usually require any capital investment or major change of process

• All employees are engaged to participate to seek the ways to improve their own performance

• It encourages the workers to take the ownership of their performance

Just-in-Time

A very similar concept to Lean and is often erroneously considered to be synonymous is "Just-in-Time" or "JIT". However there are several conceptual differences so they are not identical. Just-in-time manufacturing is focused on efficiency by reducing inventory, while lean manufacturing is focused on using efficiency to add value for the customer. Just in Time relates to making "only what is needed, when it is needed, and in the amount needed." For example, to efficiently produce a large number of automobiles, which can consist of around 30,000 parts, it is necessary to create a detailed production plan that includes parts procurement. Supplying "what is needed, when it is needed, and in the amount needed" according to this production plan can eliminate waste, inconsistencies, and unreasonable requirements, resulting in improved productivity.

Just-In-Time (JIT) is a very enticing philosophy that rather paradoxically is both essential in modern supply chain management and also almost impossible to achieve. This is because JIT sets out to cut costs by reducing the amount of goods and materials a firm holds in stock. JIT involves: producing and delivering finished goods 'just in time' to be sold.

JIT involves:

- producing and delivering finished goods 'just in time' to be sold,

- producing partly finished goods 'just in time' to be assembled into finished goods,

- producing parts 'just in time' to go into partly finished goods or

- producing materials 'just in time' to be made into parts.

The principle that underpins JIT is that production should be 'pulled through' rather than 'pushed through'. This means that production should be for specific customer orders, so that the production cycle starts only once a customer has placed an order with the producer. Stocks are delivered when they are needed and importantly this allows the producer to balance the books as the goods are turned around almost immediately, which has a tremendous positive effect on cash flow. Consequently, this is a very attractive approach for supply chain managers but it does have some caveats. JIT requires much more frequent delivery of stocks and in smaller quantities, which makes the cost per unit higher. Also any delay or disruption can cause major distress to the supply chain as there is no safety buffer. Hence, companies that do implement JIT often use it in conjunction with a safety buffer of inventory which mitigates risk but dilutes the benefits. Subsequently, developing a JIT approach requires sophisticated planning and considerable experience in this field. It also requires certain operational pre-requisites for successful implementation, such as:

- Linear and constant demand

- A fixed Bill of Materials

- Suppliers are local

- Supplier relationships are optimal

Not many companies can meet all those requirements and that is why leading companies contract out their JIT supply chain management to a specialist company like a Third Party Logistics company that are able through aggregation of demand to meet the requirements of JIT.

A further advantage of JIT is the benefit derived from eliminating line side storage of parts and the associated costs of carrying inventory as well as the "clutter" which inhibits efficient movements to/from the production line. By reducing the storage of inventory at the production line, a manufacturer is often able to increase the speed of the production line and produce more products with the same number of resources, lowering the overall unit cost of production.

Chapter 6 - Agile Supply Chain Management

The Need for Agility

Although manufacturing evolved through major eras such as the Crafting era and the era of Mass Production, the Lean principles and system of manufacturing that followed was not dominant or relevant across all industries and therefore comparable to those previously defining eras. The issue with the Lean system was although it was highly successful in certain sectors such as car manufacturing it was less suited to other industries. This was simply because Lean was developed from a forecasting based, volume production, industrial sector where the market differentiator is reliability and cost. Whereas today large parts of the global market is variety dominated and the differentiator is speed and responsiveness. Hence, lean was not a panacea after all.

The demand driven market which is best illustrated by the emergence and dominance of a new breed of enterprises such as Zara, Dell, Cisco and Li & Fung requires quick responses to volatile customer driven demand. These new style manufacturers are demonstrating different models for success when it come to responding to customers in a fast-moving environment, where life cycles are short and variety reigns. The winners in this environment are those that can respond quickly and efficiently. This renewed competitive arena calls for more nimble businesses and more agile supply chain.

It will come as no surprise that the dominant buying behaviour of customers in an agile supply chain operated environment is that of *demanding quick response*.

The known business models of *make-to-order* or *assemble-to-order* are critical for catering for such demand.

Hewlett-Packard has long adopted the practice of postponing the final assembly of its printers until the exact market demand in terms of product configurations are known.

Cisco also in early 2000 started to make-to-order on their high end configurable chassis for routers, switches and firewalls. Thus what it produced were guaranteed to be sold and not over produced and end up as items in the redundant finished goods inventory.

Similarly, Dell Computer which may have pioneered assemble to order back in the early 90's, often assembles the computers during the distribution and delivery process, so that the customer can have their bespoke computer delivered in just a few days. And for Dell, the generic components in the up part of the supply chain were produced by the make-to-forecast model where efficiency and low cost can be achieved; the assemble-to-order at the final sector of the supply chain delivers the speed and responsiveness.

Agile Supply Chain Concept

Agility is a supply chain-wide capability and a key characteristic of an agile supply chain is flexibility. An agile supply chain should be interpreted from two side of the supply chain. From an internal view of the supply chain, flexibility means configurations and structures are not fixed. Consequently, the configuration and structure may transform quickly as the needs arises. From an external view, i.e. from market and consumer perspective, the supply chain must deliver timely products and services. In addition it must deliver them at the beginning of the usually short profit windows in order to be innovative and to become the market leader.

Thus an 'agile supply chain' is essentially a design for a practical approach to managing supply networks and developing flexible capabilities to satisfy the fast changing customer demand.

In addition it is about transforming and shifting the focus of the supply chain that is typically structured around the focal company i.e. the OEM and its product categories to become a supply chain that is focused upon the end-consumers and their requirements.

Figure 6.1 - Agile supply chain framework

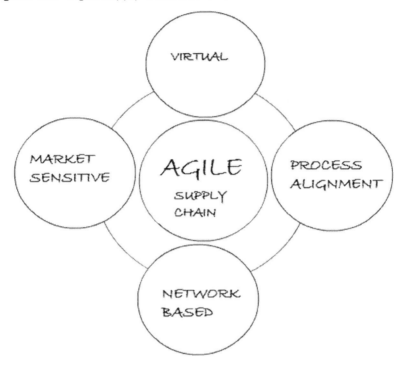

Agile supply chain is about virtual integration

The term 'Agility' implies that the supply chain is able to respond to the changes and opportunities that arise in the local market. To do this, an agile supply chain must have the capability to leverage skills, assets and other resources throughout the supply chain. To achieve this they will need to establish the common objectives, in effect the purpose of the supply chain and communicate that target to participating companies so that they all work in unity toward the common goal. The bond between organisations that have common objectives gives the appearance of vertical integration and delivers the same advantages – but without the consolidation of ownership.

Agile supply chain relies on market sensitivity

A feature of agile supply chains is that they have a high degree of market sensitivity. What this means is that the supply chain's internal metrics are sourced directly from and linked closely with the external market that the supply chain is operated in.

This is an important differentiation between traditional and agile supply chains.

Typically, we see in SCM performance metrics and business assessments being based on information generated from within the supply chain. However, if we were to apply these metrics to an agile supply chain it would probably misguide the management and drive the supply chain away from its ultimate objective of serving the market. What is required with a truly agile supply chain in terms of performance measure and operational improvement is to set up a very high level of market sensitivity by sampling metrics from the end-customer domain.

Developing a high degree of market sensitivity has two important implications. First, is with regards to the internal performance measure. In this case, every performance metric must be immediately or ultimately linked to the consumers in the market place. What this means is the supply chain metrics link internal customers and external customers to the ultimate end-consumers.

However, to be able to do this requires there is a causal mapping from what customers really care about referenced against every operation the supply chain delivers.

Second, refers to the ability to react quickly, i.e. its responsiveness. How quickly can a supply chain respond to the market change is a primary measure for the agility of the supply chain.

Agile supply improves process integration

The ability of an agile supply chain to react to changes in the end-consumer market will require a higher level of integration between internal operational processes. These internal processes such as sales, forecasting, production planning, sourcing, and delivery will need to be tightly coupled. The logic behind this is that when a sales operation senses some change of market trends it will trigger a chain reaction of responsive or corrective actions.

 These will affect many other operations in the supply chain. How fast the supply chain can react to the market change is dependent on the speed of changes in many other internal processes. Thus, it makes sense that the internal processes must be integrated so that they will perform as if they are one entity.

Agile supply chain is often dynamic network based

We saw earlier when contemplating the supply chain's architecture that SC managers need to clarify how the participating members of the supply chains are connected relative to each other. As a result we noted that the supply chain configuration can be divided broadly into two types of networks: stable network and dynamic network.

The stable network is a normal form of supply chain configuration where the suppliers and buyers are formed in tiers along the supply chain. The suppliers' involvement in the supply chain is more or less fixed. The operational guidelines are focused and formalized with respect to the OEM.

The technical role and competence positioning in the supply chain is also predefined. The style of operation of this type of network is mainly predetermined, mechanical, and predictable in its physical functions. However, the agile supply chain requires a more dynamic approach as it has a set of very different characteristics. In the dynamic network, the ties between suppliers and buyers, and amongst the suppliers themselves, are much looser and promiscuous than that of stable network.

Competing on Responsiveness

Ultimately, the validity of the agile model is tested, not by an algorithm or pre-defined formula, but by its dynamic performance against the competition in the market place. The true test of an agile supply chain is how it performs in a volatile and fast changing market environment.

The top Key Performance Indicators (KPI) for the fitness of an agile supply chain is responsiveness.

Typically high responsiveness cannot be achieved for minimal cost and often a trade-off is required.

For any agile supply chain there is always an incremental cost associated with servicing the changing demand. As agile supply chains are designed specifically to serve such volatile markets those customers who genuinely need urgent service will need to pay a premium. If the customer's demand is not urgent, they perhaps can wait or choose an alternative cheaper version which is often offered by lean supply chains. From the organisational internal structure perspective, agile supply chains also demand some structure changes. For example, there may be historically centralized operations, which may need to be decentralised to cut the bureaucracy and enable quicker response to local conditions. Similarly, in the case of multi-divisional structures it may be advisable to concentrate on the product, service, and geographical area and allow the business units to adapt to local needs.

Agile operations are more compatible with flat hierarchal structures as they tend to be less suited to tall hierarchies as the latter impedes responsiveness. Additionally, an agile supply chain thrives in an environment with a high degree of autonomy and empowerment with less formal rules as these factors are considered to be enhancements to the fundamental principles and structure of an agile supply chain.

Key Performance Indicators

An Agile supply chain differs from a traditional or lean supply chain in its goals as its focus is customer or demand centric. Therefore an agile supply chain will also need a set of its own unique key performance indicators (KPI).

The commonly used KPI in predominantly lean supply chain operating environment will not fit and often misguide the management as they are derived from internally focused metrics and goals.

An agile supply chain samples environmental conditions from the external customer market so requires metrics that align with these externally relevant goals. Hence, complimentary to traditional lean KPIs we find that the frequently used KPI for agile supply chains are:

• Design to market time
• Customer satisfaction and delight
• Production throughput
• Delivery lead-time
• Product availability in the market
• Capacity synchronization and optimization
• Cost-to-serve
• Frequency of product up-grading
• Service innovation and flexibility

Hence we can see that fundamentally the KPI for agile supply chain is the market responsiveness in terms of speed, product range and service quality. But the detailed KPI for a specific organisation, however, must always remain aligned with its top level business strategies and also remain tethered with the industry sector and product categories.

Chapter 7 - Relationship and Integration

Supply Relationship Defined

A crucial element in supply chain management is how the relationships between participating companies are established and maintained. Supply relationships are often defined as the cross organisational interaction and exchange between the participating members of the supply chain. Hence in a supply chain there are supply relationships on the upstream side with the suppliers or on the downstream side with the buyers. If the relationship is solely between one supplier and one buyer, it is called a dyadic relationship.

In supply chain management, relationship between the participating members is in fact more complicated that having a relationship or not. This is because of the various different and fluid relationship postures between companies, which can be identified, such as an arm's length relationship; short-term contractual relationship, long-term partnership relationship, and so on. It is almost like a variable that may take different and fluid values under different circumstances.

Arms-Length

The traditional supplier-buyer relationship has been limited to almost single point contact of purchasing officer on the buyer side and the sales person on the supplier side. The purchasing decision is largely based on the unit price. Information sharing is very limited if not at all in existence. These types of relationships tend to be informal and dynamic in so much as they are driven by a single factor – price.

Consequently, the relationship tends to be antagonistic and adversarial in nature with no common goals or sense of allegiance.

Close Relationship

Although the Arms-length model was the dominant relationship style in supply chain 30 – 40 years ago it was usurped in the 1980's with the introduction of a revolutionary new style - the Japanese relationship paradigm base upon fostering close bonds and common goals. Toyota first introduced this modern style of relationship building and it gained a strong foothold due to the proven success of the Japanese manufacturing industry especially in the car and consumer electronics fields. The Close Relationship model had long-term contracts and commitment at its core that encouraged stability and cooperation which was a profound shift from the short term transactional based relationships of the past. Hence suppliers and buyers started to collaborate and work towards shared goals and foster trust between the partners in the supply chain. Subsequent research has determined that it was the incremental building of trust that was to prove such a powerful catalyst in establishing the long-term relationships.

Strategic Alliance

More typically in modern supply chains today we see a shift away from the informal arms-length and the formal close relationship model, with the emergence of a new paradigm - the strategic alliance. This is a partnership that is built upon a common objective and measured with a wider range of metrics. A strategic alliance can therefore be defined as an informal or formal arrangement between two or more companies with a common business objective. A strategic alliance can be seen as recognition between inter-companies of a common goal. That common objective enables the alliance-partners to form cooperative strategies that may entail the pooling of knowledge, skills and resources. Collaboration enables the alliance partners to achieve the common shared goal which links to the individual strategic objectives of the cooperating firms. A strategic alliance usually will take one of the three structural types:

• Horizontal alliance: that is between companies on the same level of different supply chains, which is also referred to as inter-channel alliances.

• Vertical alliance: that is between the firms on the different levels of the same supply chain, which also referred to as the intra-channel alliances.

• Lateral alliance: that is developed between the client company and logistics service provider firms. Those logistics providers usually will serve many different supply chains and thus they are often seen from any supply chain as the 'lateral' rather than internal.

Companies embarked on the business of strategic alliances do so for many reasons:

• Sharing complementary resources

• Sharing market risks

• Achieve economy of scale and economy of scope

• Joint development and collaboration

- Create value through synergy as the partners achieve mutually benefit gains that neither would be able to achieve individually
- Cost saving and customer value adding

Supply Chain Integration

A further development on the model of strategic alliances between participating companies is the concept of supply chain integration. It may be looked upon as the aggregation of several strategic alliances into a larger confederacy. Conceptually, supply chain integration relates to the strategy that legally independent participating firms coordinate seamlessly together as if they are one company in order to achieve the common goal.

An integrated supply chain will in practice function as a single entity. Thus, for example, there will be a coordinated effort for the order fulfillment to match actual consumption at the end of the supply chain. Similarly, there will be a seamless effort to synchronize the suppliers' production to ensure the timely delivery of the products to the customer, at the right place at the right time and with the right price.

If we take Wal-Mart, for instance, they were pioneers in retail in sharing their point-of-sales data with their supply chain. This might not seem radical today but it was at the time as that data was considered confidential information as it included sales and stocking data. Nonetheless, its key suppliers by tracking daily sales were able to differentiate popular and fast selling from slow-moving items and to respond quickly either to replenish or to discontinue the items in retail stores. As a result, this tight coordination between Wal-Mart and its key suppliers dramatically decreased the workload on the store managers whilst also to the same extent increasing product availability and reducing inventory costs.

Figure 7.1 – Integration of Process Function in Supply Chain

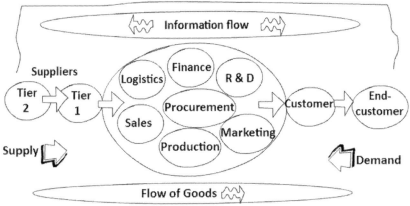

Integration of Process Control

The figure 7.1 above shows a framework of supply chain integration. It looks at the product flow that goes through a typical supply chain, which has the manufacturer as the focal company in the middle, involving two tiers of suppliers upstream and two tiers of customers downstream. On top of everything else, the information flow through the supply chain is the essential infrastructure for the integration. The contents of the integration are managed through 8 dimensions.

1. Customer relationship management
2. Customer service management
3. Demand management
4. Order fulfilment
5. Manufacturing flow management
6. Supplier relationship management
7. Product development and commercialization
8. Returns management

With the benefit of hindsight it is clear to us today that coordination among independent firms, such as raw-material suppliers, manufacturers, distributors, third-party logistics providers and retailers, is the key to attaining the goals of the overall supply chain. Moreover, the supply chain participants need the flexibility necessary to enable them to progressively improve supply chain processes in respond to rapidly changing market conditions. Furthermore a supply chain will exist in some form whether planned or not - i.e. the supply chain is inter-linked one way or the other albeit very intangible and complex - and poor coordination among the chain members can cause dysfunctional operational performance. Some negative consequences of poor coordination and lack of management include increased inventory costs, longer delivery times, higher transportation costs, higher levels of loss and damage, and lowered customer service.

Another interesting insight into the dynamics of a supply chain is that since the participating members are largely independent, a change in circumstances to any individual member is likely to affect the performance of the others and the supply chain as a whole. Thus, the performance of the supply chain is ultimately the 'integrated' performance, with or without management influence. Therefore, in order to improve the supply chain performance, requires a coordinated action. Hence, the management of the supply chain as a single integrated entity is perhaps the only effective approach to mitigate demand variability and excess inventories in the process.

If we consider that supply chain integration relates to the process of planning, executing and coordinating the interdependence of activities between supply chain members in order to create value for the end-consumer, then we can consider that supply chain management is managing the supply chain integration.

Chapter 8 - Creating Customer Centric Supply Chains

Since 2000 we have witnessed a notable shift in the focus of supply chain management in consumer retail and other demand driven industries away from *supplier centric* to *customer centric* operations. Placing the customer at the heart of the company's strategic plans and making them the focal point for sales, marketing, product development, and post-sales care was a business initiative that required reimagining the supply chain. The issue being that to become truly customer centric required a significant change in culture not just within and throughout the organisation but along the entire supply chain. A customer-centric supply chain can be achieved through:

• **Strategy**: A top down approach is the favoured method when implementing a customer oriented strategy. But it must be effectively communicated throughout the organisation. The top down approach requires that the organisation align its relationships with the suppliers and customers. This tactical approach will ensure the required levels of visibility and responsiveness to fluctuations in the end-consumers' demand.

• **Structure**: A horizontal dynamic structure that will align with products and market segment is the preferable approach. This is predominantly due to a vertical hierarchical typically having lengthy reporting lines. Implementing a supply chain modeled on the agile paradigm is a better strategic-fit and more responsive to variations in customer demand due to it inherently flexible network structure with a shallow level of vertical integration.

• **Systems**: In order to achieve integration throughout the supply chain and leverage benefits requires that procedures, processes and daily activities must be harmonised with market trends and sentiments. This requires the integration of IT systems and a 'single source of truth' as a data source. This provided the basis for sharing forecasting, reporting and marketing intelligence, which also assists in new product introduction process, which should be established collaboratively across the supply chain.

• **Shared value**: Supply chain participants must have a shared goal but it is important that they share the same customer service and customer value. Sharing the same values will become the culture of the supply chain – its voice. To this end, an integrated 'single source of truth' data system will ensure that customer orders, queries and complaints are processed equably by all participants through-out the supply chain.

• **Style**: As well as sharing values in a common culture of customer orientation it is important that the management team provides leadership and are the role models in caring about the customer. By leading by example they create a customer-centric style and 'voice'.

• **Staff**: People are the only active force in caring and serving the customer. This is true even today despite the prevalence of 'bots' in customer care call centers. Hence we must not overlook that changes in organisational culture and customer interactions is almost entirely dependent on developing people's understanding, knowledge and attitude.

• **Skills**: the skills of the workforce and the quality of service directly relate to the level of customer satisfaction, which in turn determines the organisation's and supply chain's competences in delivering quality products and services that meet customer expectation.

Adopting a customer centric strategy will necessitate a more integrated approach with tighter coupling of service philosophy and after-sales support between the participating organisations in the supply chain but that can be fraught with difficulty.

Managing Integrated Supply Networks

A common approach and a major challenge in transforming a traditional supply chain to a customer centric model is to take on the whole supply network and manage it as an integrated entity. This new competitive model places the OEM or focal-firm in the center of a confederation of partner companies with mutually complementary competencies, capabilities and culture.

Moreover, this confederacy competes as an integrated supply chain against other supply chains. But managing the confederacy requires a radically revised approach with different skills and competencies than those used in the traditional structure. Thus, to achieve global market leadership in such a networked competitive environment necessitates not just a customer focus but also a relationship management approach. One of the key cognitive characteristics of any network is its configurative structure, which specifies how a supply chain is to be constructed in terms of its flow model. A network structure's dimension determines the size of the supply base; how wide and how deep the extent of vertical integration; suppliers locations; and the strengths of the dyadic relationships, amongst other factors. Furthermore, globalization has forced some changes in supply chain network structure and configuration such as the level of outsourcing or offshoring. As a result we are seeing leading edge enterprises outsourcing more strategically important functions and dispersing them to geographically, economically and culturally remote locations. Consequently, this vertical disintegration of the supply chain has inevitably given rise to some new challenges in reimaging supply chain network management.

When contemplating the management of supply chain relationships a challenge is for the members to break free from the often adversarial nature of buyer-supplier relationships. There is now acceptance that co-operation between network partners is always the best policy to improved performance both individually and collectively.

However this is only feasible if the result of the improved performance is shared between the members of the network to achieve what's called 'win-win'. However balancing alliance-partner expectations, economically, strategically or politically is no trivial task as often it is simply about the individual partner's perception of the value of their contribution and thus the fairness of any share in the rewards.

Another significant challenge is in developing the shared information system for the network management. A common system is desirable as it is a catalyst for sharing forecasting, capacity, and production information, which can all be collectively managed to reduce the inventory levels and achieve shorter lead-time and JIT delivery.

However, whilst the supply network becomes leaner and more agile in terms of less redundant materials in the process - the material flows are gradually displaced by the information flow thus the investment in the information systems and its management gets increasingly higher.

Therefore, managing integrated supply chains is not without its challenges. For managing relationships is one thing actually integrating the technology throughout the supply chain is quite another.

This is because coordinating the IT system compatibility, software upgrading, maintenance and service across all participating parties will be an onerous task. Furthermore, it isn't just about the technical issues in interfacing incompatible systems. Often it is about forcing technology on partners who may well have their own advanced and highly customized systems and this may require partner employees duplicating work on two or more systems. Hence, it is rarely seen as a win-win at the technology level. However, despite the many obstacles in integrating supply chain partners at a technology level the gains in the much more coordinated operation and supply chain responsiveness is invariably worth the cost and effort.

Managing Risk

Of course with any level of inter-company integration comes risk, and as supply network complexity grows, uncertainty becomes ever more persistent. Risk managers therefore must keep a vigilant eye on the trade-off between the risk and the cost of building defenses and controls to mitigate threats. After all there is risk at every level when entering such an integrated strategic partnership not least the risk of missed opportunity. With so many related risks and risk-mitigation approaches to consider, managers typically do two things when they begin to construct a supply network risk management strategy.

First, they must create a shared organisation-wide risk assessment which will result in an understanding of the supply-chain risk.

Then, secondly, they must determine how to adapt general risk-mitigation approaches to the circumstances of their particular company.

Watch the Dynamics

There is however a third significant challenge to integration and that is how to survive the dynamics of the perpetually evolving supply chain. The future supply chain will face unprecedented changes with advancements brought about through emerging business models, disruptive technologies and eco-political factors in terms of structural dynamics, technological dynamics, and relationship dynamics, amongst other factors yet to emerge.

Structural dynamics

From a system dynamics perspective, the flow structure of a supply chain is typically dynamic in nature. This is as a consequence of fluctuations of demand, which can lead to overproduction, high inventory, and capacity miss-match. Demand volatility also is the root cause of backlogs of unfulfilled orders, delayed delivery, and ultimately to high levels of obsolete products in the discontinued inventory, and so on.

The problem is that the supply structure is growingly more complex, as a result of market volatility, which is also increasing due to globalization. Global scale has increased the number of factors that are continuously contributing to the increased structural dynamics. Therefore it is likely that the dynamic behaviour of a supply chain will become increasingly more volatile.

A primary factor in structural change is that companies around the world are becoming more specialised in their utilization of resources driven by competition and a need for return on investments.

 This trend towards specialization is leading to more inter-connections between specialised operations in the supply chain networks and as a result becoming triggers for dynamic behaviour. Specialization leads to a need for closer coordination in the supply chain and this in turn increases the complexity of the system.

Due to globalization the geographical expansion of territorial reach exacerbates the dynamic behaviour, as the delays in logistics and diminished visibility affects the performance of supply chains. It has also introduced instability through hard factors such as currency, technical standards, language, as well as through diverse legal, ethical and financial systems. However if that were not enough dynamic triggers there is also a myriad of cultural and religious conflicts, and other indigenous market related issues.

As an example, in the last decade or so there has been a significant awakening of public consciousness to environmental and social justice concerns around the world. Consequently, supply chains have had to contemplate their ethical and environmental positions very carefully. Public opinion on sustainability and eco-environmental issues are not something that a supply chain can ignore. Brands must be seen to promote a sustainable, ethical and Green approach to manufacturing and this has already started to reshape the world's major supply chains. Ethical production not only affects the resourcing and procurement strategies, but also the production and logistics processes. For example, the carbon footprint as a waste product has become the KPI for many supply chains across industries, which they had never heard off a decade ago. Consequently, the structure of the supply chains has had to change to meet these new standards.

Technological dynamics

Whenever we contemplate significant social or business change over the last decade it is the rate of technological advancement and disruption that springs to mind.

 Technology innovations and advancements have been a boon for the business and the consumer alike but for the supply chain a switch to new technologies can be a very painful process. All too often disruptive technology introduces dynamic change that retires the existing operating model, decimates the legacy markets and fractures supply chain relationships. The changing dynamics that have been enforced upon the supply chain can be observed from number of directions:

• Sudden change of competition landscape when the new technology advancement has helped the competitors to update their offering to the market.

• The manufacture may be forced to switch their suppliers due to the needs of the new technology in the supply base in order to keep competitive.

• Sudden requirement for new investment due to the pressure to upgrade the equipments and facilities to host the new technology.

• Surfacing of a significant skill gap in the workforce due to the unfamiliarity to the new technology.

Relationship dynamics

There is a common train of thought amongst practitioners in SCM that the operating core of supply chain management is that of managing the relationships with the suppliers and buyers including the end consumers. Hence, the external business relationship management for a company has become the centre piece of today's and arguably the future's supply chain management.

To appreciate this point-of-view we need to understand that there are typically two key dynamisms in relationship management.

The first one is the *portfolio dynamism* and the second is *longitudinal dynamism*.

The portfolio dynamism addresses - as its name suggests - a portfolio of different relationship approaches that fit to a corresponding catalogue of business models. Thus, companies will categorise a prospective partner by matching them with a discrete number of predetermined supply chain relationships. So for example, the prospect will be categorised based upon product categories, market segmentations, development strategies, and financial circumstances and so on.

The alternative approach is the longitudinal dynamism, which addresses the changing relationship posture along the time continuum. In this way the relationship management becomes a powerful instrument to achieve the supply chain responsiveness and supply chain agility.

It is anticipated that the future supply relationship management will hinge on a combined approach that addresses both the portfolio and longitudinal dynamisms.

Surviving supply chain dynamics

Professor Hau Lee (2007) from Stanford University introduced a useful blueprint to survive the supply chain dynamics called the Triple-A supply chain model:

• The triple-A stands for *Agility*, *Adaptability* and *Alignment*. The proposal suggests that a supply chain must be agile enough in order to respond quickly to the dynamics of demand fluctuations and sudden changes of supply. Thus, agility is a requirement as a supply chain capability for it handles the unexpected external disruptions smoothly and cost effectively. Agility also enables the supply chain to survive the impact of volatility in the external markets and be able to recover from any initial shocks.

• Adaptability, this capability differs significantly from agility with regards to time, as it is concerned with more long-term and fundamental changes in the overall external environment, which are often irreversible. Thus, adaptability requires a supply chain to embark on major strategic changes in technology, market positioning, radical skill upgrading and competence shift. It helps the supply chain to survive the long waves of external dynamics.

• Alignment is a capability that coordinates and balances the interests of all members within the supply chain. The utility of alignment is to address the supply chain's internal dynamics and ensure that the supply chain remains stable and cohesive.

Alignment works to marshal those complimentary resources and optimize the operational effectiveness and maintain the relationship to deliver the competitive advantage.

Chapter 9 - Technology's role in Supply Chain

Data, information and knowledge are critical assets to the performance of logistics and supply chain management (SCM). These fundamental assets provide the foundation upon which management can plan and organize logistical and supply chain processes. They are also the bases for coordination and communication amongst the participating partners. Moreover, data, information and knowledge provide the means to coordinate functional logistics activities and perform managerial control of the physical flow of material, finance and information among SC partners.

In a logistics or supply chain context Information Systems (IS) are the effective and efficient means to manage the critical assets of data, information and knowledge in order to provide sustainable competitive advantage. As far as the discipline of SCM is concerned, information technology (IT) consists of telecommunications, networking and data processing technologies – and is narrowly regarded here as the technological tools used to develop IS. For example IT provides the tools to capture or collect data, perform data analysis for generating meaningful information, and exchange and share this information with supply chain partners.

Efficiency-oriented IS / IT

From information management perspective, IS / IT is conventionally utilized in the application of efficiency-oriented SCM to increase productivity and reduce operational costs. Specifically, it is used to:

- capture and collect data on each product and service in a specific logistics activity, such as purchasing, to provide accurate, reliable and real-time raw facts;

- store collected data in a specific IS in predetermined categories and formats, such as a customer database management system;
- analyse stored data to generate meaningful information for management decision making in response to SCM events, and to evaluate SCM performance in cost reduction and productivity enhancement;
- collaborate and communicate with supply chain partners, in order to reduce information time-lag and misunderstandings, and to make the data resources available and visible to all supply chain partners;
- standardize logistics operations and data retrieval procedures, and develop generalized and rigorous information management policies;
- regulations and control measures;
- apply transaction cost theory to SCM to gain economies of scale and implement low-cost strategies.

Contemporary application of IS / IT is widely applied in the area of effectiveness-oriented SCM in order to enhance a supply chains competitive advantage, to add value and globalize operations.

In particular, IS / IT is deployed to:
- enhance the competence and positioning of a supply chain organization through designing and controlling the sharing and flow of information;
- re-engineer supply chain operations and eliminate duplicated facilities or activities, for example vendor managed inventory (VMI) instead of physical warehouses;
- manage marketing, customer, product and service knowledge or expertise developed (accumulated) in SCM, and share this with suppliers and partners, for example collaborative planning, forecasting and replenishment (CPFR);
- manage partner and customer relationships through resource-based and relational views, to stabilize supply chain structure

and enhance relations with adjacent upstream and downstream partners;

- deploy SC resources and capabilities to compete with others at worldwide level, and through international sourcing and offshore manufacturing.

The advent of Just-in-time manufacturing and a focus on consumer demand in retailing have brought significant changes to supply chain practices. Contemporary SCM attempts to achieve shorter cycle times and faster inventory turnover by tightly coupling with suppliers and to shift strategy from a pure efficiency orientation to greater coordination and integration of business processes in functional areas within the supply chain.

This strategy requires collaboration and sharing in product design and development, market research, and production planning. However, a high level of trust and the acceptance of risk are prerequisites to the extensive information sharing required for successful implementation of collaborative and integrated initiatives. Furthermore, another prerequisite to coordination of activities and sharing of resources is compatible technology.

Therefore, the integration of processes has to be built upon common technology and protocols that enables partners to interface and share information. Typically, designing and implementing a supply chain-wide compatible framework is not trivial as interfacing heterogeneous systems is an onerous, time consuming and politically fraught task.

For example, in industry the rate of adoption of new technologies, particularly in manufacturing, is not rapid due to the often long life-cycles of equipment – often 15-20 years.

Consequently, there are many legacy process control systems and the IS / IT applications that control and support their operations are still often in place. Therefore there is often huge disparity between the technologies deployed by supply chain partners. For example it is not uncommon to have one partner run all there finance, planning, administration and back office functions on spreadsheets whilst another is fully dependent on a million dollar plus ERP system. Furthermore, for true integration within the supply chain there is a requirement to have visibility and compatability at both the Operational (OT) and Informational Technology (IT) levels. Hence, to better understand the obstacles to IS / IT integration we need to recognise that the development, implementation and application of IS / IT in SCM is typically divided into four main levels:

1   IS / IT in logistics functional areas – transaction support system. Here, IS / IT is typically used for applications such as, order process and inventory management, online point-of-sale (POS) systems, warehouse management systems (WMS), transportation management systems (TMS) etc.

2   IS / IT for controlling information flows in integrated logistics operations across functional areas in an organization – intranet system, such as enterprise resources planning (ERP), groupware system and distribution requirement planning (DRP).

3   IS / IT used for information exchange and sharing between organizations – extranet system. The system is a structured and standard communication system, used to exchange logistics information among supply chain partners in certain transactions, such as ordering and trading information. Two of the most widely adopted extranet systems are electronic data interchange (EDI) and CPFR.

4   SCM system, or inter-organizational information system (IOS) – internet or network system for SC partners to exchange information, coordinate SC and logistics activities. Compared

with an extranet system, an internet system is much more flexible and powerful in information distribution and conducting logistics transactions. Typical applications are electronic banking, electronic portal, electronic procurement and customer relationship management (CRM). The internet is becoming the most useful business communication and information exchange system. It will eventually replace EDI because all information flows performed by EDI can be carried out through the internet, with low access costs and consistent transfer standards. Furthermore, it can synchronize information from all SC participants – including worldwide customers. Perhaps the most outstanding feature of the internet is that it changes information exchange from one-to-one to one-to-many and many-to-many.

Therefore, a critical SCM decision is how to develop and implement compatible IS / IT throughout the supply chain, and still maintain trustworthy, long-term relationships with key supply chain partners. For the focal company this is a conundrum because it is unlikely that they can enforce a technology standard upon a supplier as a cost of doing business. The costs to the supplier would almost certainly be prohibitive. On the other hand providing the supplier with the technology, support and training may seem to be a better approach. However, while this may encourage long-term relationships and contracts which will provide stability, the considerable investment will reduce the flexibility of exploring alternative markets, the possibility of faster growth, or increasing profits in some markets. Thus, the focal organization needs to set clear objectives and strategic planning for collaboration with other SC partners in order to share the risks and benefits, and that requires a diligent analysis of the impacts of new IS / IT.

There is little argument that IS / IT plays an important role in achieving SCM objectives. But effective SCM requires supply chain partners to act collaboratively and develop plans for coordinating the flows of goods and services. The prerequisite is that timely information is exchanged to ensure that goods and services are delivered at the right time, to the right place and at the right price.

To fully realise IS / IT potential, organizations must have an effective strategy that fits not only their organizational resources but the relationships with their partners. This necessitates that the focal company needs to work together with their supply chain partners to share the risk and costs of IS / IT development. To deliver a system, which delivers value to all partners working towards a common objective using a common IS / IT system.

Targeting Demand & the Virtual Enterprise

Since the turn of the millennium there has been a shift of attention from supply chain management to demand chain management (DCM).

This change of terminology from SCM to DCM describes the change of focus from delivering efficient supply to targeting the demand from the customer market. This has resulted in a shift from a desire for internal efficiency to one of satisfying the needs of the customer.

The fundamental change in focus required a change of thinking towards the markets, marketing and importantly to the demand end of the supply chain. Moreover, by meeting customer driven demand means aligning the operations with actual customer sales and orders, which removes a lot of the guess work out of forecasting, delivers greatly reduced inventory but with a potential risk of reduced responsiveness to spikes in demand.

The academic consensus to a solution leaned towards integrating marketing and SCM with the aim to building a new business model aimed at creating value in the marketplace and combining the strengths of marketing and supply chain competencies.

Integration of marketing with SCM provides shared market information that enables cross-functional, horizontal management along the supply chain. Further, the quality of the information shared between partners in the supply chain is even more important, making possible a responsive flow of products from one end of the pipeline to the other. This tightly integrated supply chain can then be effectively viewed as a virtual enterprise. As a result over the last decade the virtual enterprise model has become more common, but they are in fact only a series of relationships between partners based on value-added exchange of information to increase responsiveness, reliability and relationships.

The 3Rs (Responsiveness, Reliability and Relationships)

The themes of the 3Rs of responsiveness, reliability and relationships brings to the surface our assumptions regarding the 'the paradigm shift' towards partnering and strategies of cooperation, which are also very familiar in today's Industry 4.0 and in marketing.

Relationships between partners associated with the critical links between suppliers, manufacturers and customers are emphasized as companies aim to deliver more efficient supply chains. This development has led to companies focusing on their core competencies and outsourcing less strategic functions. Consequently, this tendency to focus on core dependencies has given rise to partnership and network thinking. However, there are real challenges in today's world of partnership thinking and there are many obstacles to overcome.

The challenges surface due to the fact that the path to improving interaction and collaborative planning is through the concept of integration (the virtual enterprise). Unfortunately, this type of tight cooperation is ideal in theory but can be hard to achieve in practice, as partners still want to preserve their independence.

Furthermore, if we consider that collaboration, which is the highest level of integration and requires partners to have high level of trust, commitment and information sharing, this can be even more perilous. Then the glue that holds these independent companies allegiance to the supply chain is the common objective and their shared vision of the future. The antecedent for successful adoption is trust. If trust and a genuine desire to seek common interests in IS / IT investments exist, a basis for effective IT usage is established.

Despite the inconvenient truth, which is the viability of the supply chain does not allow for too much independent behaviour on the part of individual channel participants. The evidence strongly suggests that collaboration enables information sharing, planning synchronization, workflow coordination and new business models. For example, adopting e-business approaches to coordination promises improvements in efficiency, effectiveness, service and consistency in business.

As a result we see that companies now work with many different types of supply chains and networks. This has come about due to increasing pressure from competitors and the globalization of the business environment. These factors have driven managers to look for new sources of innovation and value and the adoption and usage of technology is an obvious source of value and competitive advantage.

Assessing Supply Chain Maturity

Before you can begin to even consider improving or optimizing the supply chain you will need to know where you currently are and importantly what you need to improve.

That may be stating the obvious but often companies react to stimulus in the market such as hype over a new technology in a knee jerk manner. Similarly, a company may well know that their supply chain requires updating as it is no longer competitive in their markets but have no idea as to why it is only now underperforming. The conundrum surfaces because many companies do not understand their supply chains level of maturity. Moreover, their supply chain complexity makes it difficult to analyse and determine where areas of improvement can be identified. After all we cannot always judge the maturity and efficiency of a supply chain by the status and maturity of the focal company. There are examples of startups that have developed mature and highly efficient dynamic supply chains that exhibit all traits of the 3Rs. On the other hand there are brand-named enterprises that have long standing static SC models that are based upon an imbalance of power. Hence they are antagonistic and dictatorial and thus they reap only the minimal cooperation - above the contractual obligations - from their supply chain partners.

Fortunately, when assessing a company's supply chain maturity we can take a divide and conquer approach to negate the problem of complexity. This is because the concept of supply chain maturity can be defined by one of five distinct stages.

Stage 1 Reactive: This is a surprisingly common level of supply chain maturity especially in manufacturing. At this level the supply chains are managed in a reactive manner with managers having to fire-fight on a daily basis.

 A reactive approach requires a stable supply chain for any volatility in supply or demand causes upheaval in schedules and processing. To counter volatility requires high levels of inventory and overproduction in order to counteract and balance any temporary breaks in supply.

Unfortunately even these mitigating controls are often not present due to a reactive mentality being geared to happily solving problems as they arise. Interestingly, it is a common mistake to equate companies at this level of SC maturity with being technologically primitive luddites but nothing could be further from the truth. In fact many companies at this level are quite the opposite and are highly technologically evolved. The reason they take a reactive approach is simply due to their deep understanding of their supply chain and its supportive technology i.e. there emphasis is on development and innovation rather than planning.

Stage 2 Proactive: This level of supply chain maturity is based upon the principles of proactive management. It relies upon identifying and addressing potential problems and accepting that failure will happen. Consequently, this level of supply chain maturity is more risk averse and is designed to anticipate failure and react in a predetermined way to control the chaos through standardized processes. A weakness is that the effort is internally focused on the company rather than the broader supply chain partners. This isolated perspective can create conflicts across the supply chain. For example, one plant manager may be focused on quality of production whereas their counterpart in another factory has a mandate to cut component costs. Another significant issue with the proactive approach in the real world is getting the time to plan and document risk mitigation controls and procedures –when they are only enterprise specific - as it is often seen as being unproductive time.

Stage 3 Integrate: The preceding stages of maturity where both inward looking and worked to mitigate risk through the application of internal controls. In stage 3 the aim is to integrate and have visibility and coordination across the supply chain.

An integrated approach allows for a supply-chain wide coordinated approach to proactively mitigating risk or in the event of failure to troubleshooting.

Of course there will still be independent improvements sought inside the four walls, but managers recognise that their domain is only one part of the production system. In addition at the senior leadership level, the supply chain is treated as a holistic organism and synchronization between individual functions is prioritized.

Stage 4 Collaborate: Beyond integration and cooperation lies collaboration. At this level the supply chain really begins to harvest the benefits of tight integration and close relationships.

It is at this level that the supply chain becomes a functional seamless network that delivers value to the customer.

At this level of maturity the supply chain partners work together to reimaging their processes and activities from a focus on internal objectives to a shift towards an external common goal.

Stage 5 Orchestrate: This is the highest level of maturity that almost all supply chain leaders envision, but few will ever achieve. Collaboration is no longer one-off it is inherent and pervasive throughout the supply chain. The level of maturity has now reached the ecosystem level where all the participating partners work together to deliver value through channels geared to the needs of the customer. This level of seamless integration in all disciplines and processes creates an image of a virtual enterprise, a seamless operation, where the value of the whole supply chain is greater than the sum of the parts.

Legacy Failures in the Supply Chain

Now that we have benchmarks for supply chain maturity it is possible to categorize the existing supply chain into to these very broad stages. Interestingly, most manufacturers when honestly appraising their supply chains actually find that they are somewhere between stage one (Reactive) or stage two (Proactive).

The common consensus within the industry is that the stage to realistically strive for is stage 3 (Integrate) whilst tacitly acknowledging that the clear majority of manufacturers are still far from that lofty goals.

Interestingly, despite our knowledge that building mature supply chains requires diligent relationship building, encouraging cooperation through trust, establishing a win-win philosophy, striving for higher collaboration, and allegiance through 'Espirt de Corp'. It appears that technology is identified as being the greatest obstacle to achieving a merging of those objectives and strategic thinking. Indeed the very systems implemented to help manage the supply chain may be a big part of the problem.

The ERP Fallacy

If we contemplate the IS / IT systems in place today we can perhaps see why they are hindering the maturity of the supply chain. For example, just about every manufacturer will have an ERP (Enterprise Resource Planning) system of some sort or capability. Some may have SAP where as other will get by with open source solutions such as OpenERP or OpenBravo, other still will maintain spreadsheet workbooks that fulfill the same purpose.

The issue with ERP systems is that they were originally designed to be the transactional backbone of the enterprise. As such, they focused heavily on the financial aspect of the business such as sales orders and a financial ledger based upon a Chart of Accounts. They will also have a level of inventory management and delivery processing to help capture transactions at their source. The issue is that companies have come to rely on ERP but it is an inward facing system with a scope constrained by the four walls of the organisation. Furthermore, it was focused on finance and procurement with little or any functions to address manufacturing.

As a result Material Requirements Planning (MRP) was added as a point solution to address the needs of manufacturers. Though MRP systems were a welcome improvement they were still plant-centric with few supply chain capabilities. In addition MRP applications were focused on supply and demand of materials with little thought to capacity planning. I.E. whether the plant had the available capacity to produce a product let alone whether it would be profitable to do so.

Finite Capacity Scheduling (FCS) was quickly introduced as a point solution to make up for the scheduling and capacity planning limitations of MRP. With FCS, the production planner could at least take into account the capacity of the plant, albeit in a plant centric manner with little to no visibility of the wider supply chain.

Nonetheless, even if FCS had limited ability to incorporate available capacity across the supply chain they could then tell the planner what the factory could produce (capable to promise) albeit they still didn't provide any insight into whether the order would be profitable (profitable to promise).

Advanced Planning and Scheduling (APS) took off in the 1990s as computing power made more complex calculations possible.

Now, there was an application that enabled production planners to addressed both material requirements and capacity to optimize their production schedule. However, APS also came with limitations in that it was designed with push-based manufacturing in mind and focused on optimizing individual aspects within the four walls of the manufacturing plant and not across the entire supply chain.

As a result even up to just a few years ago there was no facility that enabled synchronized single- or multi-enterprise supply chain planning, scheduling, and execution. Nonetheless, in the last decade computing power and storage has grown exponentially and prices have plummeted. Furthermore, the introduction of SaaS (software-as-a-service) delivery models and secure cloud resources have redefined the scope of applications and put advanced applications and functionality within reach of even modest budgets.

Chapter 10 - Supply Chain Planning

The over-riding purpose of the majority of organisations is to maximize profits. As the supply chain has evolved from a tedious administrative task into a core business process with a crucial financial and operational perspective, it now plays a vital role in achieving profitability. But supply chains are complex and making profits is difficult so what are some of the key aspects of how supply chain contributes to the goals of the company?

A major contribution that Supply Chain Management brings to the business in operations and execution is its underpinning foundation of planning. Supply chains require planning in order to control production levels and balance supply and demand. Therefore it is hugely important that there is a guiding demand planning function spanning and influencing production, operations and execution. Indeed in the case of the demand plan its purpose is ensuring operations are timely, efficient, and cost effective.

The aim of planning is to ensure product availability to maximize revenues in the marketplace. But product availability must be balanced with demand as too much will increase unsold inventory, which ties up capital and incurs carrying costs. The costs of carrying or holding unsold inventory is often underestimated because many of the costs are intangible, such as the cost of finance, obsolescence, storage and transportation per unit amongst others. Indeed, in general the carrying cost of holding inventory can be estimated to be around 3 per cent of the cost. However, not holding inventory can incur far higher costs due to stock outs, which mean lost sales, lower gross profit, loss of market position, perhaps even the loss of customers and the damaged reputation of the brand. Therefore effective production in terms of profitability requires trade-offs between production and inventory. Thus an effective demand plan will require as prerequisite market demand information.

The forecasts of the potential future demand based upon historical data of products sold. This makes demand planning the most misunderstood- and most frustrating-of any supply chain planning application.

Demand Forecasting

Demand forecasting is a technique used in supply chain management to predict midterm future demand of around 10-18 months. It is the science of forecasting customer demand with the purpose of optimizing the supply so that it balances the predicted market demand. Demand forecasting involves techniques including both informal methods, such as market survey in test markets, and quantitative methods, such as the use of historical sales data and statistical techniques based on current or historical data from test markets. Demand forecasting in the context of the supply chain is used in production planning, inventory management, capacity planning, or in making informed decisions based on trend analysis or advanced data algorithms.

Regardless of the context demand forecasting is predicting future demand for a product or a service on the basis of the past events and the prevailing trends in the present. Demand forecasting and estimation gives businesses valuable information about the markets in which they operate and the markets they plan to pursue. Forecasting and estimation are interchangeable terms that basically mean predicting what will happen in the future.

Managers and business owners use multiple techniques for demand forecasting and estimation. Some are using historical data to determine the potential demand for a product or service. For example, businesses with high-end merchandise might examine census information to determine the average income of an area. Larger businesses might use test markets to estimate demand. Test markets are micro-markets in small cities that are similar in their demographics to larger markets. If the demand for a product is high in the test market, managers assume that the product will perform well in the larger market.

Demand forecasting is critical for inventory management as downstream businesses buy and manufacturers produce inventory based upon demand forecasts. For example, retail stores will increase their stock of certain items during holiday seasons because they know from past data that demand increases. If businesses do not use accurate demand forecasting and estimation methods, they risk purchasing too much or too little inventory. Similarly if manufacturers produce too many products and exceed demand then working capital is tied up in slow turning inventory. Hence forecasting is essential in all areas of the supply chain in minimizing inventory. On the one hand Manufacturers with too much inventory risk losing some of it to obsolescence but on the other downstream businesses with too little inventory will upset customers and miss sales and revenue opportunities.

Demand forecasting and estimation methods produce forecasts that are nearly always wrong but they are typically reasonably accurate and acceptable for short-term business planning. However, estimating demand for the long-term is difficult because there are many unforeseen factors that influence demand over time. For example, demand estimation might not take into account an economic recession or other financial problems. Natural disasters might also affect the demand for a business's product. To forecast long-term demand, managers must account for the social, political and economic history of their markets.

Forecasting Techniques

Such is the importance of demand forecasting that many supply chain planners are investigating new methods for improving the accuracy of their forecasts. Typically there are two avenues to explore qualitative or quantities techniques. The former includes method such as Prediction Markets, Game Theory and the Delphi techniques. The latter set of techniques has a whole portfolio of statistical and probability methods, such as, extrapolation, discrete event simulation and reference class forecasting.

However, recently there has been an upsurge in the use of Artificial Intelligence and in Machine Learning in particular. Machine learning is a branch of computer science where algorithms learn from data. The variety of different algorithms provides a range of options for solving problems, and each algorithm will have different requirements and tradeoffs in terms of data input requirements, speed of performance, and accuracy of results.

Companies are investigating Machine Learning techniques such as Data Mining; Decision Trees; Bayesian Network; Associated Rules based forecasting and even Deep Neural Networks. Machine Learning borrows from the field of statistics but it provides a variety of new approaches for modelling problems. However, in demand forecasting, the fundamental problem is how to predict new outcomes based on previously known results – historical sales. In machine learning terms, this is called supervised learning – the modeller is teaching the algorithm how to perform by giving it examples of what good performance looks like. The problem is though is that machine learning is highly data specific so what works for one business may not word for another and this is problematic for companies that expect a plug and play solution – as there isn't one.

Traditional forecasting approaches predict prospective sales from previous sales; seasonality and recurring tendencies are all in the mix, but other factors such as the product's features, attributes, value, rebates, and sales channel info are often overlooked. This is true during predicting iterations but albeit they may be accounted for in other later alterations or processes, such as S&OP.

In contrast to traditional forecasting, Machine Learning Forecasting facilitates the usage of vastly more data and a multitude of factors to be considered when processing. Hence, when making demand forecasts, traditional forecasting techniques evaluate the demand history for a particular product, group, channel, and demographic buying area. However, with Machine Learning Forecasting it has the capability to consider the history of all products, the effects of advertising and social media campaigns, together with local, regional sales advancements, and estimated demand. Furthermore, it can make these forecasts for each product in the corporate portfolio, and at every stage of their respective life-cycle making use of contemporary forecasting techniques. Some supply chain, and logistics experts believe the subsequent generation of Machine Learning Forecasting will also consist of cognitive computing where past estimates are continually re-evaluated and inevitably corrected for glitches in the prediction result.

Demand Planning

Demand planning is a business process methodology used to forecast, plan for and manage the demand for products and services. The inputs to Demand Planning are the Demand Forecasts and the output is a Demand Plan. Estimating future demand is one of the most fundamentally valuable, but difficult, challenges in supply chain optimization. Forecast accuracy is absolutely essential to planning business effectively as demand forecasting provides the crucial forward-looking picture that shapes how a company will deploy its supply chain to take maximum advantage of customer opportunity.

Demand planning" therefore is the effort to increase traditional forecast accuracy and customer service levels through better perceiving, predicting, and shaping the full range of factors that determine how well the product portfolio satisfies market needs – this is similar to what Machine Learning strives to achieve in Machine Learning Forecasting by considering a multitude of product, market, business and environmental factors as part of the mix.

A general consensus is that no other aspect of supply chain optimization is more frustrating or has greater impact on business profitability than demand planning. This is because producing an accurate forecast is nigh on impossible as it requires capturing demand close to its source and accurately predicting future demand with enough lead time and confidence to ensure maximum sales and operations performance at minimum cost. Therefore, an effective demand plan will have an acceptable error margin and will establish the fundamental parameters for balancing the higher production levels and lower inventory cost. These are the "pillars" on which competitive advantage and profitability are built.

In addition, what makes demand planning so complex is it goes beyond the basics of what type of demand are we currently experiencing for a single or even a category of products.

Instead, because for any given product in the company's portfolio, there may be independent demand, dependent demand, and service parts demand, the demand plan must consider the entire portfolio. Thus, the planning methodology requires forecasting the future independent and possibly service parts demand but all other types of demand still have to be planned for in the supply chain processes to ensure availability when required.

The problem though is that it is not just a 'one number' forecast because there is demand volatility and variation across the product portfolio. This of course means that basically every forecast will be wrong to a greater or lesser extent but generally, the more precise, timely and specific the information the planners have about the demand for the products, the more accurate the forecasts are likely to be.

For example, the bullwhip effect creates demand volatility that becomes amplified as it travels upstream along the supply chain. This is an unwelcome phenomenon compounded by independent demand forecasting within each operational silo in addition to the use of fixed stock replenishment levels. It is also an opportunity for collaboration and more timely, accurate and specific information sharing, which are the two ways to ensure a better understanding of what the real demand is. Further, demand planning is defined as "using forecasts and experience to estimate demand for various items at various points in the supply chain." But the complexity arises when the organisations product portfolio grows for the number of stakeholders also rises. The planners will require information from subject matter experts as well as sales and marketing intelligence for each individual product. To compound the problem, forecasts are also heavily dependent on the product type and where it is in the product lifecycle.

By processing and analysing vast amounts of historical data can help in identifying trends, seasonality variations, correlations and this helps build a demand pattern. But planners still need to understand the variability/volatility seen in the marketplace, and predict potential variations from the norm over a long time horizon.

Traditional forecasts then are built on information that the planners already have, historical and current and the quality and veracity of the information will ultimately determine an appropriate forecast. The forecast itself though cannot be set in stone and must be tracked for effectiveness. If the forecast's accuracy is in question then planners must take the appropriate action to apply corrective action by applying their current knowledge to produce and updated the forecast to bring it into line and this subsequently corrects the overarching demand plan. For example, should a company consistently over forecasts across several large product lines, this will lead to increased inventories and lower inventory turns. This is a case where the continuous monitoring and correction of the demand planning process can be of valuable assistance. The planning process will aid in identifying the discrepancy and provide an appropriate forecast that will target actual inventory goals and thus deliver an understanding as to the how and why. Hence providing an appropriate forecast is achieved by applying current knowledge and then re-evaluation and adaptation through ongoing analysis. The subsequent tracking of the forecast will keep it within the margins of accuracy deemed acceptable.

Now that we know about demand forecasting and the goals of the Demand Planning process in turning several individual forecasts into a single consensus forecast we can move on to consider how this is achieved. Indeed there are 8 steps that we should consider when creating a Demand Planning process:

1) Plan the Demand Process

   The first step is to define the "planning objects" – what are the key data elements and fields that need to be considered and/or forecast – as well as the time horizons that will be part of the forecasting process. It is also necessary to determine the various hierarchies that will be used (e.g., what individual SKUs belong to which product families or categories, etc.). This data is normally loaded into a data warehouse or more focused "data mart," and then transferred into the working model of the demand process itself.

2) Cleanse the Data

The next stage is to check the data being loaded into the system for completeness. For example, what is listed as "demand" may not be true demand, because the data in the system is taken from sales, and does not consider the impact of stock-outs or the data may not have captured the promotions that were used during a given period

3) Generate a Statistical Forecast: The Demand Planning software looks at the historical data

4) Prepare Forecasts for New Product Introductions: Plans and relationships for new products must be created in the system (e.g. what customers will buy them),

5) Override the Statistical Forecast with Judgmental Input: Insight from a variety of sources might be used to change the statistical forecast generated by the Demand Planning system. For example, strong input from sales channels, or changes in market conditions, might affect the statistical view.

6) Adjust the Baseline Forecast for Promotions: In many industries, especially consumer goods, promotions have a huge impact on sales volumes, and obviously need to be factored in for changes to the baseline forecast.

7) Manage VMI and CPFR Processes: If the company is involved with Vendor Managed Inventory (VMI) programs, or is using Collaborative Planning, Forecasting and Replenishment (CPFR) with its customers, there is another step to communicate that

data to both customers and internal managers responsible for these programs.

8) Generate a "One Number" Forecast: Increasingly, the first seven steps are used to provide data for a Sales and Operations Planning process (S&OP) that brings together executives from key areas of the company to ultimately agree on a single forecast number and an execution plan that will drive both the demand and supply sides of the enterprise.

One Number Forecast

In an organisation without S&OP functions planners will often work in isolation of each other, each effectively working to their own set of forecast numbers, often developed without any attempt at alignment across the supply chain.

The use of the phrase 'one number' is used as a tool to break down walls between functional areas, by conveying the image of the entire organisation working towards one goal. This single, consensus forecast is how forecasting was and still is done traditionally. However, with the advent of new digital techniques the 'One Number' approach is seen as contributing to more rather than less forecast error.

However, what we can see from the demand planning process and is of interest from the business perspective is that Demand Planning and Forecasting may well be independent processes but in order to provide real value they must be integrated into other aspects of operations. One of these processes is S&OP (Sales and Operations Planning.)

Sales & Operations Planning – S&OP

The definition of S&OP is "a process focused on ensuring a continuous alignment between demand, inventory, supply and manufacturing plans on the one hand, and between these tactical plans and the business plan on the other hand, in order to maximize operational performance."

Sales and operations planning (S&OP) is considered to be an integrated business management process. It has relevance to supply chain management as it achieves focus, alignment and synchronization among all functions of the organization. This provides the executive/leadership team with visibility in to the way that functional areas such as finance, production and sales interact.

Therefore, S&OP process includes an updated forecast of demand that leads to a sales plan, production plan, inventory plan, customer lead time (backlog) plan, new product development plan, strategic initiative plan and a resulting financial plan. The planning frequency and planning time horizon depends on the specifics of the industry but is typically mid-range at 10-18 months.

However, when short product life cycles and high demand volatility are the scenario then this will require a tighter S&OP with a shorter time-horizon than would be the case for steadily consumed products. A properly implemented S&OP process enables effective supply chain management as it routinely reviews customer demand and supply resources.

This continuous assessment forces "re-plans" where the process focuses on incremental corrective adjustments from the previously agreed sales and operations plan. The S&OP does not just take a forward looking windscreen view it also helps the management team to look back in the rear view and understand how the company achieved its current level of performance.

Nonetheless, its primary focus is on future actions and looking forward to anticipate results.The importance of S&OP cannot be over-estimated as it is critical to a business's success. The S&OP process is a strategic priority within any organization as this process provides a decision-making tool to be used in managing sales and operations.

Moreover, S&OP is important to more than just these functional areas of a business for S&OP is also an important aspect of integrating Management, Manufacturing, Finance, Sales and Marketing, R&D, and Logistics.

The reason for S&OP's relevance to so many functional areas is that it incorporates many other processes. For example, Demand Planning and Forecasting, although critical in their own right are just two important aspects of the S&OP. If we consider the Figure 10.1 we can see all the aspects that make up the S&OP process.

From the diagram we can see that S&OP integrates sales, demand, and supply planning and management. With the final output plan that links to Finance and Implementation.

The individual functions have the following detail:

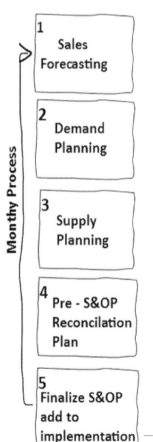

1. Sales Forecast – Gathers data on historical sales, analyses data and looks for trends and report a forecast

2. Demand Planning – examines and validates forecasts. Understands the source of forecast and variability, adjusts policies for inventory and supply.

3. Supply Planning – Asses the ability to meet demand requirements by reviewing available capacity and scheduling of resources

4. Pre-S&OP reconciliation of plans – match the supply and demand plans against the financial considerations and any constraints

5. Finalize the S&OP Plan – link it to Implementation.

Within S&OP the functions governing supply and demand are crucial aspects that make up the overall plan for managing sales and operations. The need to balance demand with supply capabilities is fundamental in SCM. For example, manufacturing needs to know what product to make, the quantities to make, and the timing of when it is needed. The supply side provides finite capacity, as well as other constraints and capabilities to accommodate those requirements. Understanding those constraints and capabilities is essential in shaping demand to more closely match the finite supply.

Therefore as demand planning is a subset of S&OP there is a common and important aspect:

"A key concept of S&OP from a demand perspective is that we are building a plan or commitment of what the sales & marketing organization will deliver."

Thus, we need to understand and create an overall plan to cater for the constraints and capabilities, and potential issues such as finite capacity and relay the subsequent information to all other parties within the supply chain.

S&OP like demand planning takes a mid-range view (18-24 months), which provides a company with increased visibility of what is expected to happen. By incorporating demand planning and forecasting into the S&OP this provides better inputs into the S&OP process and a better understanding of the demand for products, as well as improved forecasting as we look forward along the extended time horizon.

Chapter 11 - On-Demand Supply Chains

The shift from the traditional production centric supply chain to a more customer aware purpose and philosophy was the first incremental step towards a market aware supply chain. The shift in focus to the end customer brought about a profound realization that a change in forecasting demand was essential. Hence a new demand centric supply chain model surfaced. In this model it was conceived that the actual demands from the market for products should be the major influence for production. The concept was to move away from a push scenario whereby production would "push" products and services towards the market in the hope they would buy them to a new idea that the market would dictate the levels of production i.e. the market would 'pull' production. These strategies were known as "Make to Stock" and "Make to Order" respectively. This strategic model became known as an on-demand supply chain.

The Demand Driven Supply Chain

Pull manufacturing is an increasingly familiar concept to manufacturers, although it's sometimes known by other names such as flow or Demand-Driven Manufacturing. In short, pull manufacturing targets production on actual orders rather than forecasts i.e. it is demand driven. As a result pull manufacturers can improve a number of vital performance metrics such as lead times, cycle times and inventory levels. These same concepts can be applied to the supply chain for similar results.

A common supply chain problem, the bullwhip effect is an example of how creating a demand-driven supply chain can help by using pull rather than push manufacturing. The bullwhip effect describes an artificial and unwelcome amplification in demand that creates increasing levels of variability the further you move upstream in the supply chain. The result is too much on hand inventory (with its added costs and potential waste). A key contributing factor to bullwhip disruptions revolves around min/max replenishment policies and min/multi lot sizing rules that trigger replenishment at static order points rather than when actual consumption occurs.

The traditional approach to reducing the effects of the Bullwhip is by working to decrease replenishment lead times, lot sizes, and the gap between min and max when using a min/max order policy. The alternative if available is to transition to a pull-based e-Kanban system that signals replenishment based on actual demand. This allows planners to reduce lot sizes and stock buffers as much as possible – and hence mitigate the consequences of the bullwhip effect.

In a mature supply chain there is the capability to get close to the demand signal and synchronize all downstream activities and resources. Synchronizing the actual demand-signal with downstream activities works to drive end-to-end flow across the supply chain and throughout production. This not only improves other vital performance metrics such as throughput and on-time delivery but also increases capacity.

The Demand-Driven Supply Chain like demand-driven manufacturing no longer is driven by forecasts but synchronizes everything to actual orders at every level in the supply chain.

This does not mean that Predictive Analytics and Forecasting are now redundant as they still have a role in long-term decision making. Nonetheless, having everything else synchronized to customer orders, eliminates the bullwhip effect across the entire supply chain.

The Multi-Enterprise Supply Chain

In a Demand-Driven Manufacturing Supply Chain environment, everyone has access to the same real-time information, or a single version of the truth. This is the definition of visibility in the context of a demand-driven supply chains.

Visibility: The Key Ingredient of the Demand-Driven Supply Chain

Today, most attempts at real-time supply chain planning, scheduling, and execution understandably involve a single enterprise. As anything more would have required supply chain partners to create, at a minimum, a standardized format for data exchange if not actually to standardize on the system interfaces. In reality, these facilities are not available outside of the enterprise which strictly limits the visibility horizon.

In sharp contrast, in the Demand-Driven Supply Chain scenario, the production planner has insight into capacity throughout the supply chain. To do this, they do not need to exchange standard format information or access or integration to the supplier's system. They simply need access to the shared supply chain data warehouse that enables them to view and aggregate data from multiple sources. The shared data warehouse solution provides a way to consolidate the diverse companies' data streams into a single system that all partners contribute and all use as the accepted single source of truth. This enables planners in any participating partner to screen view supply chain data in real-time, such as current capacity, aggregated replenishment, as well as current inventory, and order status information.

Supply chain partners would not need to change their processes or the format of the data submitted the data warehouse handles the transform and load process. Finally, the data warehouse or as it is known in the industry an SOR, provides the supply chain partners with a platform for even tighter collaboration.

The Demand-Driven Supply Network

Around the start of the new millennia there was a shift from traditional supply driven supply chain to on-demand supply chains. This shift to a pull-manufacturing approach was the precursor of the Demand-Driven Supply Network (DDSN), which is a system of coordinated technologies and processes that senses and reacts to real-time demand signals across a supply network of customers, suppliers, and employees to improve operational efficiency, streamline and launch new products and maximize profits.

The DDSN is a supply chain driven by the 'voice of the customer', which simply means it is tuned to consumer market demand. A company pursuing this on-demand strategy will have all the inherent supply chain processes, such as infrastructure, finance, material and information flows focused to serve the downstream source of demand. This is in contrast to the legacy supply-driven chain with its focus upon the upstream supply constraints of factories and distribution systems. I.E. the DDNS is a pull rather that a push manufacturing model.

With DDSN, companies switch from a "push" method of moving product, based on incomplete or inaccurate demand information generate by forecasts, to a "pull" method, based on demand planning and dynamic response to fluctuations in consumer demand. Thus the DDSN is geared to better perfect order fulfilment, higher product customization, lower inventory and waste, and shorter cash-to-cash cycle times. However, it still requires demand forecast precision and accuracy and that, as we will see later, is no trivial task.

Ultimately, DDSN delivers results to those companies that can predict demand accurately. For example according to AMR research, companies that achieve 30 percent improvement in demand forecasting average 15 percent lower inventories,

17 percent increase in perfect order fulfilment, 35 percent reduction in cash-to-cash cycle times and an improvement factor of up to 10 times in preventing stock outs.

DDSN therefore delivers companies cost, time, and efficiency benefits and competitive advantages that boost profits through the increased levels of supply chain service such as in on-time delivery, order accuracy, and in-stock performance. This corresponds with lower levels of supply chain cost derived through efficiency gains in inventory, transportation, and materials handling.

DDSN also provides faster response to business opportunities such as the introduction of innovation with a better perfect product launch performance, which means that more new business opportunities are seized as customer or market demand evolves.

At its heart is responding to demand and Information Technology was the driving factor behind the increasing use of DDSN. Supply chain visibility, execution, and event management tools enabled companies to see across the extended chain, to track and coordinate material, and to keep it moving.

A real world implementation of a DDSN was undertaken by IBM back in early 2000. The decision to re-imagine IBM's massive supply chain was not taken lightly as IBM's supply chain incorporate at the time around 33,000 suppliers and 45,000 business partners worldwide.

Indeed at the time – early to mid 2000 - IBM offered circa 78,000 products with millions of possible configurations; ordered more than two billion component parts a year and operated 13 manufacturing locations in nine countries and, in North America alone, handled almost two million orders a year, maintaining 6.5 million client records, with an average of 350,000 updates every day.

For IBM, the on-demand supply chain was implemented as an integrated end-to-end DDSN across the company's entire operations. The on-demand supply chain could sense and respond with flexibility and speed to any fluctuation in consumer demand, market opportunity, or change in the marketplace—no matter how frequent or sudden.

One major difference was that in traditional push supply chains, companies will own and operate warehouses, a fleet of trucks, and have fixed capacity contracts with airlines. What is more these are fixed capacities that companies carry on the books as infrastructure. However in IBM's on-demand supply chain they did not have to own these assets. Instead, they worked with partners to supply them the capacity needed within a reasonable cycle time.

IBM Latin America, for example, doesn't own any warehouses. But the company still has to move product manufactured in China, via various carriers or freight forwarders, to a warehouse before delivering it to customers in that market. However, the benefits of on-demand is realised as IBM do not need to lease a finite amount of space and pay to store the goods in that warehouse, instead IBM pays a service provider for the number of times that an IBM product goes into and out of that warehouse I.E. they pay based on transactions – on-demand.

To operate its on-demand supply chain effectively, IBM required close coordination with suppliers and service providers. Their suppliers needed to see what they were doing—how much and how fast they were selling—so that they could calibrate their own operations on factors such as product inventories, transportation capacity or warehouse space. Hence in a DDSN the third-party partners need to have the same information across the network so that every participant in the supply chain is working on the same data and so are on the same page.

To build the foundation for its on-demand business, IBM did away with entrenched functional silos, bringing procurement, manufacturing, logistics, and client support teams together from almost every division of the company. It created a single business unit, the Integrated Supply Chain (ISC) division, with 19,000 employees spread out across 56 countries worldwide.

The concept was to reimagine IBM's supply chain stretching from "opportunity to cash" i.e. from raw materials at one end of the manufacturing operation, to the ongoing post-sales client support at the other end.

However, removing functional silos brings its own issues such as how to measure individual functional performance. In a supply-driven chain companies can measure execution solely within the appropriate functional silo. However, those traditional methods of measuring supply chain performance through purely functional metrics are no longer sufficient. Indeed to capture critical quantitative data across and between functions, as well as qualitative insight into the supplier and partner relationships requires a different approach.

Consequently, IBM adapted its measurement system to support the dynamics of an end-to-end operation. They retained the legacy individual metrics but they added new ones that tied the entire supply chain together with common goals and objectives.

These metrics include the following:

- Customer satisfaction. How well does the company perform end-to-end in meeting the expectations of its clients?

- Cost reduction. How much has the cost of doing business decreased through end-to-end operational integration, innovation, and increased efficiency?

- Cash generation. How well has the company created positive cash flow through end-to-end operational integration, innovation, and increased efficiency?

- Demand/supply synchronization. How well has the company created true visibility of supply and demand to effectively and efficiently manage the needs of clients and the business?

- Cycle time. Has the company been efficient and effective in driving competitive end-to-end process excellence and responsiveness?

- Salesforce productivity. By minimizing the time the salesforce spends on DDSN activity and by playing a more active/direct role in the support of its clients, how much time can the company give back to the sales force to spend with clients?

At the end of 2003, IBM had the lowest inventory levels in 20 years, and in the first quarter of 2004, it decreased inventory by another $168 million. The supply chain accounted for 50 percent of IBM's cost and expense. As part of the $40 billion IBM spent on the supply chain in 2003, they cut their costs by $7 billion. And that was just in inventory reduction. Not having that inventory frees up tremendous cash resources by improving accounts receivables and reducing inventory excess in the supply chain, which generated $700 million of additional cash. By moving to an on-demand business model IBM's supply chain reduced costs by $5.6 billion and generated more than $4 billion in cash.

IBM ultimately found that the product of all this activity in building an on-demand business was reduced cost of doing business. This was achieved by working with the business units and partners to identify any opportunity for savings. It's also about making the cost structure more variable by establishing a strong network of alliances and partnerships.

3 Steps to Building a Strong Foundation

Most manufacturers before they are in a position to contemplate planning a Demand-Driven Supply Chain to collaborate more effectively with supply chain partners will need to get their own house in order. Here are the three steps to building a strong foundation.

1) Digitize. The Demand-Driven Supply Chain runs on data—the right data in the hands of the right people at the right time. However organisations of all sizes tend to have a variety of systems that produce data from a diversity of points-of-view. For example, it's common for an organization to have two or three ERP systems in addition to several MRP point solutions for functions like maintenance, time management and so on.

There will also be CRM and Financial systems so it will be imperative to implement a platform for translation, collating and manipulating of data records from multiple sources to provide a 'single source of truth'.

2) Synchronize. A prerequisite is to synchronize everything in the organisation including processes, materials, machines, methods and data all at the customer order level. After all if the focal company is not synchronized to actual customer orders they can't expect partners to synchronize to their actual customer orders never mind the entire supply chain.

Synchronization alone can have a dramatic impact on performance.

For example, a KSB Company, GIW Materials, which is a manufacturer of heavy-duty centrifugal slurry pumps, wished to lower cycle time and improve the on-time performance. The crux of the solution was to optimize production flow and control cycle time by synchronizing everything to orders: pattern information, flasks, combination equipment, engineering revisions, and capacity. The impact was so noticeable to their customers that GIW doubled their revenue in two and a half years.

3) Visualize. Ultimately after the data has been digitized and production flow synchronized to customer orders, the aim is to put the right data into the hands of the right people. This means getting the data to your own employees in a format and standard that is understandable and convenient to use. This will eventually be extended to the supply chain partners.

There are many data visualization and communication software available that enables a manufacturer to provide visibility to both their suppliers and consumers.

Demand Management

Accurate forecasting and management underpins the success of a demand-driven supply network, but demand management is much more than just forecasting. Traditionally, forecasting involves looking at historical demand data to predict future demand. Demand management goes beyond that and supersedes it with a more fluid, ongoing view of determining demand that involves all demand-chain components. The current trend is towards real-time synchronization of the supply chain to the demand signals.

However, the trend over the last few decades has been for companies to move towards outsourcing their product distribution. This strategy is driven by a desire to keep sales overhead in check without sacrificing revenue. But, this recent trend has resulted in a dilemma for while companies can produce products more efficiently, they have little knowledge regarding what to produce, for whom and when. They now have better visibility into their supply chains but they lack the same kind of visibility into their often-fragmented demand chain.

New technologies do provide the capability to extend supply chain visibility and trusted alliances between participants support a truly dynamic collaborative internal environment. But companies are looking beyond the supply chain, such as sales and marketing, and to include end-customers in the demand management cycle.

Taking a collaborative approach to forecasting can enhance accuracy since all factors affecting the demand forecast can be viewed by all stakeholders, including customers. Thus, companies can bridge the gap between their supply and demand chains by doing the following:

1. Reshaping relationships with channel partners to ensure accurate demand forecasts. Manufacturers should implement a closed-loop process for gathering, analyzing and filtering demand forecasts from channel partners. The demand management system should be tightly integrated with management systems for entitlement and other benefit programs for channel partners. This would help to ensure that just-in-time manufacturing is performed for the right products, in the right quantity, at the right time.

2. Basing inventory allocations on real-time demand forecasts that incorporate information from all channels—both direct and indirect. This increases revenues by targeting allocations to those channels and locations that are the most effective sellers.

3. Ensuring that your own house is in order.

Having an accurate forecast of consumer demand is irrelevant if there are no supply chain capabilities that can leverage it. Thus, in order to achieve the benefits of a DDSN, companies need to get their internal demand management processes in order. For example, with the introduction of agile development the promotions group in a company responsible for creating and driving demand for a product or service is often disconnected from the operational group that produces the product. Ensuring that the different groups that have a stake in the demand process are connected is critical.

4. Ensure the presence of accurate intelligence along with collaboration and automation. New technologies enable real time flow of information within and across enterprises and the supply chain and this provides for better and faster forecasts. An enhanced ability to respond rapidly to customer requirements is all well and good but they could be exchanging bad information. Despite sophisticated statistical methods, it is impossible to eliminate market uncertainty from the forecasting process.

5. Choosing demand management applications that address the unique challenges faced by the specific business. Many existing applications fail to fulfill the specific demand management needs of companies. Some enterprise applications support fixed pricing strategies but their solutions cannot easily maintain dynamic forms or manage prices across channels. Other applications are limited in terms of other demand management challenges. Certain customer relationship management systems, such as those from Siebel Systems or KANA, assist sales personnel but lack insight into price sensitivity and supply chain capacity and are therefore of little value in terms of deciding which orders to take and which offers to recommend.

Companies successfully deploying DDSN embrace three continuous demand management strategies. These incorporate feedback loops from downstream processes and market conditions for example they link forecasts based on causal variables, like economic indicators, to current sales activity and field-level orders to create market sensitive demand forecasts that set corresponding capacity and inventory recommendations. In addition, by linking capacity to changes in demand companies can optimize service levels, minimize safety stocks and inventory levels. Importantly, as demand management is also about realizing profitable business results - not just balancing supply and demand - companies can adjust price and contract terms in line with changing market conditions.

Implementing a Demand-Driven Supply Network

Theoretically this new concept was exciting and from a business perspective it created a lot of excitement. However from a technological perspective it would mean redesigning not just the enterprise processes but the entire supply chain because a prerequisite is integration, and process visibility via transparency throughout every participating company.

Replacing their ERP and those other inward looking legacy systems was not an appealing prospect for most manufacturers who probably remembered only to clearly the pain in implementing them in the first place. Even today, many companies with legacy supply chains are still caught in this dilemma of how to reimagine not just their technology but their supply chains.

According to a study conducted by Panorama Consulting and Mint Jutras, 21% of companies defined their ERP implementations as failures. The average cost of ownership also rose from $2.8M in 2014 to $4.5M in 2016, making these projects rather costly failures at that.

Therefore, instead of the "rip and replace" approach, Gartner Research recommends adopting a phased approach that involves three levels of common supply chain planning functionality.

1. System of Record (SOR) – Establishing a SOR creates one single version of the truth – a shared Data Warehouse - that everyone across the supply chain can count on. The SOR sits on top of the current ERP to manage the manufacturing operations and supply chain. It leverages the ERP for its intended purpose, transactional data. This is the baseline level that Gartner targets in their stage three maturity, and this technology must be functioning well and stable before the organization can get to the next level.

2. Systems of Differentiation (SOD) – Once you've established a SOR across manufacturing operations and the supply chain, you can move on to a SOD. These are any other applications that help you provide differentiating value through supply chain improvements. An SOD is just another value application available through the Data Warehouse hosting the SOR.

   In Gartner's maturity model, SODs are required to move from stage three to stage four.

   Using their SOD, an aerospace and defence contractor client was able to increase their rate by 400% while reducing downtime and scrap to near zero levels. The efficiencies gained allowed them to win new contracts and, subsequently, grow market share.

3. Systems of Innovation (SOI) – SOIs move into the realm of prescriptive analytics. At this point, you're not just responding to events (however effectively); you are actually using data and analytics to predict what will happen. The Big Data and IIoT initiatives being bantered about in boardrooms everywhere often belong in this category. An SOI could well be an AI or Machine Learning engine accessed via the Data warehouse.

To clarify the Gartner Research approach the SOR, SODs, and SOIs aren't necessarily different systems. Often, it's more a matter of taking a phased approach to implementing a solution – and layering on value- by subsequently reviewing and iteratively adding functionality.

Furthermore, this approach can and should be applied to more than just supply chain planning. Supply chain plans, along with production scheduling and execution, need to be able to adapt almost instantaneously to demand changes and events in order to provide the level of responsiveness needed in the modern supply chain. One of the ways to ensure this responsiveness is to adopt a pull versus push approach to supply chain demand planning.

Advanced Demand Planning

Despite there being almost two decades of process and technology refinement, excellence in demand management still eludes supply chain teams.

In fact, Demand Planning has proven to be the most elusive function in the supply chain planning application in bridging the gap between performance and satisfaction. While companies are mostly satisfied with warehouse and transportation management, they are the least satisfied with demand planning. Nonetheless, Demand Planning despite its poor return in investments to date is the application deemed to have the greatest potential and that drives planned future spending.

Demand planning can be loosely defined as the use of analytics—optimization, text mining, and collaborative workflow—to use market signals (channel sales, customer orders, customer shipments, or market indicators) to predict future demand patterns. And here lies the first anomaly, as what is the time scale of this future period for demand planning as this will vary by industry and individual company. Nonetheless, it can be considered to be a tactical planning process – though as companies mature, the use of the forecast becomes more comprehensive and is integrated into a number of processes culminating in a more holistic end-to-end process termed Demand Management – but it typically spans a period of 10 months to 18 months.

Interestingly, in the early attempts at demand planning in the 1980s the pioneering companies steadily reduced costs, improved inventories, and sped time to market. But, the actual balance sheet results did not reflect any such improvement. Indeed very few supply chain teams have ever successfully posted improvements to their balance sheets through demand planning initiatives. This is due to the supply chain being a complex system and few companies understand that in a complex system there are finite trade-offs between areas. In the supply chain, these trade-offs include growth, costs, cycles, and complexity.

As a consequence, companies cannot make improvements in operating margin without affecting other areas, such as inventory, unless they improve the supply chain potential. Fortunately, the most effective way to increasing the potential of the supply chain is to improve the demand signal.

The challenge of improving supply chain operating margin is not a trivial task in terms of importance or scope. Supply chains have become more complex as companies span global geographies; products proliferate and demand planning grows in importance. Thus, it is not just how the data is collected and used in the demand processes that make it work, organisational, supply chain and process design, all play a major role in defining the differences between leaders and laggards.

An important factor in making demand planning accurate is in the design of reporting relationships. For instance, generally companies with reporting relationships answering to the sales organization or to marketing tend to post the worst results in demand planning as these organizations are plagued by high, and often unrecognized and uncontrolled, bias. On the other hand, the bias inherent in relationships that answer to neutral or cross-functional groups tends to not be as high as it is with sales\marketing reporting. Hence the best results, tend to be demonstrated when neutral cross-functional teams take responsibility for global planning and global/regional governance of demand forecasts, insights and data integrity for the organization.

Moreover, the compound the issue, the ability to use optimization techniques to improve forecast accuracy over large numbers of products is also getting more complex. As a result, demand volatility is increasing, demand data is becoming more complex, and the usual responses are less effective. Another issue is that demand management systems were designed to respond to demand signals periodically i.e. weekly or monthly and they processed historical data generated from completed orders or shipments.

However this data is often stale in today's fast moving world. For example, order data, by its nature, carries latency. This latency can be substantial - from one week to five weeks - based on the time that it takes to roll up minimal order quantities across the channel. Therefore, a traditional supply chain is designed to respond reactively to market changes, but this is neither proactive or flexible nor adaptable and hence the companies are not well-suited for periods of high demand spikes in volatility.

Creating an adaptable system that can predict and respond to demand volatility will require a different approach –it will need to sense changes in the demand. The system therefore will need to be designed from the outside-in as it will be tuned to sense external demand signals.

Demand Management principles require the system to be capable of sensing fluctuations in channel demand signals and to drive an intelligent response by applying advanced analytics to actively shape demand. Nonetheless, there are a number of issues with this approach for a legacy supply chain. The capability to sense demand has a prerequisite of visibility into the customer markets or at least the distribution/retail chain. Furthermore to shape demand requires tight coupling with sales and marketing, but most planners will be to far upstream to have visibility into either of these silos. Additionally, in order to find a cordial agreement with for instance sales and marketing on how to shape demand, the demand planning team will still have to identify and reduce confirmation bias and forecast errors, respectively.

There is typically a three step process for introducing modern demand sensing techniques, which is as follows:

Step 1: Revamp old techniques

The first step is to realise that the legacy techniques will have to change and the most important of these include the following:

Forget One-number forecasting: The common industry consensus today is that the one-number technique actually increases—not decreases—forecast error as it is too simplistic. A modern demand plan is a hierarchical construct built around products, time, geographies, channels, and attributes. It is a complex set of role-based, time-phased features and data, so in this context, demand planning requires the use of an advanced forecasting technology. An effective demand plan will have many numbers that are tied together in an effective data model for role-based planning and what-if analysis. This can only be found in the more advanced forecasting systems.

Dump Consensus Planning: over the last decade, Consensus Planning has come to the fore in many organizations. The concept is that each functional area within the company will add insight by participation in the process and make the demand plan better. The issue is that most companies fail to recognise that each group has its own natural bias and error typically driven by incentives. Hence, due to imbalances in the incentive structure, consensus forecasting will distort the forecast and add error.

Forecasting Supply vs. Channel Demand: The traditional technique of push manufacturing is to forecast what manufacturing should make as opposed to forecasting what is actually selling in the channel. Contrary to this approach is pull manufacturing, where actual demand –orders - dictates the amount of products made, and this is not a trivial difference. Manufacturing to order introduces potential latency and risk but accurately tracking the channel demand will reduce the production latency and risk. Moreover, ML Demand Forecasting also allows for augmenting the forecast with other demand insight, attributes and features to improve the forecast quality.

Avoid CPFR: Collaborative Planning Forecasting and Replenishment, or CPFR, was designed to align the manufacturer's demand plan to the retailer's and to reduce the bullwhip effect.

The assumption was that the retailer's forecast would provide better insights and more accurate demand forecasts for stock replenishments. The problem was that most retailers produced poor forecasts, and the CPFR process never accounted for the inherent bias and error in their forecasts. The technique did work well when retail aligned POS and Inventory data with suppliers as was the case with Walmart, but that is the exception rather than the rule.

Step 2: Buy the Right Demand Planning System

Of all of the supply chain planning applications, success in demand planning remains the most elusive. And despite the evolution of technology capabilities for in-memory processing, cloud-based analytics, and deeper optimization, very little has changed in most demand planning applications. Therefore, in order to match features with operational requirements it is critical to map the demand streams and the demand drivers. Features like causality, seasonality, tops-down and bottoms-up forecasting, and forecast of value-add analysis are essential to the selection of the technology.

Step 3: Tuning the System

To implement the demand management system correctly requires a lot of historical data and data cleansing and preparation for tuning the system. So for example, a current year forecast exercise will require processing two to three years of shipment, order, and channel data. This historic data will be used to fuel the forecast algorithm to produce a result that can be compared to a known outcome of the current year. For example, to tune a model to forecast actual output in 2017 then use historical 2014, 2015, and 2016 data. Keep fine tuning the model to close the gap between the predicted and actual results for 2017.

To further fine-tune the models, divide the data into demand streams and work each demand flow for refinement. For example, divide data into data sets for slow-moving seasonal items, fast-moving volume products, new product launches, and special promotions.

 The best demand planning implementations take time and the foundation of this effort is a carefully crafted pilot to identify the right market drivers and test the optimization engines. Many companies make the mistake of rushing the demand planning implementation and not aligning the technologies to get the best results.

Importantly, Demand Planning is not a technology implementation project that can be installed and then forgotten. The most successful companies achieve superior results through diligent tuning of their systems. Cleansing and preparation of data, the alignment of planning master data, and the fine-tuning of demand optimization engines are all critical functions of Demand Planning that cannot be overlooked. Hence, most successful organisations have a dedicated demand planning team made up of senior staff and subject matter experts that know the business.

A mindset change: Often companies fail simply because they have failed before by using the older techniques and procedures. But progress can be made by carefully articulating the path forward to drive continuous and incremental improvement in the demand planning process and by working with supply chain teams on how to better use the forecast.

Bias and error reduction: The use of forecast value-add (FVA) analysis helps companies add discipline to the demand management process to drive continuous improvement. By using FVA, the steps to develop the demand plan are carefully examined to understand if the process is improving or degrading the forecast.

Process redesign: To reduce demand volatility, design the process outside-in from the demand channel back-inside. Focus on sensing what is being sold in the channel and identifying suitable signals.

After mapping the market signals, build a demand model to forecast the channel. Focus on modeling the "ship-to" locations. Reduce demand latency to sense market variations by building strong demand translation capabilities.

Demand sensing is a radical departure from the traditional planning process of forecasting what a company needs to manufacture, but the world of demand planning has changed. The business requirements have escalated and globalisation and product customisation means it matters more than ever. Therefore it is essential to move forward by implementing continuous improvement programs to drive discipline, and re-introduce demand planning technologies to sense and shape demand.

The evolution to demand management excellence needs to be built on a program of continuous improvement focused on forecast-value added techniques to reduce bias and error. However, accurate demand planning isn't a case of picking the right technology or algorithm, it requires work.

Demand Sensing & Shaping

Amazon is pioneering many innovations for faster delivery and the potential use of drones is one that captured the imagination but another is equally astonishing. For it seems that Amazon is going to ship a customer's order before they have even completed the order process – that is right they will pre-empt the customer's order and ship their products based upon Amazon's own forecast. Indeed, it appears many other ecommerce companies are looking into doing the same thing i.e. using predictive analytics to forecast orders so that the company can ship the products to the nearest warehouse to the potential customer to expedite delivery.

Presumptuous as this might sound, it is actually an application of a technology known as *demand sensing* and it appears to be producing results albeit in specialist fields such as e-commerce. Demand sensing uses new digital technologies to analyze data sources — made up of a company's own historical data and other real-time signals — in order to determine where and when potential consumers will buy a product, and in what quantity, well before they actually do. This allows companies to get their products closer to the consumer and dramatically reduce delivery time.

Demand sensing is being portrayed as a technology that creates a better understanding of customer behaviour but it is underpinned by advanced machine learning algorithms. These advanced algorithms use categorisation, regression, probability, clustering and applied statistics to forecast customer behaviour based on their past purchasing history and importantly on the behaviour of those similar to them. Machine Learning is driving demand sensing technology and it has huge implications for the supply chain and ecommerce in particular with its high return rates. The costly return of ordered goods in e-commerce is a real problem with rates as high in some product categories as 50%. Market Intelligence has determined that a primary reason for returning goods is down to slow delivery and when one considers the changing consumer expectations for services such as instant order fulfilment that is perhaps not surprising. E-commerce retailers then are attempting to pre-empt orders to expedite the shipping times in the hope of reducing post-sale returns through demand sensing techniques.

The technology behind demand sensing relies upon the availability of new data sources impacting demand, increased computing power, and artificial intelligence – Machine Learning. Companies are using their access to new data and building up demand sensing capabilities to better understand consumer behaviour and orchestrate their supply chains accordingly.

E-commerce retailers have become early adopters as a company's sales volumes and the closer the company is to its consumers, the greater the relevance for demand sensing. However, demand sensing is becoming increasingly important for other sectors as well, such as automotive, industrial products, energy, and pharmaceuticals.

One example of a company that is a pioneer in demand sensing techniques is Procter & Gamble, which has used demand sensing for several years. It draws on internal information such as its point-of-sale (PoS) data, channel inventory, warehouse stock movements, data from distributors, and forecasts from retailers, as well as social media and app data, all of which is fed daily into an analytics engine to distil demand forecasts.

Similarly the German retailer Otto has implemented a demand sensing system that creates daily forecasts for every item based on hundreds of variables. The priority has been to distil massive data volumes into real-time decision making, and the system has resulted in a 40 percent increase in replenishment forecast accuracy per item and a 20 percent reduction in overstock.

An important aspect of demand sensing is that it is democratic as almost every company has access to the data it needs to make better forecasts as well as access to the computing power and machine-learning algorithms necessary to leverage that data, which is available as-a-service in the cloud – sometimes for free.

But the importance is that all that is required to make demand sensing work is the willingness to spend some time looking for and experimenting with potential demand signals. Then putting them into an analytics engine, and integrating the results into supply chain planning and execution.

The Demand Sensing Model

There are basically four sources of data in the model shown in figure 11.1

They are (1) structured internal data, such as direct sales transaction data from a PoS system, e-commerce sales, and consumer service; (2) unstructured internal data, for example, from marketing campaigns, in-store devices, and mobile apps; (3) structured external data, which includes macroeconomic indicators, weather patterns, geo-political trends and demographic data ; and (4) unstructured external data, such as information from connected devices, digital personal assistants, and social media.

Demand sensing captures a full range of data

Source: Strategy&

The heart of the technology is based upon advanced algorithms, which will be used to perform for example in the category of social media, message "sentiment" analysis, in an attempt to ascertain whether posts are positive, negative, or neutral — and in turn help to provide insights about consumer perception. Mobile apps are another source of market intelligence as data on product configuration apps provides insights as to which features are important in a car or mobile phone. Web forums, are another productive source of insights, especially competitor sites as any of their innovations or features that are trending – such as a new colour - will show up there first. Indeed, when sensing demand it is vital to configure some signals tuned to competitor product portfolio and their differentiator attributes and features.

However, the data in this grid does not apply uniformly in the same way in every sector. Indeed, an important aspect of the model is that it consumes structured and unstructured data from internal and external sources. This promiscuous behaviour enables the algorithms to find insights in numbers, text, photographs, videos, voice and from all sorts of data types and sources. Nonetheless, data must have context so there will certainly be regional differentiation and relevance in the stage in the product life cycle or the consumer type. Therefore a particular demand signals influence might change over time or apply differently in different contexts. For instance, a global retailer sees decreased foot traffic in its Northern European shopping Malls when the weather is hot and sunny, because people like to be outside on such rare days. In contrast in regions like South East Asia, foot traffic increases in sunny weather because stores and malls are usually air conditioned.

This underlines the fact that without understanding context or metadata – information about the data, it is not possible to properly apply the data. But once you understand the context, that knowledge serves as a key foundation for other activities as well, such as the design and implementation of new data-driven business models.

Importantly, demand sensing should be an integral part of a real-time, connected supply chain but is not a replacement for demand planning. Instead Demand Sensing should be considered an enhancement that makes supply chains far more responsive to volatility spikes in demand. Specifically, demand sensing enables automation of short-term planning by delivering the greatest value especially if its results are used in processes such as pre-emptive shipping, smart replenishment, dynamic warehousing, and real-time production scheduling.

The benefits for implementing demand sensing techniques are vast as cross-industry experience shows that it can reduce replenishment forecast error by 35 to 45 percent, leading to improved replenishment forecast accuracy and optimized safety stock levels. This has three impacts: First, fewer stock-outs lead to 5 to 10 percent higher sales. Second, because less manual planning leads to 5 to 10 percent lower operational costs. And third, on tied-up capital, having considerably lower safety stock inventory reduces overall throughput time by 10 to 20 percent.

Implementing a demand sensing pilot

The first step when implementing a pilot for demand sensing for any organization is to understand what data is available and which data points have a potential effect on consumer demand. Once a business has identified these relevant demand signals, it is recommended that starting small and adopting an agile approach is optimal. One popular approach is to start by identifying one area of the business in which there is plentiful, rich and relevant data going back at least two years. Then test the demand sensing process to discover which data sources – demand signals - have the most predictive and highest value and over which time horizon, then remove those, which have little impact.

Use the first year's data to build the analytical engine by applying demand sensing algorithms and machine learning techniques –these are freely available on both AWS and the Azure cloud. Then use the second year's data as a control to fine-tune the analytical engine by comparing it with the control data for what actually happened that year. The more data the analytical engine consumes, the more accurate the predictions become. If you have more years and more sources of data available, even better, because it will allow you to feed the engine more precisely.

By starting with a small area of the business this will achieve quick results, reduce the complexity of regional and market-specific differences, and leverage lessons from the first iterations. It is also essential to remain flexible and apply an iterative process given that this is a fast-changing environment. Some data might become less useful over time but on the other hand other new and as yet unknown sources of data will emerge that can be added as necessary.

Nevertheless, some obstacles prevent many companies from moving to demand sensing technology. One is that company leaders are simply unaware of the value that it can provide and other are downright sceptical of its worth. For instance there is much debate whether demand sensing is actually a valid technique or just a short term forecast for replenishment and optimising safe stock inventory. In scenarios where the inputs from the demand signals are limited to PoS or scanner inputs from the retail or distribution chain then that is possibly true. But when the inputs from demand sensors range in scope to cover all types of data from rich and diverse sources, such as; social media sentiment, product sensors, consumer wearables, mobile apps, personal assistants, competitor forums, and most importantly from the consumer themselves that is a much weaker argument.

Another obstacle is that many companies are wary of trusting automated systems. After all, if that is the case then the company is probably still operating a non-digital, legacy and silo-based supply chain that necessitates a manual approach to demand planning. For such companies the concept of demand sensing and demand shaping in particular are simply nonsense, as their structure does not entertain the possibility due to the inaccessible silos of functional responsibility and visibility. Also, if the planners are upstream in operations planning, then most likely they are too far removed from all the downstream marketing activities to understand those key sales/marketing programming tactics that influence demand. If the planners don't have the capability to model those demand drivers that influence demand, then it's impossible to shape future demand using what-if analysis. For example, if a planner has little or no real-time visibility into the retail chain or social media for demand sensing. Then they certainly will not be in any position or even be allowed to apply demand shaping due to that being the responsibility of sales and marketing. Its only when the entire chain is transparent, digitised and under holistic management control will autonomous demand sensing and shaping become feasible.

For such businesses that harbour doubts and remain sceptical it is worth, at the very least, running a prototype using demand inputs from those data-sets described above to see what value it can provide. Planners should deploy a pilot to test the utility and value of demand sensing as this can be easily implemented with no disruption to current operations even in a legacy supply chain. Indeed, launching a pilot to test the utility and value of demand sensing is a good and safe starting point. A side-by-side test is an even better way to develop trust by comparing the results of the analytics model with traditional demand forecasters' results in an area where historical data is available. Importantly, compare the system's predictions over time to see which are more accurate. Crucially, the automated demand sensing system will learn from its experience and human input via tweaking the algorithm and so become more accurate over time.

Over the next few years, it I likely that any company that wishes to maintain or expand its current market position will need to embrace a connected, real-time supply chain enabled through demand sensing. The pace of change is too fast and the number of influencing factors too great for traditional models, which rely on the statistical analysis of historical data, to remain serviceable.

Moreover, a significant benefit of demand sensing underpinned by Machine Learning is in preparing the ground for a wider digital transformation and enabling a truly connected end-to-end supply chain. Thus, demand sensing not only delivers substantial benefits in material sourcing, manufacturing, warehousing, and distribution, but also lays the foundation for new data-driven business models with increased consumer interaction. In addition, demand sensing also generates early buy-in across the organization because it proves the value of new tools and typically delivers rapid, tangible benefits. It can boost confidence in digital technology and lower the barriers of entry for further digital initiatives along the entire supply chain, such as integrated planning and execution, smart manufacturing or even a digital supply chain.

Chapter 12 - Digitizing the Supply Chain

A Digitized Global Supply Chain

The goal of any company that digitalizes the supply chain is to achieve optimized cost, agility & speed while minimizing risk by comprehensively addressing the global supply chain network to achieve competitive advantages. In this context, digitalization relates to optimization rather than digital transformation which we will introduce later.

The fact is that global expansion is a reality for many organizations, whether they are digitized or not, in the manufacturing and production environment. This has been deemed necessary to alleviate the pressures of shrinking product margins and increasing competition in the home markets. However, organizations are expanding their global sourcing markets as well as their sales operations. As a result organizations need to increase their visibility into the expanded supply chain and this requires a holistic digitized network and integrated approach that combines product development, sourcing optimization, supplier management, holistic risk, and quality assurance into account. By increasing their visibility into their digital supply network they can coordinate activities throughout the supply chain in order to reduce costs, lower risk, enhance agility and improve speed-to-market. Moreover, the prospective utility and value of digitization makes it enticing for companies as it makes it feasible to share knowledge, undertake collaboration, automate processes, and introduce machine learning analytics via the information flow. A digital model of the global supply chain creates the ability to swiftly and easily adapt to the real world and that produces flexibility.

Furthermore, the digitizing of global trade management (GTM) processes can be aligned to entire business policies and objectives. This is in stark contrast to the legacy methods of outsourcing processes and/or managing disparate systems. Instead, leading companies have been able to challenge the traditional mindset of GTM - being a cost of doing business - as they have leveraged opportunities from the logistics, legislation and financial functions.

Drivers for Digital Transformation

Collaboration

The value of Collaboration has been amply covered but it is still challenging when more than one communication method, protocol or non-standard interface is used to connect supply chain partners. Disparate systems can usually cause operational inefficiencies, bottlenecks and introduce labour intensive activities. However, by democratizing the flow of information across the end-to-end network it will improve real-time cooperation via visibility and then accelerate time-to-market by, amongst other factors:

• Sharing product specifications with suppliers
• Communicating cross-border transaction data with freight forwarders and customs brokers
• Receiving trade agreement details about a product
• Making electronic bookings with international carriers
• Filing information with customs electronically

Automation

The automation of recurrent processes particularly in sourcing, procurement, logistics, cross-border trade and compliance can improve operating efficiencies and financial performance.

With the information flow digitized, it can also handle exceptions and be processed quicker and be executed in a timely manner with added transparency.

Where digitization can make the difference is with:

- Purchase Order alerts that are in danger of delays or other issues
- Determination of carrier rate, schedule, and booking
- Alert supply chain resources when an interesting event has occurred
- Determination of import regulations of a product to a given country
- Determination of trade agreement eligibility

Analytics

The collecting and storing of data from business processes and systems only provides added value if it is analyzed in such a manner to produce information that has inherent value. Therefore the aim is to digitize information in such a way as to analyze performance metrics for insight. Of course this requires that you have a clear idea of the specific insights you are looking for. For example, by prioritizing data analytical efforts for the intent of identifying opportunities and risk that furthers the improvements in supply chain efficiency.

To achieve these goals data scientist must aim to identify typical KPIs for supply chain performance that relate to the following metrics:

- Measure the multi-tier supplier relationships upstream and downstream
- Historical analysis of carrier/3PL performance
- Historical analysis of supply chain performance relative to specific products, countries, ports and more
- Identification of opportunities for duty savings through trade agreements or other government programs
- Identify potential supply chain risk factors

Flexibility

When the supply chain is digitized, the result is flexibility.

This is because information is centralized – within a shared SOR, a Data Warehouse - and hence malleable, which allows it to be adapted to meet the changing business or regulatory environment. A digital supply chain provides the versatility needed to compete successfully in volatile and fast paced customer markets. Some examples of this flexibility are:

- Ability to swiftly swap in/out suppliers when needed
- Quickly handle corporate acquisitions and divestitures
- Easily change logistics partners as desired
- Efficiently access new sourcing and sales markets
- Accommodate non-standard requirements

Value Factor

Agility

Agility is another value factor to be gained by digitizing the supply chain. Previously it has been demonstrated that the advantage of a centralized perspective of the end-to-end supply chain will create a 'control-tower' like visibility. This high level point-of-view provides a planner with the real-time awareness and insight they need to take effective action. The benefits that agility provides include:

- Quick access to information for effective and faster decision-making
- Straight-through processing to increase speed, while reducing cost and errors
- Predictability by visibility: supply chain alerts, lower dependence on safety stock and in-transit inventory
- Real-time communication with globally-dispersed suppliers and internal teams

Moreover, dynamic change is to be expected in this rapidly evolving environment, which makes supply chain agility more important than ever. By having the capabilities to quickly recognise and manage change is the key to sustained success in the face of increased volatility.

Risk Reduction

Digitizing the supply chain can mitigate several risk areas such as in ethical sourcing. As collaboration with supply chain partners can result in cooperation in audit, inspection, and testing. Hence, companies can create transparency and when information is clear the reliance on disparate manual systems that are prone to delays and failures are eliminated. Moreover, the supplier and product risk areas become visible and auditable, which ensures corporate, ethical, and quality standards are maintained.

Logistics: Real-time, in-transit shipment monitoring provides for immediate visibility and notification of supply chain events. Event notification systems can automatically initiate actions to keep goods moving in the case of planned and unplanned events. Increased real-time visibility and real-time alerts help reduce the risk of supply chain bottlenecks and create a more agile global supply chain.

Import/Export: The manual processing of import/export transactions is not only very labour intensive, but increases compliance risk. By implementing process automation for import and export transactions this provides assurance that every cross border move has been validated against its respective country regulations. In addition, Automation Trade Risk provides global standardization, which reduces regulatory compliance risk and creates efficiency.

The benefits include preserving your brand's reputation, improving product quality, and protecting the flow of goods.

The Intangible Benefits of a Digital Supply Chain

A 2015 study by investment bank Ocean Tomo revealed a surprising transformation in the way that we value companies. In their estimation in January 2015, the tangible assets –buildings, equipment, and so on - comprised 16% of the combined value of the Standard & Poor's 500 Index, meaning that today, 84% of the S&P's value is made up of intangible assets—things like a company's intellectual property, its customer relationships or its proprietary way of doing things.

What we can deduce from these figures is that today's companies are largely the sum of their intellectual properties, ideas and solutions. And those solutions increasingly come from their expertise with digital technology, which enables them to perform better and faster than their competitors. Digital technology permeates along every link of the value chain delivering more transparency, efficiencies, agility and connectivity and many other intangible benefits that companies can leverage to build faster, responsive and more precise supply chains.

Now, if we consider that the goals of business are to make a profit then how is this accomplished from a supply chain perspective. To understand this we need to look at some of the key aspects of how supply chain contributes to the goals of the company.

Every company faces a different set of needs and challenges when contemplating supply chain considerations. However one commonality is that when defining a digital supply chain strategy, it is critical to work from the outside-in i.e. start with the customer and work backwards to the suppliers. This is the case even for a business-to-business (B2B) company, where the key opportunity might be to try and mimic the flexibility and agility that drives the efficient business-to-consumer (B2C) customer experience that retailers like Amazon have excelled at.

After all, if Domino's Pizza customers can track an order from oven to doorstep, why shouldn't business customers expect the same level of transparency and convenience from their suppliers?

One thing the digital revolution has indisputably brought is enhanced Customer expectations and increased competitor performance in the global markets. Applying digital solutions across the supply chain is a powerful way for businesses to deliver quick results along both these dimensions – customer experience, and competitive advantage. But not all businesses are technically savvy or inclined to follow every digital fad or trend going. Where most companies fall behind and become laggards is they make the assumption that a digital supply chain will need vast investment as they will need to reinvent themselves entirely while investing heavily in digital technology, knowledge and expertise. Often however, digitizing the supply chain is simpler and less expensive than it might seem. The critical set of tests for any digital investment is will it serve the organisational an business strategy, add value for existing customers and/or open the door to new ones?

Company executives, especially in sales, marketing and operations planning recognize that their customers are demanding the flexibility and agility realised via a digital supply chain. Furthermore, they know that the market for digital technology will only get busier, more complex and confusing as a plethora of digital products emerge looking for a problem to solve. They also realise that their companies' can no longer procrastinate as the competition will likely not, and seize the initiative to digitize to gain the advantage.

Chapter 13 - Digital Supply Networks (DNS)

Up until this point in the book we have contemplated supply chains as being linear constructs with a discrete progression through the stages of *design, plan, source, make,* and *deliver.* Contemporary digital designs however are becoming considerably more complex with many nested and interdependent relationships. As a result, the traditional lean supply chain is transforming from a staid but comprehensible sequence of predetermined activities and events into a dynamic, interconnected networked system.

The result is a dynamic digital supply network that can autonomously discover and incorporate ecosystem partners and evolve to a more optimal state over time. This shift from linear, sequential supply chain operations to an interconnected, open system of supply operations are the foundation for how companies compete in today's digital markets.

The Digital Supply Network

This interconnected, open web of relationships is referred to as a *digital supply network* (DSN). DSN's collect and integrate information from many different sources and locations to drive the physical act of production and distribution. The result is the creation of a virtual world, an extension of the concept of the virtual enterprise, as it mirrors and informs the physical world.

DSN's leverages techniques that merge the next generation of disruptive technologies and digital thinking with legacy data analytics. The confluence creates the merger of sensor-based data sets including unstructured data and the aggregation of process control (Operational Technology) along with informational data to construct the physical environment.

The Internet of Things and all it delivers - automation, big data analytics, and revolutionary new business models, amongst others enables process planners to integrate a clear view of the supply network.

For example, there are many organizations already on the path to creating Digital Supply Networks. Their strategies are aimed at shifting focus away from managing and optimizing discrete functions, such as procurement and manufacturing. Instead, the modern analytical approach is to use the DSNs to focus holistically and autonomously on how the supply chain can achieve the business objectives. While also informing and influencing the corporate, business and portfolio strategies.

Indeed, DSNs have enabled supply chains to become an integral part of strategic planning and decision making. To this end, organizations will often take the approach of developing and leveraging multiple DSN's in order to complement different strategic targets tuned to effectively deliver the ultimate business objectives.

Handling Big Data

The digitization of information and the application of advanced innovative technologies to supply chain planning will present the opportunity to drive business value throughout the supply chain. Hence, it is no coincidence that data scientists handling big data and supply chain professionals in DSNs manage similar data criteria. Notably the "five Vs" (volatility, volume, velocity, veracity and visibility) as they attempted to optimize results across a series of objectives that include total cost, service, quality, and support for innovation developed with new digital technologies. These traditional priorities are not likely to change, but going forward, supply chain decision makers should be able to achieve higher levels of performance with supply chain capabilities that build on advanced data analytics and disruptive technologies.

Additionally, supply chain professionals can help create new sources of revenue by providing new and faster insights into production processes, product design and access to markets, while also supporting the innovation behind development of smart products. Such opportunities add creation of revenue to the existing list of objectives for the next generation digital supply chain.

Moreover, digital disruption can change supply chains in any industry. Importantly, as the shift how is toward direct competition between supply chains it will be imperative that business leaders avoid becoming a victim of disruption. Hence the need for executives to understand these seismic shifts in the environment brought about through digitisation and adapt accordingly. In order to do so they must be aware of the presence and potential of next generation supply chains and DSNs in particular by familiarizing themselves with:

- Tracing the technological evolutions that enable the rise of the DSN
- Defining what the DSN is, along with its role within a wider business strategy
- Examining the trade-offs inherent in a typical supply chain, and identifying the characteristics that can mitigate those trade-offs
- Considering how to build a DSN

The Rise of Industry 4.0 and the DSN

Industrial digital technologies have radically changed the competitive ecosystem in recent years by effectively levelling the playing field. Driven largely by three key developments: Cloud computing, which has delivered lower computing costs, cheaper storage, and ubiquitous access; SaaS (Software as a Service), which has brought enterprise software to small medium business (SMB), and the IoT, which has accelerated M2M (Machine-2-Machine) communication and full scale process automation via the collection, processing and analysis of real-time sensor generated data streams. The availability of these cost effective technologies has brought about a sharp operational and capital cost decline which has made it possible for companies of all sizes to invest less and still reap the benefits of digital technologies on a wider scale.

The confluence of these technologies has brought about significantly lower costs, and improved power and technical capabilities. This has led to the combination of information technology (IT) and operations technology (OT).

The merger of OT & IT has brought the real world –sensors, machines and processes - into convergence with the virtual world of advance data analytics and process control. These improved processing capabilities now augment human thinking to analyse more data in real time, which has brought about the era of Industry 4.0.

Industry 4.0, or the fourth industrial revolution, is characterized by the merging of the real (OT) and the digital (IT) worlds through new IoT technologies. Diversity in the industrial enterprise has come about because OT and IT have taken distinct evolutionary paths determined by their unique characteristics. OT is machine and process orientated and this requires real-time speeds ≈50ms response, deterministic-performance, continuous-operation, high-availability, reliability and robustness. IT on the other hand is practically the reverse as it is orientated towards human on-demand style of interaction where real-time is around sub-second at best. These represent profound operational differences in the approach to troubleshooting, maintenance and support. Despite these significant operational hurdles, industrial organisations still strive to achieve convergence because the promise holds such rich possibilities.

The promise of OT-IT convergence is that data gleaned from machine sensors will provide insight into the internal status of the machine's health or the processes under its control. If that data could be understood and ingested by the IT systems then the possibilities for utilizing big data, Artificial Intelligence and machine learning algorithms to gain valuable process insights are limitless.

At the IT layer OT-IT convergence produces linked data, which creates value when it is shared throughout the value chain. The linked data can be synthesized by all manner of intermediate stages in the value chain and business units such as finance, Human Resources, R&D, stock control, sales, production management, logistics and quality control amongst others.

Post convergence, OT and IT systems are connected for automatic and seamless data exchange between them, without any human intervention, with this, OT systems can monitor the process plant and send large volumes of data about the condition and status of critical assets back to the IT systems seamlessly in real time. The IT systems can synthesize or analyse the big data received from OT generate critical insights/visibility into the behaviour of plant assets and automate quick actions to optimize plant performance. However, the benefits of OT-IT convergence do not stop there. There is also the potential for sharing linked data with subsidiaries, partners, vendors and even customers, which provides both visibility and allows elements and systems to 'talk' to one another throughout the supply chain. This can result in tremendous opportunities for innovation and in reducing costs while improving the operation efficiency of the entire supply chain. Indeed sharing this linked data with the supply chain creates the ability for automation of Supply Chain Management and 'just in time' ordering of components or raw materials from vendors.

Merging the disciplines can be seen as coupling real-time access of new and existing data sources with powerful analytics tools, such as visualization, scenario analysis, digital twins and predictive learning algorithms. The merged environment enables companies to harvest vast data sets from physical assets and facilities in real time, and then perform advanced analytics to generate new insights, and enhance executive decision making.

These tactical decisions can then be actualized by the capabilities of advanced physical technologies, such as robotics, drones, additive manufacturing, and autonomous vehicles. This digital revolution is transforming the way products are designed, created, and delivered to customers. Although Industry 4.0 may have its provenance in manufacturing and the Smart Factory it also has a tremendous impact on the modern supply chain.

Impacts of technology disruption: Smart DSN

The function of any supply chain centres on the movement of materials, sub-assemblies, capital, and other assets from place to place, as well as the production of finished goods. At their core, however, supply chains consist of many transactions: the exchange of time, money, information, or physical materials for some other unit of value. Nonetheless, there have been dramatic technological and digital developments, brought about through greater computing power and lower overall costs, which have impacted the traditional supply chain in several key ways, including a reduction in transaction costs and increase in innovation related to the production process itself.

Reducing transaction costs

The increase in the efficiency of new technologies has been amply demonstrated by reduced transaction and operations costs both internally and externally. It is no longer prohibitively expensive or time consuming to gain insight into operational processes, or analyse customer or supplier demand patterns. The advent of Industry 4.0 meant that acquiring inexpensive and easily manipulated information enabled supply chains to incorporate and utilize increased intelligence. For while the physical linear flow of designing, creating, and moving physical goods remains unchanged, the data collected from sensors and processes now flow through and around the participating nodes of the supply chain, dynamically and potentially in real time. These new interconnections between nodes controlling processes and sub-processes have transformed supply chains into efficient and predictive networks. This creates an opportunity to dynamically control networked supply chains, for when the costs of transactions fall - whether that be counted in time, money or capacity - the ability and capacity to transact with more and different partners increases. Hence, companies can simply dynamically connect and negotiate with other suitable partners when and where necessary in order to deliver substantially increased value.

Innovation in production

The process of production is evolving as a result of technological improvements in both the process by which materials can be manipulated for example 3D printing and the way that embedded computing power (RFID tags) can assist in production. Similarly, the improvement in the flexibility and capability of capital equipment has led to less of it being required to commence production. When less capital is required, the minimum efficient scale comes down as well, and production is allowed to scatter, locating closer to demand.

Demand can also be fulfilled in a more flexible manner as productions lines can be reimagined and reassembled into other configurations quickly and easily. By having flexible production lines allows for small production lots, potentially lots size of 1 and hence greater product variety.

Furthermore, lower capital costs and investment allows for smaller and more nimble players to enter the market. These lowering of the barriers to entry or the shifts in the level of the playing field are being addressed both strategically and operationally by focal supply-chain companies. They are re-evaluating the criteria for supplier relationships as they look to optimise their supply chains to deliver maximum value.

The shift from linear to dynamic networks

Ultimately, the concept of a linear supply chain masks a complex web of interrelationships and interdependencies which surfaces in the form of a Smart DSN. This heralds the shift from a traditional, linear supply chain consisting of staid nodes towards a set of dynamic networks established on a real-time, needs and opportunistic basis. Furthermore, these opportunities allows for increased product or service differentiation for the organization that is able to harness and leverage them. For increased digital and technological capabilities reduce the latency between decision making and material action as this relates to information flow.

In traditional supply chains, the information flow travels bi-directionally but linearly, with each step dependent on the one before it. Therefore, inefficiencies in one step will affect the following step resulting in a wave of inefficiencies and delays rippling along the supply chain. Stakeholders often have little, if any, visibility into other processes, which limits their ability to react or adjust their activities. To operators, this manifests itself as the dreaded "bullwhip" effect, in which inventory fluctuations due to changes in customer demand are amplified beyond recognition on the journey towards the products source, and thus are less predictable and more volatile further upstream in the supply chain.

Nonetheless, as each supply node becomes more capable and connected the supply chain changes into a dynamic, integrated supply network. Indeed DSNs mitigate the effects of the Bullwhip characteristic by sampling real-time demand data close to the customer source. This feedback mechanism realises better informed decisions, provides greater transparency, and enables enhanced collaboration across the entire supply network.

Figure 13.1 represents the shift from the traditional supply chain to a single SDSN. It is important to note, however, that organizations will likely have more than one SDSN.

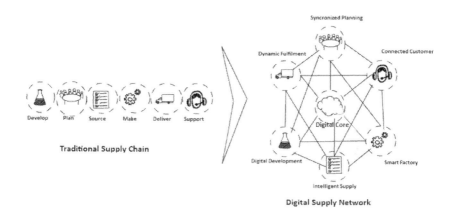

In figure 13.1, the interconnected lattice of the new SDSN model is clearly visible, with digital at the core. The network mesh topology provides the potential for connectivity between each node to every other point of the network. This mesh arrangement of potential interactions allows for greater connectivity among areas that previously did not exist. In this model, communications, for example, are multidirectional rather than bi-directional, creating connectivity to areas and functions where traditionally there had been none. For example, drone video monitoring of remote work sites enables site optimization analytics and rapid issue detection, while on-site 3D printers rapidly make component or spare parts replacements to reduce downtime. While there are a multitude of underlying Internet of Things technologies that would enable this process and others like it the key to achieving these improvements is in identifying how to communicate, aggregate, analyse, and act upon the available information. Hence, the transition from linear to network often requires the organization to embrace a new way of linking physical and digital assets – the merging of OT & IT.

Traditionally, linear supply chains (IT) rely on batch processing to produce periodic relayed forecasts and plans, which become increasingly outdated—and thus inaccurate—with each stage. By connecting all the stages in a mesh network via advanced technologies, a smart DSN can minimize the latency, risk, and waste found in linear supply chains. Furthermore, as companies have adopted Smart DSNs and leveraged their potential for connecting the real (OT) and the digital (IT) worlds, the traditional barriers of time and space have shrunk. Companies are able to achieve new levels of performance, improve operational efficiency and effectiveness, and create new revenue opportunities.

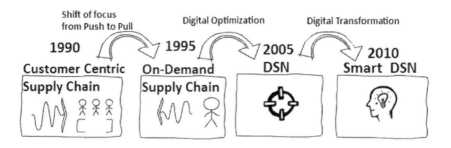

Figure 11.3 – Supply Chain Evolution

As noted previously, organizations will likely have more than one DSN as organizations have the opportunity to match DSNs to commercial or to business strategy and update them for the needs of the specific part of the business they will support. Hence, there are often concurrent DSNs which may form parts of others—for example, they may share distribution facilities—but other pieces of the DSN would be diverse and specialized, as in the case of manufacturing a different product or subassembly. However, it is this capability of mixing and matching that allows DSNs to better serve the strategic needs of the organization by being more nimble, flexible, and customizable.

Thinking strategically about Smart DSNs: What makes them different?

What separates smart DSNs from traditional, linear supply chains or indeed the standard digital supply network is the fact that the smart DSNs are intelligent, always-on, dynamic, integrated networks characterized by a multi-dimensional continuous flow of information that facilitates autonomy, generates value, improves workflow and analytics, and importantly they generate valuable insights. With the ability to ascertain information in real time, many of the latency challenges inherent in linear supply chains can be avoided.

For example, Tesco, a multinational grocery retailer, strives to maximize revenue and minimize waste by reducing the latency in the supply chain. An example of how Tesco achieves this by feeding external weather data into its predictive analytics tool to forecast demand of weather-dependent products (such as sun lotion and ice cream). The predictive analysis output automatically adjusts inventory and supplier orders in advance on a store-by-store basis to minimize missed revenue. Such predictive analysis saved the company approximately $140 million, mainly through the reduction of wasted stock. The benefit of the predictive analysis must be considered to be only partial, for a local grocer may have had the foresight and used the weekly weather forecast to also adjust orders when warmer weather was forecast. The full benefit therefore to Tesco was only realised when the local grocer's traditional supply chain latency did not have the responsiveness to allow a fast-enough reaction time to prevent a stock-out or to minimise waste.

A standard DSN would also have sidestepped that latency by making changes based on data, communicating changes throughout the supply network in real time but where the smart DNS comes into its own is due to its inherent intelligence, which facilitates holistic and autonomous decision making.

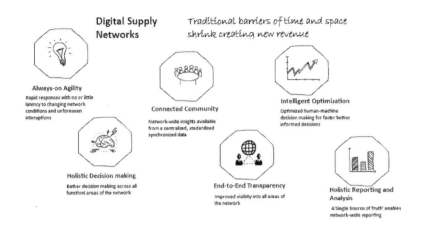

Figure 11.2 – The Smart Digital Supply Network (SDSN)

Hence we can see in Figure 11.2 the main characteristics of the smart DSN, which are: always-on agility, connected community, intelligent optimization, end-to-end transparency, and holistic decision making. Each of these characteristics plays a role in enabling more informed decisions and can help organizations address the central question in their strategic thinking: *how to win.*

Since the DSN is always on, sensors and other location-based tools can continuously transmit data to provide integrated views of multiple facets of the network with little to no latency. At the same time, each of the attributes in figure 11.2 enables the DSN to address many more issues within the supply chain beyond simply overcoming latency challenges. Indeed, the five main characteristics of the DSN describe much more than faster data transmission. They illustrate how companies can develop a far more complete picture of the total supply network—which can foster more informed strategic decisions.

Connected

Smart digital supply networks give senior management and their operations team an unprecedented level of real-time visibility into all aspects of the manufacturing and distribution process. This visibility supports more effective collaboration within an enterprise, and throughout its ecosystem of partners and suppliers.

The connected community allows multiple stakeholders—suppliers, partners, customers, products, and assets, among others—to communicate and share data and information directly, rather than through a gatekeeper. Being connected in this way allows for greater data synchronicity, ensuring that stakeholders are all working with the same data when making decisions, and allowing machines to make operating decisions.

Intelligent

Smart digital supply networks utilise innovative technologies such as analytics, smart devices, M2M, mobile and Cyber Physical Systems to deliver actionable insights in areas ranging from delivery times to quality control. Industry 4.0 and SDSN foster the automation of manual processes, which helps to reduce labour costs and improve quality control by reducing the opportunity for errors that would otherwise require rework. Intelligence in the context of Industry 4.0 and the supply chain is the capability for machines and humans to work collaboratively, sharing data that can be analysed to optimize decision making.

Visibility

End-to-end transparency of the supply chain can provide instant visibility across multiple aspects at one time, providing insights into critical areas and improving decision making. Increased visibility enables a SDSN to track material flow, synchronize schedules, balance supply and demand, and analyse transactions and financials rather than having to view discrete, siloed batches of information from multiple sources. This holistic view represents a full map of the supply network, where companies can see how all components interact and relate to each other.

This map enables holistic decision making, with regards to better supply and demand balancing. Its contribution to strategic planning is that it better informs organizations in decision making as they can clearly see and understand the trade-offs any decision may entail.

Holistic thinking enables broader strategic transformations: Instead of planning incremental improvements within the supply chain, organizations can contemplate how the supply network can be leveraged to drive growth across the business. For example, Nissan looked to improve the manufacturing capabilities of its cars by using product life cycle management (PLM) software, which enables collaboration among production teams around the globe. The PLM supports a virtual production process - incorporating the collaborative input from the designers in various diverse facilities - that enables the testing of design feasibility to be performed in real time. Nissan create a final design in 20 percent less time, what is more this process helped them design a car that was ultimately named the 2014 UK Car of the Year.

Making SDSN an integral part of business strategy

As organizations seek to determine optimal ways to achieve their business strategies, they have tactical choices to make. With any tactical choice, however, come trade-offs: these are the choices or capabilities that are often surrendered to pursue the preferred option. This is the risk of missed opportunity. For example, one tactical choice may be to focus on agility and speed to market, however that must be balanced against other options such as quality. Therefore, the choice is made in the understanding that this selection can close off other options. Manufacturers would often like to develop strong capabilities in multiple areas, as focusing on one area can often mean sacrificing capabilities in another. In this scenario, trying to do too much can serious effect the cost of the goods as each additional function is likely to have not just added value but an added cost. Perhaps worse the situation may arise where trying to do too much will result in not being able to do anything particularly well.

The strategic decision-making process can be particularly tense, as making inopportune choices can impact the outcome. The common approach has been on focusing on the maxim — where to play and how to win— as this marketing focus can help identify major marketing considerations and their relevant stakeholders. Taking a market focus on the product development can streamline the process, and enable companies to prioritize their efforts. However, not all production or marketing choices are intuitive sometimes it is quite the reverse. An example of this is the poor security associated with IoT consumer products. Manufacturers of these household IoT devices assumed that consumers would not be prepared to pay an extra 10$ on adding security to the product. They were probably right, unfortunately when these IoT devices, for example a Wi-Fi baby-cam monitor, was subsequently discovered to be so easily hacked that it could be snooped upon and accessed from the internet, the customers' were rightly furious. There have been a myriad of other IoT products that suffered similar security failings. Building security features into the product had been strategically rejected due to perceived lack of customer value and the added cost. However, had a SDSN approach been applied on a demand driven bases the designers would have been better informed as to the changing expectations of the consumer and made better informed decisions.

By answering pertinent strategic questions aligned to the market, organizations can better understand their and the consumer's needs and make choices, which are specifically geared toward the overall strategic goal and aspirations. In addition the SDSN can assist in making the correct tactical choices by answering the strategic questions as it evolves to enable more transformative decisions.

Smart DSN capabilities can impact strategy by enabling organizations to achieve multiple priorities, thereby lessening or eliminating trade-offs while still maintaining competitiveness. Since organizations can deploy multiple DSNs, several can be implemented to address each area of strategic priority identified. Depending on the specific DSN, transformations can address a variety of considerations.

It helps to examine the specific attributes of the DSN that can make this possible, and understand the importance of involving SDSN planning in all stages of the strategic development process.

Trade-offs to customization

What we have been able to determine so far is that due to the interconnected nature of the DSN, it has the inherent capability to theoretically at least see and sense what is happening at any particular node in the network at any given time. Companies can deploy many DSN to match organisational strategies and not all will be or require to be smart. In this way, a DSN can serve as an integral part of business strategy, enabling the business to negotiate and in some cases even avoid trade-offs.

When companies make choices regarding the products they wish to produce and the customers they want to serve they will typically customize their supply networks to address specific customer goals. Thus companies can take segments of the supply network and align them to what is most important to current needs, which may include getting the products sooner or at the lowest possible cost.

Further, integrated DSN also allows an organization to compete on a variety of differentiating factors, such as speed or service, and apply those criteria across all the traditional nodes of the supply chain as required. This works because, different stages of the supply chain communicate with each other via connected, Industry 4.0–driven technologies or through an existing SDSN. Hence, priorities identified during the strategic decision-making process can be distributed and addressed at every node. In effect, this gives DSNs (and supply chains) new powerful and distributed strategic decision-making abilities unlike anything they have had before.

For example, Rolls Royce changed one of its business models from designing, manufacturing and selling engines to providing an entire suite of services, which provided engine flight hours as a service. The new approach was measured by active flight hours in so much as the customer paid for the use of the engines and Rolls Royce undertook to provide the engines and all servicing and support as part of the service. The performance management of the engine was managed by adding a myriad of sensors to the aircraft engines that collected and transmitted data. In effect Rolls Royce built a Digital Twin of each engine and monitored the performance and stress of each virtual component. As a result Rolls Royce didn't have to take engines out of service and in for routine maintenance as they could accurately predict using data on the twin as to when servicing was required. By using advanced predictive analytics Rolls Royce was able to lower maintenance costs reduce inventory and engine downtime by minimising unnecessary servicing. Thus offering increased economic value to the customer and a lucrative new continuous revenue stream for Rolls Royce.

Transitioning to a Smart DSN: Shifting strategic choices

Transitioning to an always-on, holistic DSN allows companies to shift their strategies and to compete across different nodes of the supply chain simultaneously. However, once organizations have determined their strategic objectives they should then contemplate how to effectively configure their supply networks to reflect their desired objectives. One of the main benefits of a DSN is its agility, and the multitude of options companies can pursue to build one. Thus, as companies contemplate the strategy they wish to pursue, they should focus on identifying the type of supply network, which will be needed to achieve it. Only then can they determine the capabilities their supply network will require.

To configure and realize a SDSN-driven strategy requires that large companies can execute multiple different supply chain transformations. However, it is important to reiterate that many large organizations will often find the need to deploy multiple supply networks, depending on the demands of their customers and stakeholders. In these cases, organizations might require multiple transformations i.e. one for every supply chain, depending upon their requirements. For instance, a supply network that focuses on quality as its main differentiator might want to be more agile, and mitigate some of the trade-offs associated with planning and inventory inefficiencies by dynamically sourcing materials with the lowest failure rate and best post-sales support.

EasyJet, for example, employs augmented reality smart glasses to enable two-way communication between its network of remote maintenance technicians and the central engineering team. Virtual step-by-step walkthroughs in real time enable technicians to effectively perform complex maintenance tasks and reduce downtime. EasyJet also uses drones to perform efficient and immediate visual safety inspections of the exteriors of its plane bodies, reducing the time the plane is out of service, how much hangar space is required, and the amount of inspection labour.

Alternatively, a supply network focused on service might want to use DSN transformation tactics to mitigate some of the trade-offs around operations efficiency and supplier collaboration. In one such example, Spine Wave utilizes Medical Tracking Solutions' iTraycer to create a device-focused inventory management system. Sensors are placed on each piece of spinal implant equipment, enabling Spine Wave to remotely track each piece within a spinal surgery kit. Spine Wave can then immediately replenish inventory, and automate invoices at the point of use. In contrast, most hospitals today must return the surgical kit to the company, which identifies which parts must be replenished and triggers invoicing.

Implementing an SDSN: The physical-to-digital-to-physical loop

When it comes to transforming the traditional lean supply chain to a SDSN model it is common for business leaders accustomed to traditional linear data and communication, to experience the shift to working with real-time data and intelligence, fundamentally transforms the way they conduct business. For example, once an organization makes the strategic decision to adopt a SDSN and utilise the various Industry 4.0–driven technologies that empower it, it is a prerequisite to develop the processes of information creation, analysis, and action as a continuous cycle. The integration of digital information from many diverse sources and locations drives the iterative processes of manufacturing and distribution.

Hence, the real-time access to data and intelligence is fundamentally driven by the continuous and cyclical flow of information and actions between the physical and digital worlds. This cyclic flow occurs through an iterative series of three steps, collectively known as the physical-to-digital-to-physical loop:

- **Physical to digital**— At this stage the focus is on the capture of analogue raw data from the physical world and the creation of rich information derived from the physical data
- **Digital to digital**— At this stage the onus is on sharing information and surfacing insights using advanced analytics, scenario analysis, and artificial intelligence

- **Digital to physical**— To circle the process algorithms translate information into decision-making and effective data for action

  and change in the physical world

Making the DSN real: Building and powering the digital stack

In traditional supply chain design, data tends to be siloed in separate information clusters. Traditional silos of information in manufacturing will often have ERP, CRM, MPC, amongst other databases harbouring the customer engagement data, sales and service customer operations data, core operations and manufacturing data, and supply chain and partnership data but these are all kept in isolation. This isolation of core customer data leads to missed opportunities as organizations cannot see where these areas intersect or align.

An integrated DSN can enable the free flow of information across information clusters. This network, or mesh of digital interconnections, provides a single source to access near-real-time operational data from multiple sources, such as products, customers, suppliers, and after sales support. This singular digital repository includes multiple layers that synchronize and integrate operational data into a stack that supports and enables informed decision making.

Building a Smart DSN

Smart Digital Supply Networks represent the evolution of supply chains, which provides an interface between the digital and the physical worlds. Seamless access to information, computational abilities, and innovative technologies have connected and collapsed the formerly linear and siloed supply chain. As a result, there is now a confluence of real-time information and insights, which are available through shared access across the entire supply network to drive better informed and actionable decisions.

The business advantage that is derived from the integration of operational and informational data applies across all industries. In addition and accompanying these changes comes opportunity. These events surface through the ability of SDSN to align strategic decision making to the requirements of individual customers and markets. Therefore, to start building a functional SDSN, organizations can follow a common roadmap:

Think big

The first step in transforming a traditional supply chain into a SDSN should be to pause and contemplate what drives the need to change. Often the motivation and drivers are unclear and change is undertaken based on a technology fad or in some oblique way to differentiate goods or services. However, when executives clearly understand how they can optimise and why they want to differentiate, organizations can examine real-world supply chain applications that suit their business objectives.

- **Immerse in innovation.** Explore the art of the possible to push the organization to understand the application of various technologies and their potential impacts on the business.
- **Build an ecosystem.** Assess the organization's digital maturity to understand what might be feasible, and what steps should be taken to build the technological capabilities necessary for a functional SDSN.

Start small

The journey of a thousand miles begins with a single step. Consider ways to make the transition to SDSNs a manageable and realistic one.

- **Scale at the edges.** At times, it makes sense to start with smaller stakes, where strategies can be tested and refined with relatively fewer consequences. Selecting projects at the "edges" of the organization can provide greater latitude for building SDSN capabilities, and can also help individuals feel less afraid to fail, which ultimately leads to greater innovation.
- **Start with one or two transformations.** Prioritize areas that can unlock several waves of potential value, and build on those successes to continue to establish SDSNs where they make strategic sense. At the same time, it can be essential to act with growth in mind: Focus on areas that might unlock several waves of potential value, creating a ripple effect that leads to exponential growth.

Act fast

Don't wait for "perfect." Exponential growth techniques are rapidly evolving, requiring constant iterations. Establishing a competitive advantage requires the willingness to join the fray, but you should do so quickly.

- **Prove it works.** Small successes can serve as proof points, leading to a greater willingness to take a chance on more substantive investments. By starting small and moving quickly, organizations can generate success stories that prove the value and importance of the SDSN.
- **Market your successes.** Success generates success. Sharing examples of successful SDSNs can evangelize skeptics within the

organization. It can also demonstrate to customers that the organization is at the forefront of technology and is focused on their needs.

Advancing to an "always-on" SDSN is not about a single technology implementation; it is more about developing an agile supply culture and promoting a more strategic approach to meeting customers' needs. Investments in SDSN technology and tactics can become key differentiators in not only supporting but also advancing business strategy.

Chapter 14 - Industry 4.0 and the Smart Supply Chain

"A phenomenon in which emerging technologies of the physical, digital and biological worlds converge altogether to revolutionize the organization of value chains globally, disrupting business models, reshaping production, distribution and consumption" (Schwab, 2016)

The term 'Industry 4.0' was coined to mark the fourth industrial revolution, a new paradigm brought about by the introduction of the Internet of Things (IoT) into the production and manufacturing environment. The vision of Industry 4.0 places emphasizes on the concept of a global networks of machines in a smart factory, which are capable of autonomously exchanging information and controlling each other's actions in order to fulfil a common activity.

This cyber-physical system – a combination of real and virtual technologies - allows the smart factory to operate autonomously. For instance, a machine will know the manufacturing process that needs to be applied to a product and what variations may be made to that product. But if the product can be made intelligent via RFID tags for example it could uniquely identify itself, its production history and its product type during the manufacturing process. The machine would then know exactly what variations in the production process to apply to any of the product variants on the production line. Not only does this realise multi discipline and variant production lines it also removes low batch size restrictions – theoretically to a batch size of 1 - by transforming the product into an active entity whose configuration and route in the production line is unique.

The introduction of Industry 4.0 into manufacturing has many impacts on the supply chain and to realise the benefits collaboration between suppliers, manufacturers and customers is crucial. The critical task is to increase the transparency of all the steps from when the order is dispatched until the end-of-life of the product. Therefore, when we consider the impact of Industry 4.0 on the supply chain we must analyse it in its entirety.

Fundamentals of Industry 4.0

The term Industry 4.0 has its provenance in German manufacturing and has come into the technical lexicon for many industries over the last decade. Conceptually Industry 4.0 is the confluence of several key sub concepts such as automation, transparency, digitization, modularization, socialization and mobility amongst others. Hence in order to define Industry 4.0 we need first define each of these conceptual modules.

Digitalization – To have any sort of smart supply chain requires that the participating companies' internal processes, product components, communication channels and all other key aspects of the supply chain are digitized as the digitalization process itself is the most important characteristic feature and underpins all the other characterizing features of Industry 4.0.

Autonomization - A key feature of "industry 4.0" is that catalyst technologies enable machines and algorithms to make decisions and perform learning-activities autonomously i.e. without any human intervention. Further, this autonomous decision-making is built upon advanced M2M communication, embedded intelligence and machine learning algorithms. Entities that are a convergence of physical and virtual are defined as Cyber Physical Systems or CPS and these enable whole factories and manufacturing facilities to work with minimum human-machine interaction

Transparency – Today, global supply chains are characterized by highly complex structures, which is only beneficial to SCM if there is visibility between participating partners. The latest "industry 4.0" technologies being deployed in supply chains are increasing the visibility through the whole value creation process. This increase in transparency drives collaboration and efficiency, which in turn drives faster better decision-making. Transparency when applied well does not just apply to production processes but extends through to post-sales and service supply chains and even into the customer domain.

Mobility - the ubiquity of mobile devices has revolutionized communications over the last decade or so, data sharing and the generation of value is made possible globally. Indeed, the mobility of devices is changing the way customers are interacting with companies, and M2M communications have accelerated as the interaction of machines in the procurement, production and logistics processes are now prevalent throughout the smart supply chain.

Modularization - The "industry 4.0"-technologies enable the modularization of products and services through the whole value creation process, e.g. manufacturing facilities. The concept of modular production facilities can be adjusted in their quantity autonomously, which is increasing the flexibility of the production processes and realising the promise of individualization and lot size=1 in production. The importance of modularity in supply chain and manufacturing is displayed in building modular products with a fixed Bill of Materials (BoM) for the common subassembly then allowing customer individualization through a selection of semi fixed BoM optional components.

Network-collaboration – An extension of transparency and M2M communication takes the form of network collaboration. Networks must integrate and provide a platform for collaboration, through visibility and even mutual provisioning. The companies' processes will be defined and activities will be decided through the interaction of machines and processes with minimal human interaction within specific networks that span across the participating companies organizational borders.

Socializing - The visibility and the collaboration introduced by shared networks is enabling machines (not only smartphones) to start communicating and interacting with other machines and/ or humans in a socialized manner. Hence, the collaboration with machines is socialized, since humans are able to get into a conversation with the machines.

Cyber Physical Systems (CPS) – This entity is almost peculiar to Industry 4.0 and refers to any entity that is a combination of the physical and virtual worlds. For example a machine with embedded intelligence, a factory with robotic vehicles, a modern airliner or a human with a smartphone - these are all valid examples of a CPS.

Industry 4.0 – Hence we can now understand Industry 4.0 as being: *The sum of all disruptive technologies and innovations derived and implemented in a value chain to address the trends of digitalization, autonomization, transparency, mobility, modularization, network- collaboration and socializing of Cyber Physical Systems that product smart products.*

The Smart Factory

 Industry 4.0 involves a radical shift in how production shop floors currently operate. Typically Industry 4.0 can be thought of as a global transformation of the manufacturing industry by the introduction of the concepts of Industry 4.0, digitalization and the Internet.

After all these are the key elements that deliver improvements in the design and manufacturing processes as well as the optimization of operations services and manufacturing. A smart factory is referred to as the use of new innovative developments in digital technology including;

"Advanced robotics and artificial intelligence, hi-tech sensors, cloud computing, the Internet of Things, data capture and analytics, digital fabrication (including 3D printing), software-as-a-service and other new marketing models, mobile devices, platforms that use algorithms to direct motor vehicles (including navigation tools, ride-sharing apps, delivery and ride services, and autonomous vehicles), and the embedding of all these elements in an interoperable global value chain, shared by many companies from many countries".

Within the context of Industry 4.0, the smart factory of the future will enable the connection between machines and human-beings in Cyber-Physical-Systems (CPS). These new systems focus their resources on the introduction of intelligent products and industrial processes that will allow the industry to face rapid changes in consumer demand.

Industry 4.0 also promotes the use of big data, IoT and Artificial Intelligence (AI) for advanced data analysis as well as adaptive, predictive and prescriptive analytics. This revolution envisages an environment whereby smart machines can communicate with one another, not only to enable the automation of production lines but also to analyze and understand a certain level of production issues and, with minimal human involvement, to solve them. Even though this revolution is initially considered to affect mostly manufacturing industries, these innovations will affect retailers, operations companies as well as service providers.

In order to understand the utility realised by Industry 4.0 it is helpful to consider several of its key features.

• Vertical networking of smart production systems: This type of networking is based on CPSs to build reconfigurable factories that are flexible and react rapidly to changes in the customer demand.

Manufacturing processes in a smart factory enable true mass customization. It enables "not only autonomous organization of production management but also maintenance management.
Resources and products are networked, and materials and parts can be located anywhere and at any time. All processing stages in the production process are logged, with discrepancies registered automatically".

• Horizontal integration via a new generation of global value chain networks: The implementation of the CPS within the smart factory requires strategies, networks and business models to accomplish a horizontal integration, which subsequently provides high levels of flexibility, enabling the company to respond faster. The transparency within the value chain allows the manufacturer to identify changes in customer requirements and to reflect them in all of the production steps, from development to distribution.

• Through-life engineering support across the entire value chain: Innovation and technical improvements in engineering are present in the design, development and manufacturing processes. These enable the creation of new products and production systems utilizing a large amount of information (big-data).

• Acceleration through exponential technologies: The implementation of innovative technologies enables companies to reduce costs, increase flexibility and customize the product. Industry 4.0 involves automated systems including Artificial Intelligence (AI), robots, drones, nanotechnologies and a variety of inputs that enable customization, flexibility and rapid manufacturing.

While Industry 3.0 focused on the automation of single machines and processes, Industry 4.0 focuses on the end-to-end digitalization of all physical assets and integration into digital ecosystems with value chain partners. The involvement of value chain partners is a major differentiator between itself and other digital concepts such as the Industrial Internet of Things.

Industry 4.0 takes a holistic approach that incorporates vertical and horizontal value chains within its scope. Hence, the concept of value share amongst partners is fundamental to Industry 4.0. Consequently the generation, analysis and communication of data throughout the supply chain provides the foundations on which the gains promised by Industry 4.0 are realised.

While the term Industry 4.0 has many definitions as it has been adopted as a catch phrase to address industrial digitization, and a whole host of technologies, in the context of supply chain we can loosely define Industry 4.0 as being driven by:

1) Digitization and integration of vertical and horizontal value chains

At a fundamental level Industry 4.0 supported by its concept of delivering the Smart Factory through digitizing and integrating processes vertically across the entire organisation, from the seamless merging of Operational and Informational Technology, coordinated product development and procurement, through to manufacturing, logistics and service.

Under the approach of Industry 4.0 a typical plant will have all data about operations, processes, process efficiency and quality management available and shared between departments and business units to support operational planning. This vertical integration of value amongst internal units provides real-time operational control and optimizes production through a coordinated enterprise wide effort.

However, with regards supply chain the focus shifts way from the internal vertical value stack towards the horizontal plane. For it is along the horizontal where sharing and cooperation stretches beyond the internal operations from suppliers to customers and to all key value chain partners. In addition to information sharing there will be a shift towards embracing new technologies from track and trace devices to augmented reality and IoT sensors to enable the merging of real-time integrated planning with process execution.

2) Digitization of product and service offerings

Over the last decade there has been a major shift toward digitization and specifically the benefits reaped through the digitization of products. These benefits may include the enhancement of existing products, e.g. by adding intelligence via smart sensors or communication devices that can connect with data analytics tools. However it also relates to the creation of new digitized products which focus on completely integrated solutions.

By taking advantage of the opportunities to harvest the new methods of data collection and analysis, companies are able to generate data on their product's use and hence refine products to meet the increasing needs of end-customers.

3) Digital business models and customer access

Another business benefit derived from Industry 4.0 is that industrial companies are able to expand by providing improved and more efficient data-driven services and integrated platform solutions.

These digital business models will be focused on generating additional digital revenues and optimizing customer interaction and access. These models deliver because digital products and services are designed to serve customers with complete solutions in a distinct digital ecosystem.

Digital Supply Network: the visibility challenge

One of the obstacles to the DSN metamorphosing into its Smart automated form and thence to transform via Industry 4.0 into Supply Chain 4.0 was despite its network structure and the increased visibility and transparency with its collaborative sharing of information throughout the supply chain. There was still a lack of true integration at the automation and provisioning level. Operators and planners could visualise and troubleshoot processes but not provision changes. This was due mainly to the existing gulf between industry realizing that the industrial and supply chain transformation goals of Industry 4.0 and Industrial IoT on one hand brought potentially huge benefits, and the reality of overcoming natural competitor reluctance in actually building supply chain automation and collaboration on the other, are rarely compatible.

Therefore, despite the concepts of Industry 4.0 being highly seductive to industry and this can be witnessed especially in their eagerness to implement them internally within the vertical value chains of the enterprise there is still a lot of resistance to be overcome in deploying automated provisioning in the horizontal external supply chain. Hence, successful deployments of Industry 4.0 can be witnessed in smart factories and enterprises. However, along the exterior supply chain there is still sub-optimal communications and a lack of true collaboration between participating companies. Thus it is common in manufacturing that despite the desire to implement Industry 4.0 principles the information sharing across the supply chain does not yet happen. Indeed, partners still tend to communicate not through the DSN but through email, EDI and fax. Hence, although Industry 4.0 has been a hot topic in manufacturing over the last few years the promised end-to-end smart chain with seamless information flows has still not materialised in the majority of deployments.

The road ahead towards Supply Chain 4.0

Industry 4.0 still has yet to be fully realised and most organizations are only starting to tentatively explore the possibilities and importantly assessing the risk of close collaboration and information sharing required by smart logistics and supply chain management. Technology is often touted as being the savior that will mitigate risk and enable collaboration in an adversarial environment more accustomed to dog-eat-dog type competition.

Nonetheless, it cannot be just about the technologies, even if newer technologies keep surfacing, for example, blockchain, which has recently gained much publicity due to its inherent capability to act as a secure and trusted ledger. Blockchain therefore could provide the answers to many trust issues within the supply chain such as with contracts, shipping manifestos and border/customs documentation. However there are also new advancements in AI and machine learning, better drones in logistics, collaborative robots, and autonomous guided vehicles but these don't necessarily promote trust and collaboration between partners sometimes the threat posed by emerging technologies manifests quite the opposite.

Therefore despite technology being disruptive enablers to many aspects of supply chain 4.0 it is not the entire solution. Logistics and supply chain management needs all stakeholders, to realise that flexible, smart supply chain decisions, enabled by humans or machine are what make the difference in gaining competitive advantage. Indeed, technology can actually create information silos and disconnects even more so that any legacy issues. For while IoT and cyber-physical systems are increasingly being successfully adopted within the enterprise the same is not true of smart and digital supply chains. Where technology undoubtedly delivers in the enterprise, its ability to enhance visibility and provide a platform for collaboration and for information sharing between partners in the supply chain is not so promising.

Chapter 15 - SCM and Logistics 4.0

The human element in supply chain management transformation

Supply Chain 4.0 is enabled through the context and technologies of Industry 4.0, which in turn places a lot of importance on the dual concepts of decentralization and automation. Indeed demonstrating autonomous control being distributed at the edge rather than having a central point of control is prevalent in Industry 4.0 thinking. However, there remains an important human element whereby supply chain management is changing in the decentralizing context of Industry 4.0 as it nevertheless needs people to plan and take actions as not all actions can be or should be automated.

To meet the idea of decentralization behind Industry 4.0 requires an intelligent, automated and preferably an autonomous flow of assets, goods, materials and information between the point of origin and the point of consumption. The problem arises though as supply chain management is contrary to the principles of decentralization as SCM by its nature plays a centralized role. As intelligence and autonomy are moved to digital platforms located at the edge, the decisions and tasks of supply chain management become strategically key as they must monitor and collect insights across the network including the furthest peripheral activities. Therefore, the additional core tasks of smart logistics and supply chain management in the Industry 4.0 context of logistics then become:

- Adding the right level of autonomy and intelligence to logistics in order to make logistics more efficient, effective, connected and agile/flexible as it needs to be more intelligent in order to deliver a far more connected economy and an increasingly real-time economy.

- Create a balance between self-organizing and (semi) autonomous systems and human planning. Starting with a focus on action and intelligence whereby the collaboration between man and machines and the end goals are crucial.

- Transforming the ways of working and managing in line with Industry 4.0 requires the development of real-time capabilities and agility with a shift from centralized organizational and planning to on-demand planning and managing uncertainty in far less pre-determined logistical scenarios.

The very concept of Industry 4.0, the Internet of Things and the digital economy has at their essence the premise that connectivity and the free flow of information is critical. The ability to leverage data to produce information and knowledge and to connect and share that meaningful intelligence and insights with various key partners within the supply chain is a prerequisite for digital supply chain. However, many manufacturers just aren't ready for Industry 4.0, let alone for the realization of a digital supply chain.

For example, a November 2017 report by Sapio Research - based upon a survey of 330 senior managers within a range of manufacturing sectors across Europe and South Africa - reveals the state of the digital supply chain, digital supply networks and supply chain visibility and collaboration. The report reveals a serious lack of end-to-end supply chain visibility and access to information, which stands in the way of the goals of manufacturers.

"At present, manufacturers state securing meaningful intelligence from their end-to-end supply chain as a challenge (80%), dealing with-real time information (75%) and the ability to deal with the intelligence – as significant hurdles that need to be overcome" (Zetes, November 2017)

While the survey shows that manufacturers do want to improve supply chain visibility and collaboration, increase agility, mitigate risk, and to be more efficient, they still find it difficult to respond to customer demands. This is due to the fact that the demand-driven manufacturing environment requires end-to-end control, real-time visibility and agile process execution. However, in order to achieve demand-driven manufacturing, seamless collaboration and real-time information requires visibility and exchange of information for efficient process control. Yet, according to the report, the majority of manufacturers are not able to achieve this.

While 89 percent of responding manufacturers perceive a single view of the supply chain as a key priority, 70 percent have no end-to-end visibility.

According to the survey only 29 percent of manufacturers admit that they really understand what having a digital supply network *(DSN)* is. Less than 15 percent of respondents are implementing a digital supply network and expecting DSNs to become the norm for the business in the next 5 years.

More worrying is that 68 percent of responding manufacturing decision makers state they don't have access to the right information and insights to make informed business decisions and that 67 percent are struggling to share key information between/with their suppliers, partners and even their own departments.

"Manufacturers know that across the industry there needs to be greater focus on speed, accuracy and agility within the end-to-end supply chain, if they are to remain competitive and achieve the nirvana of Industry 4.0.

The only way they are going to be able to reach such heights is to optimize processes between legacy and new systems as well as providing key stakeholders with meaningful insight from real-time data sources".

Chapter 16 - Supply Chain 4.0

Often Digital Transformation is confused with the digitization of analogue processes or products though utilization of the internet or the IoT however that is considered to be optimization. For example by embedding intelligence and connecting the cloud into nodes within a DSN will provide the optimization for it to be considered a Smart DSN. But to take the next step to Supply Chain 4.0 requires a full Digitization or Digital Transformation (DX) in the context of Industry 4.0. This doesn't necessarily mean applying the latest disruptive technologies: it means aligning digital initiatives with supply chain goals and adopting a Digital Operating Model to find the untapped potential of existing resources and capabilities thus resulting in a higher level of performance, integration and automation.

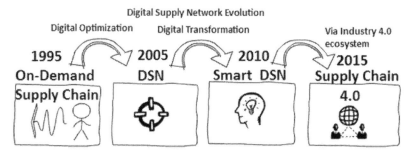

Figure 16.1- Digital Supply Network Evolution

Embarking on a DX program must be a collaborative effort between the information technology (IT) organization and other lines of business. At its core, DX is about reimaging business and operating models through the application of modern digital technology. Consequently, realising this model requires a partnership between the line of business and IT. For the supply chain organization forging this partnership is critical, as this establishes the strategic partnership to ensure that business process and operating model transformation are designed, enabled and supported by the correct digital technologies.

To effectively deploy DX in the supply chain, business, marketing and the IT organizations must define a strategy and ultimately a roadmap to modernize their existing business and operating models through the application of suitable digital technology. A typical roadmap and strategy for manufacturing would be a bias toward a convergence of IT with operations technology (OT) and the subsequent merging of the business process, with minimal disruption. In essence this means that an organization must be equipped with a strategy for driving change, while minimizing the impact of such disruption on the organization.

Digital transformation (DX) today is the term that is driving organizations of all sizes to consider how they will evolve in order to maintain their competitiveness in a volatile and connected environment with the constant risk of technological disruption. The idea supporting DX emerged due to the advent of digital technologies, specifically in the way which modern digital technologies are enabling business to better compete in the modern business environment.

Supply chain leaders are no exception and must be aware of what is happening from a DX perspective. This will require proactively planning a DX strategy to revolutionize how their supply chain operates. In practice, this will entail contemplating the steps in the supply chain process and re-evaluating how the business is positioned for DX in relation to:

- Internal collaboration, aligning the vertical value chain connecting all aspects of supply chain operations across the internal organization from product lifecycle management to customer fulfillment.
- Supply base management, leveraging digital technology and redefined processes to connect with suppliers, and improve upstream alignment and collaboration for downstream efficiencies.

- Distribution network management, leveraging digital technology and redefined processes to improve collaboration with downstream business partners to improve the flow of information from the distribution network though the supply network.
- Customer insight, strategizing around modern digital technology to improve the relationship with customers, enabling improved customer service while keeping a finger on the pulse of the market to drive agile response relative to changes in the market.

Driving change on the scale of DX requires organizations to rethink their approach to leadership relative to DX. As DX is inherently driven by technology, there is a strong relationship between the IT organization and the effort to digitally transform. To address the need for effective leadership, the principles of leading in the 3D framework acts as a model for driving digital transformation through the IT organization with line-of-business partnerships that enable an organization to:

- Innovate with business to create digital innovations.
- Integrate newly created digital capabilities with the enterprise platform.
- Incorporate new techniques and technologies into the IT organization.

Leading IT to Innovate

Traditionally, the relationship between IT and Marketing, Finance and Manufacturing would have been based on a service basis. However, recent changes have disrupted the way IT relates to the business and more often it is being seen in progressive companies as an essential source of innovation. This modern approach is most often encountered in businesses that operate a "DevOpSec" environment whereby the three pillars of Development, Operations and Security are merged into a single department. However, where a legacy relationship remains the task of leading IT to innovate will be of strategic importance. Changing the way IT operates will require a shift away from the service mentality towards building a digitally savvy and innovation-inspired culture. This will often be an onerous task and a top-down approach is required to place pressure on management to develop the right people and skill sets. It will also require a change in the way IT will define governance, change controls, information structures and best practices in order to align innovative skills and competencies with operational excellence. Leading IT to innovate requires uprooting the traditional culture and replacing it with a mentality geared to welcome and embrace innovation as a means of enhancing the performance of the business.

Enabling Technologies in Supply Chain 4.0

Digital technologies make it possible for companies to transform the way that their supply chains operate at every level. At the enterprise level, digital transformation can mean deploying data analytics, artificial intelligence, augmented reality, autonomous robotics, the Internet of Things, and many other advanced technologies to support the supply chain's objectives. A supply-chain digital transformation will strive to establish a platform for digital applications which will be designed to improve service, cost, agility, and improve inventory levels. A DX program will also act to consistently implement process and organizational changes that use these new technologies.

An example that illustrates the benefits of a DX comes from an advanced industrial company. The company was implementing a new ERP system and set up data streams from sources within its organization and across its supply network. Despite this they struggled to monitor activity across every part of its supply chain and diagnose systemic problems affecting the supply chain's performance. The problem was that the company hadn't linked related data sets together in ways that would allow it to glean useful insights such as delays in the component-manufacturing stage were likely to make a particular customer's order late.

The solution was to merge the data streams by feeding them all into a common processing engine. Then the incoming data from different sources could be interrogated to reveal causalities such as how activities and decisions in one part of the supply chain would influence operations in another. Within a few weeks the company's new data processing engine had uncovered several systemic issues, such as mismatched lead times and past-due purchase orders that prevented reliable indicators of future demand from reaching suppliers. Ultimately, the new approach to processing incoming data enabled the company to reduce its inventory by 20 percent and improve the productivity of its planners by 20 to 30 percent.

An interesting aside to this example was that the improvements in the data processing aspect of the DX process was easier to set up and use than deploying the ERP system. Collecting and analysing data streams from their supply chain was an almost trivial task using cloud-based offerings, for example, Microsoft Azure Data Warehouse and Analytics. Indeed, many new technologies are also simple to integrate with existing cloud systems. Additionally there are off-the-shelf S&OP software packages, for example, that can be connected to legacy ERP systems using standard application programming interfaces (APIs) that provide the latest in Machine Learning and AI data analytics and advanced algorithmic functionality.

Hence, we can consider that improving supply-chain performance isn't solely down to deploying new systems or software. Supply-chain management can be an incremental and collaborative endeavour, which uses new technology and techniques to enhance existing processes and models. Indeed, the most successful efforts to improve supply-chain performance involve small incremental changes to the ways that employees and partners share information, collectively contemplate problems and opportunities, reach collaborative decisions, and then execute actions they agree on.

Moreover, the latest digital technologies integrate better with existing solutions using standard APIs or other methods for collaboration into a company's existing processes. By enhancing existing operational procedures there is greater employee acceptance of the new technology and this prevents a company's disillusioned employees from regressing to the old, less effective methods in due course.

Planning an effective digital transformation

An effective DX will likely depend on a creative concept for the future supply chain. This means forward-thinking in order to align the transformation with the business objectives and goals of the company. This will need to address trends, risk and changes that could influence its competitiveness, as well as the changing expectations of its customers. This has largely always been the case but what's new is that the DX vision must now address the myriad of pressures and opportunities that surface in an increasingly digitized economy.

Once a company sets out a vision for its supply chain, it should articulate that vision in terms of business and technical capabilities. These might include the following:

- *Better decision making.* Machine-learning systems can provide supply-chain managers with recommendations for how to deal with particular situations, such as changing material planning and scheduling in response to new customer orders.
- *Automation.* Automated operations can streamline the work of supply-chain professionals and allow them to focus on more valuable tasks. For example, digital solutions can be configured

to process real-time information automatically (for example, automated S&OP preparation and workflow management), thus eliminating the manual effort of gathering, scrubbing, and entering data.

- *End-to-end customer engagement.* Digital technology can make customer experiences better by giving supply-chain managers more control and providing customers with unprecedented transparency: for example, track-and-trace systems that send detailed updates about orders throughout the lead time.
- *Innovation.* A digital supply chain can help a company strengthen its business model (for example, by expanding into new market segments) and collaborate more effectively with both customers and suppliers (for example, by basing S&OP decisions on information that is automatically pulled from customers' ERP systems).
- *Talent.* Digitally enabled supply chains have talent requirements that can be quite different from those of conventional supply chains. At least some supply-chain managers will need to be able to translate their business needs into relevant digital applications.

Adjusting performance goals and setting new KPIs complete a company's vision for its transformed supply chain. Setting performance goals requires a company to gauge its current performance and then determine achievable improvements. Goals can be defined in terms of agility, service, capital, and cost measurements. A company that aims to reduce lost sales by a specific amount, for example, would need corresponding supply-chain performance goals—for example, improving the speed and reliability of shipments to customers.

Assessing the supply chain

The vision for the digital supply chain provides a company with reference points for the second step in transformation planning: a comprehensive assessment of the supply chain's business and technical capabilities. To make the assessment simpler, companies might ask the following questions to find capability gaps in five overlapping categories:

- *Data:* Do we collect and generate all the data we need to enable our vision? Is that data stored in a manner that makes it easy to access and use?
- *Analytics:* Do we have the analytical capabilities to extract useful insights from the data that we collect?
- *Software and hardware:* Do our software and hardware systems enable the analytical and process capabilities that the company requires?
- *Talent:* Do we attract, develop, and retain the "digital native" talent needed to run and transform our supply chain? Does our culture and organizational model encourage experimentation, innovation, and continual improvement?
- *Processes:* Do we have the right processes in place across different supply-chain sub-functions? Are those processes clearly defined and well understood by everyone who is involved in them?

Traditional methods of conducting supply-chain assessments rely heavily on management interviews and surveys of employees and business partners, with a lesser dependency on manual data analysis. With digital technologies however, companies place the emphasis on data analysis as it can perform deeper, cheaper, quicker and more insightful assessments. Indeed with off-the-shelf or cloud based analytics-as-a-service applications these can be used to make sense of large, detailed sets of transactional data and extract insights that are more reliable than insights based on traditionally processed data samples. Having said that though we must not lose track of the effectiveness and importance of the management and employee interviews as these provide the strategic and tactical bias to the operational data collected and processed.

For example, a company may have to undertake the study of several years' worth of transactional data in order to understand trends affecting service levels. Previously this would have been an onerous and time consuming task however now it can be accomplished in just a few minutes using a data analytical engine.

The availability of cheap data storage and bountiful amounts of memory mean that vast arrays of data can be collected and processed using cloud based assets and technology. Indeed, such is the pervasiveness of advanced data analytics and Machine Learning algorithms companies of any size can now delve into and process their historical and even real-time data to harvest insights. These initial analytics efforts can have benefits far beyond the assessment phase, too. Companies can leave in place the applications they install for their initial assessments and continue to use those as benchmark applications or as "one click" diagnostic tools for ongoing performance monitoring.

Creating a transformation road map

The final step in planning a supply-chain transformation is to develop a road map projecting several years into the future. That means identifying operational improvements and digital solutions that will build on the company's existing capabilities to produce the capabilities described in its vision. Here root-cause analysis is an essential tool in identifying and exposing the problems that underlie performance shortfalls. Once a list of possible changes has been established, the company needs to prioritize them and weigh the expected value of a change against the ease of implementation. This is still an effective way to prioritize change but it should also be updated according to the complexities of digital transformations.

Value remains relatively easy to quantify in terms of agility, service, cost, and capital but it is not so straightforward when trying to balance the ease of implementing changes.

This is partly because technology is continually advancing and issues that may be tedious to address today, can and often will be prioritized as a vendor update, hence what is impractical today might become trivial in the next service release. Nonetheless, a common approach is for most companies to target the "no regrets" changes. These are opportunities for change which have high value and few barriers to implementation. These changes will be easy to accomplish and demonstrate the project teams capabilities while preparing to make other changes that come with greater uncertainty, at a later date.

Once the company has identified and prioritized potential changes, it is often politically advantageous to pursue the 'low hanging fruit' – easy obtainable but strategic targets - in order to gain early and demonstratable success for the project. As the easy pickings and the no-regrets projects are progressing, a company may well build upon the early success and goodwill by introducing a multiyear road map that targets making changes in other areas, such as talent and processes, as this will set the stage for future digital-transformation efforts.

A major benefit from the advances in digital technology is that it enables companies to improve their supply-chain performance both rapidly and cost effectively and with modest technical resources. The appeal of these technologies is that their ease of deployment and user friendliness has led to rapid deployments. However, this has encouraged some over-zealous companies to mount poorly considered and thus ultimately disappointing, digitalization projects.

Industry experience suggests that companies reap greater benefits when they develop a comprehensive vision for the future of their supply chains, carry out a disciplined assessment of existing performance, and draw up a long-term transformation road map.

Importantly, the company should also recognize that supply-chain transformation is not just about deploying technology it must always extend to bridging technology and operations.

Thus, it is companies that employ a considered, informed approach when addressing supply-chain DX that will stand a better chance of harvesting the full value that digital technology can provide.

Five Pillars of Excellence

The five pillars of excellence in DX resonate increasingly in the executive suite and in the boardrooms as the critical drivers of supply chain excellence.

These 5 pillars that form the foundation of the new digital supply chain are not new but they are undergoing a revival.

1. Talent is the first of the five pillars driving supply chain excellence. Simply put, if you don't have the right people, you can't build a digital supply chain strategy. Moreover, if the company fails in producing an appropriate strategy due to a lack of talented people then they will also not have the people to execute it. Finding talent for supply chain positions has unique challenges due in large part to the cross-functional and cross-company pressures supply chain executives face today.

2. Technology is always critical, but the real key is making sure you choose the right supply chain technology and successfully implement it. Improperly understood or implemented technology can cause severe damage rather than improvement. You must be careful in how you select and apply the latest supply chain technologies, especially given the extremely complex nature of today's global supply chains.

3. Internal collaboration means that each function in your firm plays a critical role in building a successful supply chain. Effective internal collaboration will help you develop a clear vision for how all the functions can work together to achieve supply chain excellence. The New Supply Chain Agenda includes a self-assessment worksheet you can complete to honestly evaluate your process for aligning the demand and supply sides of the firm.

4. External collaboration focuses on how your company can achieve breakthrough results by collaborating externally with both your suppliers and your customers. Best practices for collaboration exist and are being applied by more and more firms.

5. Managing supply chain change is the last but equally critical pillar of a supply chain excellence strategy. If you don't execute

change successfully, everything else is for naught. You need to learn how to increase your chances of success on the path to supply chain excellence. Because of their cross-functional, cross-company nature, supply chain projects are more difficult to implement than those in other functional areas.

If the promise of Industry 4.0 is to become reality, then the evolution of traditional supply chains toward a connected, smart, and highly efficient digital supply chain ecosystem will be a critical element in achieving this.

Despite the advances and research in and around SCM today's supply chain typically remains a series of largely discrete, siloed stages. The path through these silos meanders through engineering, marketing, product development, manufacturing, logistics and distribution, before eventually reaching the end-customer. However, digitization can remove or bridge many of the barriers that prevent harmonisation so that the flow becomes a completely integrated ecosystem. The removal of silos creates a transparent system for all the partners — from the suppliers of raw materials and components, as well as to the transporters of those supplies and finished goods, and finally to the end-customers.

To realise this network will require the digitisation of enterprise processes on a number of key technologies: integrated planning and execution systems, logistics visibility, autonomous logistics, smart procurement and warehousing, spare parts management, and advanced analytics. Digitisation ultimately will enable companies to react to disruptions in the supply chain, and even anticipate them by adjusting the supply chain in real time as conditions change.

Once built the digital supply "network" will offer a new degree of resiliency and responsiveness enabling companies that get there first to beat the competition in the effort to provide customers with the most efficient and transparent service delivery.

Chapter 17 - Supply Chain 4.0 Ecosystem

In most industries, it is common for products to be delivered to customers through a very standardized legacy process. A walk through the workflow would illustrate that marketing analyzes customer demand and tries to predict sales. Based upon Marketing's forecasts and conclusions manufacturing will order the necessary raw materials, components, and parts to meet the production capacity. The Distribution department will then make adjustments to cater for the upcoming changes in the amount of product coming down the pipeline, and finally customers are informed as to when to expect shipment. If all goes to plan, the gap between demand and supply at every point in the system is small.

The trouble is that it rarely goes to plan as forecasting is an inexact science, dependent on data which can be inconsistent and incomplete. To compound the problem a basic lack of transparency means that none of the silos in the supply chain really understand what any other is doing, or their requirements or constraints. Inevitably, the orderly flow from marketing to customer is disrupted and in reality we see a decoupling whereby manufacturing operates independently from marketing, from customers, and from suppliers and other partners.

However, with the advent of the smart digital supply network, silos dissolve and every link will have full visibility into the needs and challenges of the others. Supply and demand signals will originate at any point and travel immediately throughout the network. Low levels of a critical raw material, the shutdown of a major plant, a sudden increase in customer demand — all such information will be visible throughout the system, in real time. That in turn will allow all players — and most important, the customer — to plan accordingly.

Better yet, transparency will enable companies not just to react to disruptions but to anticipate them, modeling the network, creating "what-if" scenarios, and adjusting the supply chain immediately as conditions change.

The goal of this digital supply ecosystem is ambitious as it demands building a new kind of supply network that's both resilient and responsive. But if companies do make the digital supply ecosystem they can't just gather technologies and build capabilities they must transform their entire organization. Thus, the digital supply ecosystem will likely consist of eight key elements: integrated planning and execution, logistics visibility, procurement, smart warehousing, efficient spare parts management, autonomous and B2C logistics, prescriptive supply chain analytics, and digital supply chain enablers. Companies that can assemble these key components into a coherent and fully transparent unit will gain huge potential advantage in customer service, flexibility, efficiency, and cost reduction.

The evolution of the digital supply network

Behind the grand potential of the digital supply chain (DSN) is Industry 4.0, the fourth industrial revolution. Industry 4.0 then is about digitization and how companies orientate themselves to the customer through e-commerce, digital marketing, social media, and the customer experience. Ultimately, if the vision of Industry 4.0 is to be realised then virtually every aspect of business will be transformed through the vertical integration of internal business units such as research and development, manufacturing, marketing and sales, to create new business models.

In effect, we are evolving toward the complete digital ecosystem with Supply Chain 4.0 as we can see from the diagram 17.1 below.

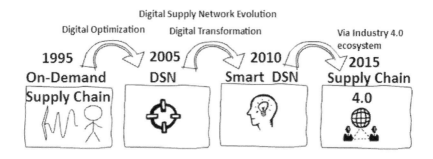

Digital Supply Network Evolution

This supply chain ecosystem will incorporate a wide range of digital technologies — the Cloud, Big Data analytics, the Internet of Things, 3D printing, Augmented and Virtual Reality, Blockchain, Artificial Intelligence and Machines learning and many others. Together, they enable the digitization of products and services, through the digitization and integration of every link in a company's value chain: the digital workplace, product development and innovation, engineering and manufacturing, distribution, as well as the digital sales channels, and after sales and reverse logistics including customer service management. All this activity underpins the digital supply chain, as it is vital to the operations of every manufacturing company - the supply chain is the business.

The supply chain extends the vertical integration of all intra-company functions to the horizontal external dimension, connecting relevant partners through a network of IoT sensors and social technologies, overseen via a central control tower, and managed through an overarching data analytics engine.

Such is the interest companies are rushing to deploy across all industry sectors and there are some already heavily active in developing their own versions of the digital supply ecosystem. In a recent PwC study on the rise of Industry 4.0, a third of the more than 2,000 respondents claim that their companies have started to digitize their supply chains, and fully 72 percent expect to have done so by 2020.

With regards Supply Chain 4.0 the economical and commercial drivers for investment are clear. Supply chain professionals expect digitization in the context of Industry 4.0 to bring significant benefits. For example, companies with highly digitized supply networks and operations can expect efficiency gains of 4.1 percent annually, while boosting revenue by 2.9 percent a year according to PwC study.

Nonetheless, some industries are going to adapt quicker than others but most industries are already working to digitally transform their supply chains, as are even asset-intensive industries like chemicals and Oil & Gas. Electronics manufacturers, for example, are early adopters as they have learned a great deal about building and managing DSNs through their long-standing efforts to create outsourced manufacturing networks. Customer facing industries on the other hand such as retail and fast-moving consumer goods, which are still vulnerable to serious disruptions in their supply and distribution networks are proving to be slower to adapt.

Core elements and new technologies

Traditional supply chains follow the well established SCOR process — of plan, source, make, deliver, return and enable. However, each of these elements is being reimagined through technology.

To understand the part technology plays in the Digital Supply Chain we can segment it into eight key areas: (1) integrated planning and execution, (2) logistics visibility, (3) Procurement 4.0, (4) smart warehousing, (5) efficient spare parts management, (6) autonomous and B2C logistics, (7) prescriptive supply chain analytics, and (8) smart supply chain enablers

All of these elements are interrelated, and they supplement and embellish one another. Consequently, a digital supply chain strategy needs to take a holistic approach and consider all of them in order to leverage the full benefits of digitization. Let's look more deeply into each of these critical elements.

Integrated planning and execution

The business objective of the digital supply chain is to deliver the right product into the customer's hands at the right time. To achieve this goal requires a responsive and reliable supply chain, which is fully integrated, and seamlessly connects suppliers, manufacturing, logistics, warehousing, and customers, through a central command tower. When a digital supply chain has this level of integration, signals that trigger events in the supply chain can emanate from anywhere in the network and alert all participants to issues affecting supply or demand, such as shortages of raw materials, components, finished goods, or spare parts. Today, customized manufacturing is becoming the norm, and customers are becoming ever more demanding, hence the fully responsive supply chain in the context of Industry 4.0 is not just desirable but essential in modern industry.

A supply chain network delivers transparency, awareness and enables collaboration along different time horizons on the strategic, tactical, and operational levels. Increasingly modern supply chain integration platforms have core planning capabilities that can support "what-if" scenario proactive planning.

As an example, planners can be notified in near-real-time to changes in customer demand. The planners can run simulations or what-if scenarios to immediately assess impact on inventory, capacity, supplies of raw materials, or the effects on other customer orders. In addition, the projected results can be evaluated against business KPIs to identify the optimal solution. This solution is then immediately available to the supply chain partners for acceptance or further refinement.

To this end there are business networks and collaborative cloud-based platforms emerging that have social network style interfaces. These internet applications allow companies to interact fully and quickly with supply chain stakeholders. All the participating partners sharing the network can now exchange information about demand, inventories, and manufacturing and logistics capacity, and provide near-real-time feedback on changes such as potential bottlenecks that may occur along the supply chain.

This level of integration encourages partners to plan collaboratively, using the same data – single source of truth - to run scenarios and estimate potential trade-offs against criteria such as capacity, cost, margin, delivery performance, and fill rate. The resultant workflow can be modelled to contemplate and integrate all the collaboration processes which will provide a rapid exchange of reliable information about when finished products will be delivered to customers.

By integrating data across the entire supply chain, in real time and often without human intervention, delivery lead times can be significantly reduced and freight and inventory management optimized, which boosts the agility of the entire chain.

Logistics visibility — seeing into the network

As we have learned the key to success for any supply chain is efficient and rapid exchange of information. The traditional supply chain is fraught with friction, caused primarily by breaches in the communication channels. These disruptions to the information flow lead to a lack of reliable and timely information exchange. Consequently there is high potential for disruption caused by sudden shifts in demand, lack of raw materials, or even natural disasters and these elements can wreak havoc on even the best laid plans. Furthermore, the outsourcing of many of the processes in manufacturing only makes it harder to understand the supply chain in its entirety making it difficult to address and fix problems as they occur.

That's why visibility has become one of the most important elements of digital supply chain management. Increasing visibility opens up the supply network for all to see. This desire for increased supply chain visibility is evident in the B2C markets where companies are demanding that partners provide this level of visibility, such as information about shipment arrivals with real-time updates. Similarly, in B2B networks, producers expect timely status information on their supply shipments as these are often linked to production plans. They will also require access to reliable transportation information as this can significantly improve customer satisfaction.

However introducing a high degree of transparency into the system is a non-trivial task, requiring both technical sophistication and a fair degree of intelligent human intervention. But once it is achieved, the benefits are significant, and not only limited to inventory savings and planning improvements.

A typical framework for transparency would be to ensure that:

- Data from internal and external sources, such as transport tracking devices, process control data and customer demand, is brought into a single platform.
- The data is consolidated and enriched with cross-referenced information, such as supply chain events impacting supply shipments. Relevant external information is sourced from weather, traffic, and news feeds. Even social media networks such as Twitter are monitored
- This enriched information is then linked within the platform and put through additional analytics and simulation runs, allowing various levels of strategic optimization such as route network

improvements and carrier performance reviews. If all this information is to be really useful, it must feed into a control center that monitors and manages logistics activities and applies advanced analytics and prescriptive algorithms to the equation.

- The resulting "single source of truth" lets companies optimize their choices under different conditions, using the information to alert factories, warehouses, and customers to endangered arrival times and engage in mitigation actions. Visibility into both transport status and expected external impacts on lead time, and the ability to change plans accordingly, will be instrumental for companies looking to use their supply chains to competitive advantage, and to manage more carefully the many risks associated with supply chain activities.

Eventually, machine-learning algorithms will become smart enough to automate even this kind of human intervention, allowing managers and other stakeholders to make better and more informed decisions daily. These prescriptive algorithms will offer mitigation advice and proven routine solutions from the past, when available. Benefits will include workload reductions and even greater increases in supply chain efficiency.

Chain visibility is often illustrated using examples from the Transportation & Logistics segment (T&L). With legacy supply chain systems it was possible to track shipments as they passed through specific points in their journey such as at a harbour or at a customs facility. However, the new breed of technology in use in T&L depends on an effective "track and trace" (T&T) system that enables partners to determine the actual real-time location and status of any given shipment at any point in its travels. Transport data and status information is available regardless of the type of transport as it is captured from sensors connected via carriers, either through direct connections or via third-party portals. Partners access this data through the T&L partner's enterprise resource planning systems typically through a web portal, an API connection or an internet feed. In addition, advances in the miniaturisation and cost of GPS technology enables companies to check the exact shipment locations of products, while field sensors monitor environmental conditions such as temperature, vibration, shock and humidity. But because data is arriving from many different sources — suppliers, transporters, warehouses, distributors — quality and interoperability of the data is critical, and still a significant technological barrier that a wide range of companies are working on.

Track-and-trace technologies

The adoption of track and trace technologies to monitor the movements of supplies and products through the transportation system has evolved significantly in recent years. This has been necessitated by the globalisation of markets and subsequently companies increasing their reach across the globe, as much as to falling prices. Radio frequency identification (RFID) and Bluetooth technologies are being used to monitor inventory and track the location or movement of items indoors, such in factories and warehouse monitoring systems. 3D printers generate readable sensor tags that can be attached to cargo and capture temperature and humidity conditions throughout the shipment or in the warehouse inventory. Global system for mobile communication (GSM) and satellite tracking are used in road, air and maritime transport, and a myriad of sensors monitor engine and core component performance.

The command centre for these remote-sensing activities is the control room or logistics visibility platform, akin to a traffic control tower. The great virtue of the control room is that it can provide executives and senior managers with a dashboard view of the company's supply chain performance, and this supports the decision-making processes needed to keep the flow of parts and products running smoothly.

Procurement 4.0 — sourcing on demand

A critical component in the digital supply chain ecosystem is the efficient integration and management of suppliers of raw materials and parts. This is termed procurement and the digitization of procurement is a priority to most companies. Indeed, the digitalisation of procurement is well under way with most companies already using a variety of big data tools and techniques to connect with suppliers. The goals are typically to further improve and aid the planning process, improve sourcing, actively manage supplier risk, and boost collaboration. The results typically are measured in lower costs and faster delivery throughout the supply chain as it becomes increasingly automated.

Nonetheless, a true digital supply chain will have several other key consequences for the procurement function. Primarily, the overall industry shift towards Industry 4.0 will require companies whose supply chain needs have been limited to physical goods to become equally adept at making or buying digital supplies and services. For example by creating and issuing RFQ for software specifications and requirements (SRS), software development contracts, and in acquiring third party developers and digital procurement platforms. In addition, the millions of sensors and other electronic components needed to run the digital supply chain itself are another obvious procurement requirement. As all those IoT sensors being deployed will need interfacing with new software and applications.

The real challenge, however, will come as software and services become pervasive and products have AI and cloud based IoT analytics embedded and this become a significant feature of differentiation. Already, the advanced software embedded in some products, from electronics to cars to industrial machinery, is actually of greater value than the physical products that they go into — and this provides the competitive edge and differentiation that companies need to win.

Smart warehousing — robots at work

The warehouse and logistics functions have been the vanguards in utilising IoT and advanced technologies to an extent that they have become a strategic tool in the way that companies operate and generate value for their customers.

The warehouse for instance has changed radically over the last decade with the adoption of technology aimed to improve efficiency and safety. This has come about through the automation of virtually every ordinary warehousing activity. Indeed, the Industry 4.0 warehouse looks and operates nothing like the traditional labour-intensive buildings of the past.

The transformation of the warehouse in the context of Industry 4.0 begins with inbound logistics. Trucks on the way to the warehouse communicate their position and arrival time to the intelligent warehouse management system (WMS), which selects and prepares a docking slot, optimizing just-in-time and just-in-sequence delivery. RFID sensors will reveal what's been delivered, and send the track-and-trace data horizontally across the entire supply chain. The management system will automatically allot storage space for the delivery, and assign the appropriate autonomous equipment to move the goods to the right locations.

Inside the warehouse, the management software will constantly update inventory in real time, through the use of sensors embedded in the goods and the system will deploy flying drones to aid in taking inventory and regularly assessing the whereabouts of goods through sensor data.

In addition to enhanced inbound logistics, autonomous transportation, and optimized logistics processes, other emerging innovative technologies will transform such mundane jobs as picking goods to fulfill and order. Already, companies are experimenting with wearables and augmented reality systems to aid in this expensive, labour-intensive process, which is often still carried out using manually using paper and prone to human error.

DHL recently conducted tests on an augmented reality system at a warehouse in the Netherlands owned by Ricoh, the Japanese imaging and Electronics Company. The employees equipped with smart glasses containing software from Ubimax, navigated through the warehouse along optimized routes guided by the map on the glasses' graphics display. The Augmented reality display enabled them to find the right quantity of the right item much more efficiently, and with reduced training time. Over the three weeks of the test, 10 order pickers succeeded in fulfilling 9,000 separate orders by picking more than 20,000 items. The resulting productivity improvements and reduction in errors increased the overall picking efficiency by 25 percent.

Moreover, once the proper products are picked, they will be packaged for shipment by robots that can handle a broad range of product sizes while taking into consideration data on the product and the customer's packaging requirements. Software will also control the internal warehouse environment, including setting the proper temperature, light, and humidity according to predefined requirements. By shutting off the lights and heat in areas where all the work is being done by robots and autonomous vehicles, for example, energy consumption can be reduced significantly.

Efficient spare parts management — with 3D printing

The warehousing link in the supply chain is expensive, labour-intensive, and fraught with potential error. Digitization will certainly eliminate much of its inefficiency and integrate the process into the entire supply chain. Meanwhile, 3D printing is poised to transform this critical link in the chain even further. Consider for example the problem of spare parts. In many warehouses, more than half of all orders shipped are one-time requests for spare parts, and the demand for them is highly erratic and almost impossible to predict. That's why companies typically maintain huge inventories of parts, many of which must be kept for decades.

Nonetheless, digitization is revolutionizing the warehousing and the distribution of spare parts. Sophisticated analytics software allows demand for spare parts to be forecast much more precisely, through solutions such as predictive maintenance of industrial vehicles and machines. That in turn allows companies to optimize spare parts storage and distribution, as a great deal more information can be integrated, such as social media, geo-political news, traffic and weather data, on which demand and distribution depend.

Then if we also take 3D printing into consideration spare parts can be manufactured as needed at facilities maintained locally — even on-site, if demand is high enough or critical enough. For 3-D printing all that's needed are the printers, software, a blueprint with the right specifications for each part, and the materials needed to produce it. The specifications for any part, including parts from machines too old to have the specs on file, can be created using 3D laser scanners and automatically translated into code readable by printers.

The benefits of 3D Printing include dramatic reductions in spare parts inventories and associated carrying costs. Just as important, customers can count on much greater uptime for critical equipment, as problems are anticipated and spare parts arrive much more quickly. Indeed, the capacity to add predictive maintenance services to industrial equipment, and the ability to deliver parts in a timely fashion, is instrumental to the shift to Industry 4.0.

Autonomous and B2C logistics — robotic transport

The futuristic perception of the digital supply chain can be best represented by the rise of robotic autonomous transport. The notion of driverless cars has already captured the imagination of the public. But it is not just Google and Uber driverless cars that are becoming reality, indeed all manner of driverless vehicles and other robotic innovations will come to the fore and play an increasing role in moving goods around the world.

The most common use of autonomous vehicles in logistics will be driverless trucks. Self-driving or autonomous trucks will depend on mapping software and short-range radar to assess the vehicle's surroundings. Wireless connections to other vehicles and to the road itself will provide additional information that will speed up traffic flow and reduce roadway congestion and accidents.

The possibility of autonomous truck convoys or platoons which is really just multiple trucks forming a line reduces the need for human drivers and allows the trucks to drive more closely together. The benefit of such vehicles are obvious as they realise faster and more reliable delivery times, lower labour costs, the elimination of human error, and reduced emissions. These benefits are rapidly realised through more efficient operations, routing, and convoying of trucks.

Last year, the U.S. state of Nevada licensed two of Daimler's Freightliner Inspiration Trucks for use on public highways. Equipped with radar, advanced cruise control, and mapping software, the trucks, in autonomous mode, free their drivers to concentrate on more value-adding logistical tasks such as routing and route logging, making the job more attractive, safer, and less monotonous.

Another major area for deploying process automation is last-mile delivery that expensive and troublesome part of getting products into the hands of the customer. Because last-mile delivery is so labour-intensive and requires some customer interaction, it is often a major pain point for businesses leaving them open to ideas for lowering costs and providing greater customer value. Some of the ideas being discussed, include crowd-sourcing apps to employ non-professional drivers to deliver packages along their typical commute routes; self-driving delivery robots moving at pedestrian speeds that distribute packages along flexible routes; using drones to drop packages from the sky onto customers' lawn; using drones to deliver to intelligent mailboxes – ones that it can lock/unlock.

Nonetheless, despite the keen interest for deploying technical solutions to address the last-mile conundrum it is actually within the production facilities themselves that autonomous on-site vehicles are becoming the norm. Autonomous robotic vehicles routinely are moving raw materials, parts, and components around without human interference, and choosing the best route despite constantly changing conditions. These are tightly integrated with the company's ERP system, so that the vehicles are able to determine independently which supplies are needed to complete an order, which components need replenishing anywhere in the production process, and they can also pick up and deliver parts or packaging. The vehicles are utilising contactless sensors and laser safety bumpers to significantly improve on-site employee safety. For examples of this type of automated vehicle there are systems from companies such as Germany's Still. Their vehicles even operate as a team, coordinating with one another as well as their human overseers to determine the best routes and most efficient use of the team's assets in a dynamically changing environment.

Prescriptive supply chain analytics — decision support for managers

If the goal of the digital supply chain is to fully integrate and make visible every aspect of the movement of goods then the key to this is big data analytics. Companies are using tools to visualise and describe much of the current state of their supply chains. For example to visualise where specific goods are located, where the demand for specific items is located, and when items are likely to be produced and delivered. Moreover, many companies are learning to PREDICT critical elements of the supply chain with unprecedented accuracy. Using Big Data and predictive algorithms allows that variations in demand through the chain can be better anticipated. This is down to sampling more data from the market to extract more sophisticated triggers, which translates to demand for production capacity, storage and logistics, and corresponding changes in requirements of raw materials.

Nonetheless, despite these data analytic advancements in forecasting it is the development of supply chain analytics that can prescribe that will be the most important. The capability for algorithms to prescribe how the supply chain should operate is the ultimate in Industry 4.0. The goal isn't simply to optimize demand planning, production, distribution or the management of inventory and spare parts. Instead, the ultimate goal is to optimize any number of factors that may arise across the entire chain, depending on circumstances, and then be able to actively modify the chain accordingly.

Hence the Prescriptive analytics systems provide decision support to supply chain managers and can even act autonomously on routine decisions. To improve the quality and efficiency of such decisions, companies will be able to include external information such as economic indicators and employ self-learning algorithms to aid in automating the decision-making process.

Prescriptive analytics, big data and complex algorithms

When contemplating planning scenarios, planners will ask questions of te network such as what would be the best way to optimize the supply chain to minimize costs, setting aside other considerations such as on-time delivery or the best way to speed up delivery time, no matter what the effect on cost might be?

Fed enough quality data the analytics engine would produce a minimum-cost scenario showing not just how much money could potentially be saved but also how to achieve this objective. This scenario could be adjusted to account for other factors. Ultimately, prescriptive analytics will be able to offer scenarios at a very fine level of detail, describing how shifting to a new supplier might affect product quality, or even whether the introduction of a new colour of mobile phone would increase sales through cannibalizing other similar products.

This degree of utility for prescriptive analytics will depend entirely on the ability of companies to use data to build a map of all the key elements, functions, processes and rules of the supply chain into an integrated whole. The next logical step will then be to automate standard activities and processes within the supply chain based on the recommended methodologies and workflows. This would be an incremental step toward fully orchestrating the entire chain and managing exceptions to standard processes autonomously.

Smart supply chain enablers — success factors

Companies setting out to build the smart supply chain face a difficult task, one that will likely prove impossible unless they develop a clear strategy that is fully responsive to the opportunities on offer in a fully digital environment. It must be based not just on the company's current operations and business model but also on new business models available once digitization has been implemented, such as creating direct sales channels and leapfrogging levels in the value chain.

Once the strategy is determined, companies must put into place several key capabilities needed to carry it out, in addition to the supply chain applications discussed above. These key capabilities include the following:

- **Processes.** Establish the new end-to-end processes connecting suppliers and customers that digitization makes possible, such as how to collaborate on cloud-based platforms.

- **Organization and skills.** This requires generating an end-to-end understanding of the mechanics of the value chain. For example, switching from a reactive mentality to becoming a supply chain "orchestrator" — seeing, managing, and optimizing the entire chain. Achieving this goal will require a digital transformation that promotes communication across different media, programs, and user groups and in developing the digital talent and expertise needed to build the technology and carry out the new supply chain operations.

- **Performance management.** Developing a straightforward set of business rules covering the management of the supply chain, and suitable key performance indicators needed to measure outcomes that are compatible with the business plan and objectives.

- **Partnering.** Focus on boosting partner relationships with other companies, as the fully integrated supply chain cannot be built without collaborating with a wide variety of suppliers, distributors, and technology providers.
- **Technology.** Devise a digital road map for the many technologies, old and new, that will underpin the digital supply chain, including the information integration layer, database and analytics capabilities, as well as the cloud.

Supply chain maturity

Few companies have reached anything close to complete maturity in their efforts to put together the fully digital supply chain. To develop a supply chain strategy and organize their ensuing efforts in a coherent fashion, it is critical that companies understand their starting position. The process leads through four stages of maturity:

1. **Digital novice.** These companies have yet to embark on the journey. Their supply chain processes remain discrete, carried out by individual departments and business units.
2. **Vertical integrator.** Companies at this stage have managed to integrate their supply chain processes internally, across departments and functions.
3. **Horizontal collaborator.** Here, companies have learned to work with their supply chain partners to set business goals, define and carry out common processes, and achieve a fair degree of transparency into the chain.
4. **Digital champion.** These companies have achieved the highest level of collaboration with partners and transparency into operations, while developing mutually beneficial processes and analytical techniques for optimizing the entire supply chain.

The digital supply chain road map

The key to becoming a digital champion and reaping the full benefits of the potentials of the Digital Supply Chain ecosystem lies in developing an orderly process for implementing and integrating the many technologies and capabilities required. Typically, companies need to take five primary steps:

1. **Understand the current position:** Review the current maturity along the four stages of the maturity model and identify areas for improvement.
2. **Define the strategy:** Determine the desirable target maturity level and the supply chain vision that best supports the business strategy.
3. **Develop the appropriate road map:** Settle on the necessary implementation steps and work them into a detailed road map.
4. **Deploy small pilots with end-to-end scope:** Many applications that make up the digital supply chain represent a radical change for most organizations, so companies should first carry out smaller pilots that showcase benefits and help develop the right capabilities. These "lighthouse" projects should aim at testing the end-to-end flow for a specific supply chain, rather than implementing a limited set of technologies on a broader scale.
5. **Segmented rollout and capability development:** After a successful pilot, the rollout should start with those supply chains where expected benefit is highest. This could involve key customers, key regions, or some other supply chain segmentation criterion. The capabilities required will need to evolve along with the rollout.

Supply chains are extremely complex organisms, and no company has yet succeeded in building one that's truly digital. Indeed, many of the applications required are not yet widely used. But this will change radically over the next five to 10 years, with different industries implementing DSNs at varying speeds. Companies that get there first will gain a difficult-to-challenge advantage in the race to Industry 4.0, and will be able to set, or at least influence, technical standards for their particular industry. The advantage will by no means be limited to the greater efficiencies. The real goal will be the many new business models and revenue streams the digital supply chain will open up.

Chapter 18 - Supply Chain 4.0 - Enabling Technologies

There has been a lot written about the Internet of Things (IoT) and how it will affect nearly every global industry and that is especially significant when we consider the global supply chain. Industry 4.0 and the very similar Industrial Internet of Things (IIoT) are built upon the foundations of technological capability that the IoT delivers.

The Industrial Internet of Things

Indeed, the IIoT is set to revolutionize the global supply chain with both operational efficiencies and revenue opportunities and this has become feasible through the transparency provided by the myriad of IoT sensors and data points that are ubiquitous in the IoT ecosystem.

Contemporary markets require supply chains that can do more than just keep track of products they have to deliver an edge on competitors and provide the goods or service differentiator in order to build the company's brand. It is to this end that industries across the board have embraced the concepts of Industry 4.0. The IIoT in turn also provides the connectivity and data sharing measures that enable supply chain 4.0 to deliver on the promises of Industry 4.0.

IIoT Operational Efficiencies

When it comes to operational efficiencies, the IIoT offers many tools that can be deployed to leverage operational benefits and differentiation:

Asset Tracking: Tracking numbers and bar codes were traditionally the standard method for managing goods throughout the supply chain. However along with the IIoT come RFID and GPS sensors which can track products from cradle to grave. Manufacturers can use these wireless sensors to gain granular data like the temperature, humidity and location at which an item is being stored, how long it spent in the warehouse, any excessive vibrations or shock during shipment and even how long it took from the time it went on the shelf to the time to be sold. The type of operational and environmental data gained from IIoT sensors can help companies get a tighter grip on quality control, on-time deliveries, and product forecasting.

Last Mile Delivery: in home deliveries the most expensive and unpredictable section is referred to as the last mile. One of the biggest frustrations for both the customer and the delivery agent is arranging a mutual time to deliver a package to a customer's home. Not only does this add significant delay it adds costs typically through missed appointments. Amazon though has come up with another innovation that might just remove this bugbear. The Amazon Key is a door lock and video cam system that can be attached to a house door or locker and connected to the internet so that a delivery agent can open the door and complete the delivery. This may not be anything new as several IoT devices allow this operation. The difference with the Amazon Key is that Amazon deliveries will now have a unique code which can be used to open the door by the delivery agent - with the customer's prior permission and opt-in to the service with the video cam recording the event - and thus be able to make a delivery securely even when the householder is not present. In addition there is also version for a car so that the delivery can be placed inside the vehicle if it is parked in an area accessible by the public.

Another Amazon supply chain innovation based on IoT is their recently-introduced "Dash" button which enables users to order basic household supplies at the touch of a button embedded in a label that can be conveniently attached close to where the product is use or stored. This innovation as multi-value as it is convenient for the customer to order an have the product delivered to their home the same day – depending on location within the hour. But it also provides Amazon with a wealth of real-time data from which they can gain even more specific information about when demand for a product will rise and fall, so that they can adjust stocks accordingly.

Vendor Relations: The data obtained through asset tracking is also important because it allows companies to tweak their own production schedules, as well as recognize under-performing products and vendor relationships. According to IBM - the developers of the Watson AI technology, which has become a major resource on the supply chain scene - up to 65% of the value of a company's products or services is derived from its suppliers.

That's an important metric, which provides a clear incentive to pay close attention to how partners in the supply chain are adding value to the product. Higher quality goods mean better relationships with customers—and better customer retention overall.

Forecasting and Inventory: IIoT sensors provide far more accurate inventories than humans can manage alone. For instance, Amazon is using WiFi robots to scan QR codes on its products to track and triage its orders. Others are using indoor drones to count inventory by flying along aisles in the warehouse and detecting the RFID or QR SKU (stock keeping units) tags. These automated methods of stock counting and inventory management allows for companies to track their inventory in real time at the click of a button and that precise data can be used to find trends to make manufacturing schedules even more efficient.

Connected Fleets: As the supply chain ecosystem continues to grow—upward and outward as it incorporates more enterprise supply chains—it is imperative that all carriers, be it shipping containers, suppliers' delivery trucks, or last mile vehicles are connected. Collecting location and environmental data from T&L enables manufacturers to get products to their customers, faster and in better condition.

Scheduled Maintenance: The IIoT's use of predictive maintenance algorithms and the concept of digital twins to virtually replicate machines and processes enable companies to leverage the use of smart sensors on their manufacturing floors to manage planned and predictive maintenance and prevent expensive down-time.

Revenue Opportunities

The ability to source business intelligence that lets planners know more—and understand more—about customers, their buying habits, and the trends associated with them is invaluable. It allows businesses to form tighter connections with customers and, inevitably, market to them in new and better ways.

 In addition to using data for improved efficiencies businesses can get creative with supply chain transparency. A popular customer demand from suppliers is for ethical and sustainable products. To that end, producers can build a reputation of social responsibility by allowing customers to access the product history through blockchain and AR technology and see where their product came from, who made it, and the conditions in which those workers lived.

Research shows 70% of retail and manufacturing businesses have already begun to transform their supply chain processes due to the concerns of the consumers about where their clothes were made. Fashion clothing and sport shoes have got a long unsavory history in exploitation of child and extreme poverty labour. New technologies such as Blockchain may be the answer to audit tracking ethical products.

However, when it comes to the global supply chain, this is far from being a level playing field. For the IIoT to be truly effective, all members of the global supply chain must be connected.

However, many companies are only just now embracing the concept of mobility so taking the necessary steps towards digital transformation could be some way off. Nonetheless, some technologies like blockchain and edge computing will continue to take form, and new IoT technologies surface each year, so there is still a lot further we can go in making supply chains even more productive, efficient and creative than ever before.

Blockchain

Blockchain, which is most famous as the technology that supports Bitcoin, is a secure protocol for a distributed digital ledger that enables proof of ownership and the transfer of ownership from one entity to another without using a trusted third party intermediary (like a central bank). The information – the value - that is transferred can also move through an extended supply chain while ensuring that what occurs at each point in the chain can be chronologically recorded and not edited or deleted. As a result of this inherent security Blockchain technology has found several use cases in supply chain management and in logistics.

For example, a use case in logistics is a blockchain pilot program involving Maersk and IBM, which created a digital distributed ledger to create a single electronic record store where all the myriad documents related to a shipment, could be stored securely. This use case is of profound importance in Transportation & Logistics as blockchain could very effectively carry the customs documentation and international authorisations on a scannable label on a consignment. This could enable drive – through customs and borders as each consignment would be detected and scanned via the blockchain ledger. In addition even without cross-borders administration a truck could load and unload much quicker, resulting in fewer delays, if all the necessary paper work was readable on a blockchain ledger.

In a similar vein, in another project a company called T-Mining, utilised the blockchain distributed ledger as an authorative record giving clearance for personnel such as a truck driver to pick up a load.

In both examples the projects made use of one of the key advantages of blockchain, which is that its ledger has an audit trail which is unchangeable so it is much more secure than traditional IT solutions.

The security of the digital ledger is robust as to change or edit an entry would require finding and then hacking every node in the distributed network, which is frankly unfeasible.

Consequently this makes Blockchain highly secure and as the information stored cannot be changed it has a complete authenticated and irrevocable record of all transactions undertaken.

One organization called Kouvala Innovation has an even more audacious vision for blockchain – the uberization of shipping. Their idea is that transport pallets are fitted with RFID tags, which communicate their requirements to get from point A to point B by a certain date. The carriers running "mining" applications would bid for the right to move that load. The RFID tag would award the business to the carrier that bests meets a shipper's price and service needs. Then as the move progresses, the blockchain would continue to track the shipment.

It is also thought this technology might find many other use cases such as in enhancing food and drug traceability and for reducing costs associated with factoring. Provenance, a U.K. software startup, looks to use blockchain technology to establish the authenticity of food. For example, Provenance is testing the technology to authenticate tuna caught in Indonesia but subsequently delivered to Japanese restaurants. In this implementation the blockchain takes information from IoT sensors or RFID tags and records it on the blockchain to track the fish from "hook to fork." Indeed, IBM is also interested in food traceability, and has announced a consortium with several major food producers and retailers to track food from "Farm to Table".

Another use case for blockchain is being pursued by The Sweetbridge Foundation, a non-profit governance body, which is aiming to use the technology to lower the cost of doing business in global supply chains. The principle here is that in global supply chains, it is common for a big firm to buy goods from small manufacturers, but then to take many months to pay. As a consequence of this, small suppliers must engage in price factoring arrangements to insure they have enough cash flow to continue operations. This increases costs not only for the supplier, but across the end-to-end supply chain. By utilising blockchain the premise is that it could greatly reduce the financial costs associated with strategic procurement as the accounting process would be visible to all in the supply chain via the audit trail.

Blockchain has great advantages in terms of cybersecurity but there are several challenges associated with maturing this technology for supply chain purposes:

- The technological talent is scarce and expensive; much of it has been scooped up by fintech startup firms.
- There are network effects associated with deriving value from blockchain in logistics. The more entities that participate, the more valuable the solution is. But this network effect makes things difficult at the start.

- It is likely that to get to scale, large companies will need to require their supply chain partners to participate. But this could hinder the drive to create the necessary standards. Further, while several organizations are seeking to play the necessary role of standards body; none has yet achieved the necessary scale.
- "Miners" are used to validate that the data added to a blockchain is valid. With Bitcoin, this process can take several minutes. There are supply chain processes where less latency would be very desirable.

Blockchain is certainly an intriguing technology and is creating a lot of broad interest across many industries that are generating ideas and potential use cases.

On the other hand, many businesses are waiting to see what develops because blockchain is a back-end technology, hence most companies don't need to proactively invest in exploring its value as it will be the applications riding on top of the technology that will determine its success.

Artificial Intelligence & Machine Learning

Before addressing what AI can do in the context of supply chain, it is critical to first understand what it is. AI has created a lot of hype over the last few years but it has been around since the 1950's. In the simplest terms, AI is mathematical intelligence delivered via algorithms and exhibited by machines that matches or ideally betters human thinking. Thus Artificial intelligence is an area of computer science concerned with developing programs that are intelligent, or can do intelligent things. The scope of Artificial Intelligence is vast but one area of interest to supply chain involves learning, e.g. machine learning. A.I. may involve other concerns such as reasoning, planning, memory, and much more, but currently the focus of interest is in learning algorithms. This could encompass diverse types of learning such as:

- Developing code to investigate how to optimally plan logistics.
- Developing code to investigate how to determine sentiment from a paragraph of text.
- Developing code to investigate how to pick a product based upon a photograph

These algorithms permit machines to mimic or ultimately to exceed and replace intelligent human behaviour, such as problem solving, product picking or in learning how a product is being received on social media. In essence, AI is machines making autonomous decisions based upon algorithms feeding on data whether that is in controlling a self-driving car, autonomously controlling industrial processes or learning how to adjust an order forecast based on changing demand.

AI has shown great promise in improving human decision-making processes and achieved success through subsequent increases in productivity in various business endeavors. This success is due to its ability to recognise business patterns, learn business phenomena, distill information from large scale data, and analyse the data intelligently. Despite its widespread acceptance as a decision-aid tool across many industries, AI has up to now seen only limited application in supply chain management (SCM).

Like so many other technologies before it AI has been a victim of excessive hype that has led many companies to rush to implement it, but with ill conceived expectations and thus with disappointing results. Machine learning, which is a subfield of AI, on the other hand has a much longer history in industry as M2M communications and robotics have a distinguished record of achievement. Machine learning is another field of computer science concerned with programs that learn.

The field of machine learning is concerned with the question of how to construct computer programs that automatically improve with experience. — Machine Learning, 1997.

There are many types of learning, many types of feedback to learn from, and many things that can be learned. This could encompass diverse types of learning, such as:

- Developing code to "learn" how to identify and manipulate demand trends in the consumer market.
- Developing code to "learn" how a robot on the production line "learns" in response to stimulus from other robots or products.
- Developing code to investigate how to "learn" patterns and detect correlations in historical data.
- Developing code to investigate how autonomous vehicles in a warehouse "learn" the optimal path from their base to the storage bays.

We can see from these esoteric examples that machine learning is a broad and far reaching program of research. Another reason that Machine Learning has found a niche in industry an the supply chain is because of its close relationship to Applied Statistics which planners have depended upon for generations.

Statistics, or applied statistics with computers, is a sub-field of mathematics that is concerned with describing and understanding the relationships in data. This could encompass diverse types of learning such as:

- Developing models to summarize the distribution of a variable.
- Developing models to best characterize the relationship between two variables.
- Developing models to test the similarity between two populations of observations.

Many methods used for understanding data in statistics can be used in machine learning to learn patterns in data. These tasks could be called machine learning or applied statistics.

The major problem with Artificial Intelligence and Machine Learning is that despite their age they have been mercilessly hyped since around 2010 as a new wonder technology and a panacea for all the world's ills. Thus we see products embedded with AI and ML capabilities flooding the market and the understandable rush by executives to onboard these 'new' technologies with often little or no real understanding as to why they are deploying them. Indeed often the case is that organisations in their zeal to deploy Machine Learning for example dive straight into employing Data Scientists and expertise that in not aligned to their business model or purpose. For example Machine Learning is a huge academic field but thankfully little of it is of relevance to industry or the supply chain. So planners should remember a few things when deploying Machine Learning solutions such as they are not in the business of academic research in Machine Learning or trying to create an intelligent agent as in artificial intelligence or even why variables relate to each other in data as in applied statistics.

Furthermore, when it comes to learning relationships in data most industry practitioners need to remember that they:

- are not investigating the capabilities of an algorithm
- are not developing an entirely new theory or algorithm
- are not extending an existing machine learning algorithm to new cases

Therefore they need to keep use cases simple and well defined and this means deploying AI and Machine learning to address the problem you are trying to solve and in terms of the solution you require.

In short: "Find a model or procedure that makes best use of historical data comprised of inputs and outputs in order to skilfully predict outputs given new and unseen inputs in the future."

The importance of taking this highly specific approach is it first of all, discards entire sub-fields of machine learning, such as unsupervised learning, and focuses on one type of learning called supervised learning and all the algorithms that fit into that category.

Second of all, it gives you a clear objective that dominates all others: that is develop the model skill at the expense of other concerns. Thirdly, framing the problem in this way fits neatly into another field of study called predictive modeling. That is a field of study that borrows methods from machine learning with the objective of developing models that make skilful predictions and is often referred to as predictive analysis. The art or science if you like of demand and supply forecasting is making heavy use of predictive analytics.

Why AI & Machine Learning can fall short

Typically businesses that are new to AI and Machine Learning do not fully understand how they derive value from the technology and its myriad of algorithms and use cases. Nonetheless, even if following the highly specific approach outlined earlier and within the context of SCM systems today there are several reasons AI has fallen well short of the hype. For example, AI in general and ML in particular falls short of expectations due to the inconvenient truth that there is not just one super algorithm or set of parameters for a particular use case as they are data specific. Furthermore, because algorithms are so data specific even the experts can't tell you what algorithm to use. To compound the problem it is not a case of writing code to solve the problem. In fact, problems of this type resist top-down hand-coded solutions. If were feasible to write some if-statements to solve your problem, you would not need a machine learning solution. It would be a programming problem. Thus the best type of machine learning methods that you need will learn the relationship between the inputs and outputs in your historical data. But that requires:

- a well considered use case with highly specific objectives that are aligned to the overarching business plan
- the expertise from data scientists and subject matter experts to ask the right questions or understand the functional tasks
- data scientists to tweak the algorithms and prepare the training data and then make sense of the results

Furthermore, Machine Learning initiatives will fail due to:

- Objectives are actually in conflict with other functions of the business and/or partners
- They will often miss potential opportunities and correlations hidden in the network because they overfit the data
- Correlations and causations are often misunderstood due to a lack of involvement of a process Subject Matter Expert when analysing results
- Often the algorithms are fed stale or overly bias data and thus promote or reinforce poor decisions
- Often algorithms are deployed using over-simplified models that do not relate to the real world

These SCM limitations to using AI have severely suppressed return on AI investments. Despite this however recent market-research conducted by IDC predicts that by 2020, 50 percent of mature supply chains will use AI and advanced analytics for planning, and to eliminate sole reliance on short-term demand forecasts.

As a result it is believed that supply chain planning and optimization, including demand forecasting, will become a key areas for AI research and deployment. This is mainly due to the complexity of global supply chains as they are affected by so many variables. Hence it may be that AI will become essential in identifying and predicting problems and potential solutions. Consequently, companies are already applying AI-based machine learning to automatically analyse the vast amounts of supply-chain management data, in order to identify trends and predict problems and potential outcomes. The benefits for global supply chain management include reductions in forecasting errors through the application of machine learning capabilities that can automatically detect errors and make course corrections.

Indeed Industry 4.0 has at its core this capability for processing real-time data streams for predictive and prescriptive analytics.

Therefore, AI an ML will not just predict outcomes it will be able to prescribe solutions. Furthermore, with supply chain processes already generate mountains of data that can be used to train the ML algorithms. This data is used to train the algorithms to learn where things went wrong, and how to fix it.

However, AI and predictive algorithms have only been adopted mainstream for stock and inventory optimisation but there are also applications that enable "anticipatory logistics". This is the field within supply chain concerned with shortening delivery times and the improvement of efficiency by predicting demand before a request or order is even placed. Amazon and the global logistics provider DHL are actively participating in this area and Amazon has some patents pending for shipping before sales. The potential is that global supply chain managers could use AI systems to predict orders and jump-start the shipping process in order to minimize delays. The way this works is that supply chain managers who have analyzed and predicted their customers' purchasing behaviours might also move goods to distribution centres that are closer to the customer, allowing faster delivery.

However, it predictive analytics is not just limited to transportation as there is a use case within warehouses. For example, machine learning systems may be able to recognize common scenarios and trends, and link these to specific customers and then predict orders. By anticipating the content of an order, these ML systems would then pre-pick-and-pack without first waiting for orders to be placed, which again pre-empts an order but hastens the delivery.

Key Requirements for AI in SCM

Despite the many potential use cases for AI and Machine Learning in SCM it is felt that there are eight key criteria that are mandatory for a successful AI implementation in a supply chain management scenario.

For the AI solution to offer optimal value in supply chain, it is critical to ensure the following:

1. Real-Time

Traditional enterprise systems undertake batch planning using historical data and to improve on these systems requires that an AI systems use real-time data. It is essential to remove the issue with using stale data as without real-time information an AI tool is just making bad decisions faster.

2. External facing

AI and ML solutions require a holistic view of market data hence it is essential that market data that is relevant to the industry is made available to any type of AI, Deep Learning or Machine Learning algorithms. Similarly, the AI tool must have access to all supply chain partners data so it can see the forward-most demand as well as the downstream supply, and all relevant constraints and capacities in the supply chain. Without this visibility the results will be no better than that of a traditional planning system.

3. Realistic

The end-customer is the only consumer of true finished goods and the single source of money. Hence, the supply chain partners will also want the full value that comes from optimizing service levels and cost to serve as increased consumer sell-through drives value for everyone.

Consequently, the objective function of the AI engine must be consumer service level at lowest possible cost.

This is not to say that the decision algorithm may not support enterprise level inventory issues or decide individual enterprise business policies it must support global consumer-driven objectives when faced with constraints within the supply chain.

4) Incremental

Ideally the decision processes should be incremental and contemplate the Cost of Change.

This means minimising re-planning as regular change without diligent process of weighing the cost of the change will create more costs than savings and reduces the ability to effectively execute. Hence, an AI tool should consider trade-offs in terms of cost of change against incremental benefits when making decisions.

5. Continuous

The decision process should be designed to be continuous, self-learning and self-monitoring. The AI system must be looking at the problem continuously, in real time and benefiting from the volatility of data within the multi-party network. It should also continuously learn the effectiveness of the produced "analytics" it derives and then apply what it has learned.

6. Autonomous

ML algorithm must be trusted to make the intelligent decisions and also to execute them.

Furthermore, they need to execute not just within the enterprise but where appropriate, across supply chain partners.

This requires your AI system and the underlying execution system to support multi-party execution workflows.

7. Scalable

For the supply chain to be optimized across an entire network the system must be able to process huge volumes of data in real-time. Hence as network supply chains can have millions of stocking locations and SKUs. AI solutions must be able to make smart decisions, fast, and on a massive scale.

8. Transparent and Interactive

AI should not operate in a "black box" fashion as the tool must give users visibility to decision criteria, propagation impact, and enable them to understand issues that the AI system cannot solve.

Therefore the users must have a way to engage with the system to monitor and provide additional input or to override AI decisions when necessary.

A.I. Delivering Value in SCM Today

Laying the proper groundwork through the application of the principles above will provide a firm foundation for deploying AI. There's no doubt that AI offers vast promise and there are significant benefits waiting for companies that focus on the fundamentals and put AI to use today. The beauty of AI-based solutions is that they self learn are autonomous and drive continuous improvement over time i.e. they get more precise and sophisticated as they mature by processing more data and learning through more experience.

Artificial intelligence is therefore starting to be deployed more in global supply chain management in order for companies to analyse and extract insights into their global supply chains' vast data. Gartner identified 10 notable areas where AI was providing value in supply chain.

1. AI improves automation via improved data quality and reduces the need for manual intervention

2. AI senses, samples and shapes market demand through direct customer engagement i.e. social media and sentiment analysis

3. Conversational Artificial Intelligence offers interactive user experience via existing technologies i.e. chatbots, Robo-advisers

4. AI improves performance and extends transportation capacity i.e. via augment reality and route planning

5. AI identifies hidden patterns in market data through machine and deep Learning – via categorisation and regression algorithms

6. AI capitalizes on IoT data to create an intelligent digital twin in manufacturing

7. AI extends existing Supply Chain planning capabilities – via predictive analytics

8. AI identifies Risk Exposure and offers actionable mitigation strategies – via anomaly detection, pattern recognition and machine learning

9. AI supports improving Customer service levels in Post-sales interactions via pre-emptive, proactive support and despatch, omnichannels interaction by bots, RPA and robo-advisers

10. AI supports efficient processing of supplier RFP responses via RPA and character recognition and machine learning

However, while machine learning and other AI technologies are indisputably important and disruptive in other industries, there are sizable challenges when deploying in the supply chain. Some notable examples are; the shortage of the high level technology skills required, the need to integrate multi-party data sources across the chain in order to gather data and execute algorithm solutions; and of course any global regulatory hurdles that may need to be overcome to enable widespread adoption.

Wearable Technology/Smart Glasses

Wearable technology is a broad category of sensors, computers and peripherals that can be attached to the wrist, ear, torso, over the eye or embedded in clothing.

For example, wearables range from smart glasses that provide heads-up displays of data to personal sensors that can detect fatigue or abnormal changes in vital signs and even exoskeletons that give the wearer increased strength and durability.

Smart glasses, have become pervasive in many supply chain use cases so they can fall into several categories: virtual reality (Vr), augmented reality (Ar), and mixed reality (mr).

Augmented reality and mixed reality maintain and present the viewer with an existing physical reality, but augment reality with a digital element to create a superimposed layer of virtual simulation on top of the real world. This is contrary to Virtual reality, which completely immerses the user in a computer-generated and simulated environment. More specifically, Ar takes advantage of the person's natural view of physical objects and enhances them with an overlay of digital information (e.g. text, simulated screens).

Mixed reality, Mr, on the other hand, brings virtual and real worlds together to create new environments. In these newly created environments, the virtual and the real worlds coexist and interact with one another. Nonetheless, it is not just smart glasses that can support Ar, Mr and Vr, indeed the success of the technology is because a smart phone, tablet and PC applications can also superimpose virtual information over a real world environment making the technology cheap an fast to roll out.

Some supply chain applications are emerging such as:

Microsoft Hololens: an MR product being used for a range of applications in the supply chain, especially for training in hazardous environments. For example, it can project holograms of unsafe conditions in an existing DC. A person wearing the headset can walk through the DC and identify safety problems. These headsets cost in the region of $3,000.

Similarly, Google glass, Vuzix Smart glasses, and Apple are all examples of companies with hands-free Ar headsets focused on augmented reality solutions on industrial applications.

These companies provide a wide range of industry solutions including applications in warehouse pickers, manufacturing, quality assurance, remote support, healthcare, training, utility/field service, and warehouse logistics. The Apple application is targeted for 2018, and will connect to an iPhone for processing. Such applications are being tested by DHL and are being piloted in the US and Europe.

DC pick, pack, and ship applications: DC applications are most commonly seen in pick and pack, using hands-free Ar solutions such as smart glasses. Warehouse pickers can identify and pick components more quickly and efficiently while reducing mistakes. Such applications are being tested by DHL and are being piloted in the US and Europe. The use of smart glasses improves the process of manual order picking, incoming/outgoing goods, or sorting and packing of goods, as well as inventory.

Smart glasses have the potential to positively impact the warehouse of the future in a number of ways. The technology will need to reduce in price, have multiuse capability, and make performance of repetitive tasks more efficient and accurate.

Some examples of current use case applications are as follow:

Dc customization applications: Smart glasses are used to enhance many DC processes such as when providing faster ramp-ups and improved quality and productivity by providing relevant information, confirmations, and documentation directly to workers' field of vision.

Work optimization through experience sharing: Smart glasses can assist other workers during training as the 'head's up' display alerts the user to a list of steps required to perform a task, to a better way of doing any number of tasks, or importantly, how to avoid unsafe conditions. Virtual digital assistants like Siri, Alexa, and Cortana can be added to help answer questions with a visual demonstration.

Service and repair: A repair technician can bring up instructions on their Smart glasses and can also connect with an off-site expert. Ar is especially helpful during troubleshooting and maintenance as it can superimpose a CAD image on to an object identifying the components an the steps to be taken.

Order picking optimization: Smart glasses are used to display the shortest, safest path to the next pick, and then highlight the specific item to be picked.

There is some interest in adding a scanner into the glasses as well as integration with the warehouse management system interface. An example of this is Vuzix integration with SAP's WMS. Some envision linking two wearable technologies: smart glasses and smart watches having multiple forms of data available and as well input options.

Engineering design: Smart glasses that create virtual environments will be useful for engineering applications. A remote design engineer can see activity in real time on the shop floor. An engineer can virtually walk through a new DC layout and modify it.

Temporary workforce management: Smart glasses will be able to provide step-by-step instructions for complex tasks or temporary workers. This is potentially a major benefit in using this technology as it accelerates the training and onboarding of temporary workers. This application of the technology could be especially useful when large numbers of such personnel are hired for seasonal, holiday and e-commerce volume spikes.

Other wearable technology: Sensors may be put in clothing to judge fatigue and motivate safety and other wearables could monitor vital signs (e.g. employee biometrics), warn of movement into a dangerous area, or even be able to shut down a forklift or robot if necessary.

The Smart glasses being produced today have a voice component and a vision component to enhance speed and accuracy. Gesture control could eliminate the need to a voice response. Despite, all of the perceived advantages Smart glass and augmented reality may not be for everyone as there are a few obstacles;

Wearability: Smart glasses must be comfortable to wear for eight-hour shifts. Designs will need to become lighter and smaller. Another issue is that they will have to coexist with personal, prescription glasses. In addition some people find the smart glasses were unsafe and obstructed their view of obstacles whereas others reported disorientation, headaches, and vertigo.

Augmented & Virtual Reality

Thanks to recent innovations in artificial intelligence and the distributed ledger technology known as blockchain, augmented reality is poised to transform the software used to manage supply chains. Augmented reality (Ar), which overlays information onto the real world, will now help truck drivers, warehouse workers, and management keep track of products from the second they leave the factory until the moment they arrive at the destination.

With over one billion AR-enabled smartphones and tablets already in use, companies don't have to wait for low-cost augmented reality glasses to start reaping the benefits of augmented reality. There are five ways that AR is transforming the supply chain into a nimble tool for global distribution:

1) Pick-and-Pack Services

Augmented reality is being used in warehouses to more efficiently locate products and pack them in outgoing boxes. One of the costliest parts of running a "pick and pack" service is training new workers to navigate a large warehouse and find the one product they are searching for.

 AR glasses can paint an imaginary line on the warehouse floor to simplify the searching and training.

For example, during the peak holiday season, temporary workers need to be on-boarded quickly. AR shortens the learning curve by providing new hires with constant feedback on their glasses about how they are doing and what can be improved. Picking and packing becomes more like a game, in which workers must gather the correct items before time runs out.

Field tests of AR pick-and-pack systems have reduced errors by as much as 40%. Some AR glasses can even be used to provide graphic overlays of packages on shelves, thereby minimizing the time needed to find and identify items to be picked. Once packed, the AR software can instantly provide carriers with handling instructions and anticipated shipping times.

2) Collaborative Robotics

This type of robot is the ultimate in human augmentation. Workers sitting comfortably at their desks can wear AR glasses that let them see what a robot in the warehouse sees. By wearing these AR glasses a human operator can now navigate robots through the maze of a warehouse and then use the robot's strength to lift and move heavy cargo.

Similarly, an operator can utilise a collaborative robot to undertake any dangerous or repetitive tasks, such as loading a truck. By utilising AR the operator can delegate tasks to robots that require human supervision when loading shipments to achieve the maximum load. Additionally, logistics robots are able to scan each product for damage, check its weight, and abide by any package shipping instructions. By connecting robots with office managers through an AR interface ensures that customers can be automatically alerted of any products that aren't available before the truck even leaves the warehouse.

3) Maintenance

Fixing a problem before it happens is the most cost-effective form of maintenance.

With many aircraft engines now transmitting usage data via Wi-Fi when they are on the ground, augmented reality is assisting maintenance crews in reducing engine downtime by comparing engine data with historical data from similar avionics systems.

These algorithms can suggest maintenance before a problem is likely to occur. For planes that spend most of their ground time at distant locations, AR can also enable more experienced maintenance teams at the airline's hub to see what local technicians are dealing with and provide timely live support.

4) Last Mile Delivery

In logistics, the last-mile of delivery to customers is the most expensive and problematic. AR can save money by cutting the time spent on last-mile delivery nearly in half. According to a DHL report, drivers spend 40% to 60% of their day searching inside their own truck for the correct boxes to deliver next. Augmented reality is used to identify, tag, sequence, and locate every parcel and this saves considerable time as the driver no longer needs to search for a specific item. AR glasses can also navigate the driver to the proper door in multi-tenant residences for delivery. These systems will record each and every delivery so that new drivers will benefit from past driver experiences.

5) Procurement

The distributed ledger capability of blockchain is being combined with augmented reality to bring transparency, consistency and traceability to procurement. This is because with a growing demand from consumers for ethical and sustainable products the entire supply chain falls apart when customers can't be assured of a product's origin or authenticity.

Using AR to identify and track each shipment from the source of raw material through to the manufacturer then to end consumer is a way to help solve customer concerns. Recording each transfer of ownership on a blockchain that will be instantly readable via Ar glasses can also assist procurement practitioners in verifying the origin of pharmaceuticals, food or the source of harvested crops.

In addition, AR will come in handy in three main areas across industries: product development and design, manufacturing and assembly, as well as support, maintenance and inspection.

6) Product development and design

In automotive design, AR imaging is being used to work out vehicle dimensions before prototypes are created. With the ability to visualise life-size computer aided design (CAD) models of a car through AR headsets, designers can now interact and test design changes without going through unnecessary and expensive prototyping. This helps to lower cost by eliminating the need for unnecessary scale models, while improving the efficiency and speed of the design process.

7) Manufacturing and assembly

In an aerospace assembly trial conducted by Boeing, technicians donning Google Glass headsets carried out complex wiring tasks by using voice controls to query for specific instructions which were then displayed on the headset displays.

8) Support, maintenance and inspection

In a motor workshop, technicians can use AR applications on a digital tablet to display detailed locations of hard-to-reach components. Repair instructions and special tools requirements will be overlaid onto the live camera image, enabling workers to quickly assess and identify the cause of malfunctions. This allows the workshop to increase productivity by improving the speed and quality of repairs.

Big data drives the decision making behind the world's distribution of products throughout the supply chain. Augmented reality is now poised to exponentially increase the speed at which data can be analyzed and acted on.

The insights augmented reality bring to the supply chain can be used to power the next generation of the supply chain, which will feature autonomous vehicles and delivery drones.

Drones

Last mile delivery is a conundrum that supply chain professionals today struggle to address. They expend great effort continuously searching for ways to achieve the next step improvement. Drone delivery may or may not be the answer but it is no longer the madcap idea it first appeared to be. Indeed long after the Amazon announcement in 2013 of drone delivery services and the subsequent patent filings for its multi-copter delivery devices – and the bemused market response. The idea is still very much alive with Amazon's confident of reaching their vision of a thirty-minute delivery service by Amazon Prime Air. The drone delivery would likely pilot in low-population rural areas with new Amazon stores in hundreds of locations serving as drone airports. Indeed Amazon has already carried out live residential deliveries in the UK.

For example, Amazon started Prime Air residential delivery for a few customers in December 2016 in Cambridge, United Kingdom. The trial delivered packages of up to five pounds in thirty minutes or less (thirteen minutes in one trial). In that region of the UK, Amazon was granted approval to fly at 400 feet fly and beyond the line of sight (the drones have sense-and-avoid-technology to avoid collisions). Customers were required to place a small QR code sign on their lawn to serve as a landing pad for the drone. Such drone delivery concepts are evolving rapidly, and all of this is still very much in the experimental stage. Nonetheless, other retailers are following Amazon's lead and are also experimenting with drone delivery, and one claims to have made many successful deliveries in the US in an FAA-sponsored experiment.

Some other drone delivery concepts in the planning or pilot stages are:

- Drone delivery from a truck: UPS and Fedex are considering a program where a drone will fly from a UPS/Fedex truck to deliver the last few miles. In a similar idea, Matternet (a maker of drone delivery systems) and Mercedes-Benz have a partnership to dock drones on a moving vehicle. The vehicle gets close and the drone lies from its roof to make the final delivery. The drone can also deliver while the truck continues to make its rounds.

- Drone landing: hosts of delivery methods are envisioned. One includes having an RFID tag on a locked mailbox that would be activated by the delivery drone. A DHL model delivers to a locker station in the neighbourhood, and then sends the customer a text with a code to open the box. Another idea proposes dropping packages via a controlled parachute rather than landing the drone.

- Special applications: UPS is testing drone delivery for emergency medical supplies. In a Google Project Wing test (initiated in 2012), the five-feet long, single wing drone hovers thousands of feet in the air and lowers packages to ground delivery robots. These drones would also have radio transponders that mark their location relative to other aircraft. Google reportedly is testing this concept in Australia. Such a drone could also be used for disaster relief scenarios once fully viable.

- Drone delivery from a store: Drone startup Flirtey has successfully completed a number of delivery experiments and these include a Domino's Pizza delivery, and a delivery from a 7-eleven to a private residence one mile away in Reno, Nevada, in July 2016.

According to 7-eleven, the goods were packaged in two containers separately flown to the home. The initial delivery included a chicken sandwich, donuts, coffee, candy, and Slurpees. Once the drones arrived at the residence, each container was lowered to the ground to the waiting customer.

In a later trial in December 2016 Flirtey made seventy-seven successful drone deliveries from the 7-eleven. Despite these successful pilots or proof of concepts the jury is still out on how rapidly this technology will roll out. It will be more likely that drones will find their role in internal supply chain usage such as in:

Warehouse and logistics: A number of companies are already using drone applications for internal use within supply chain operations. These prospective use cases seem to be in supply chain operations, especially in the following categories:

Inventory monitoring: Drones are used to track inventory in a warehouse. DroneScan and Corvus robotics are two examples. With these applications, a drone navigates the warehouse and does a physical inventory by scanning QR codes, reading RFID tags or using image recognition technology to identify and track inventory. One example is Walmart who used a drone to verify inventory in one of its large distribution centers (DCs). The drone reportedly checks the entire one-million-square-foot Walmart facility in a day, as opposed to the month it takes for a human. Furthermore, the drone can do this every day continuously updating the inventory. This application improves operational efficiency, increases inventory accuracy, and helps provide better customer service.

Inspection: Drones are also increasingly being used in industry to perform difficult or dangerous task especially in the field of inspection. For example, in 2016, BNSF railway began using drones to inspect tracks, bridges, and also to monitor air quality around rail yards. The company has 32,500 miles of track which needs to be inspected multiple times per week. The use of drones makes inspection feasible without increasing congestion on or around the tracks. The dromes capture data with cameras and sensors (e.g. laser profile sensors) to detect any anomalies and the data is fed into a predictive analytics engine in an attempt to forecast potential problem areas.

The drone reportedly checks the entire BNSF railway using multicopter drones for short duration applications (i.e. less than thirty minutes).

However for longer flight times of up to six hours the company also partners with the FAA on long-range drones. The drones have the advantage over human inspectors as they can work around the clock and can access areas which are difficult to get to, such as beneath tall bridges.

Similar to this idea of using drones for inspections, energy companies are using drones to inspect their power stations and high voltage lines and Oil and Gas companies have them deployed to inspect Oil rigs and pipe lines. Another inspection application could be using drones to survey roofs, outside walls, and areas around distribution centers.

Transportation assets, such as heavy goods trucks, spend an estimated 40 percent of its total transportation time sitting idle at either the point of origin or destination. That is why yard management systems are critical to tracking and optimally managing large amounts of truck and inventory assets.

Service and repair: Drones are being pressed into service to deliver spare parts to remote areas, such as sensors for IoT applications.

In addition to these use cases, many industries are conducting research projects with drones in the expectation of the potential in the development and application of affordable, autonomous drones. The key to widespread drone usage in the supply chain will come down to developing autonomous drones which can fly out with a handlers eyesight as well as to take of, fly, land, and return without human intervention.

From these early use cases, it can be seen that the use of drones in the supply chain is arousing a lot of interest.

Robot Process Automation

The technology of software driven Robotic process automation, or RPA, is the use of programming code to replicate human physical interaction such as typing or using a mouse or a GUI to mimic a human interacting with a program.

Despite being a software application the essence of RPA is automation technology, which allows an application to connect via systems through their user interface. That is importantly, despite being software why it is called robotic -- it mimics what the human would do at the keyboard.

RPA applications are highly beneficial when deployed to undertake high-volume repetitive and tedious tasks that previously required humans to perform. Indeed RPA is making a name for itself within the FinTech open banking industry as screen-scraper applications that can mimic a user's behaviour and hence automate remote banking services. This is because RPA applications were designed to mimic human interaction with an application so by watching and learning a human interact with even a complex application an RPA can soon learn the intricacies, nuances and learn how to replicate the user's actions. Indeed some RPA applications are so good that highly sophisticated anomaly detection systems cannot tell them apart from the genuine user.

Or at least that is what they were originally designed to perform today RPA technology enables companies to automate manual processes in the supply chain using software robots to interact with humans via text or voice and handle customer care or technical support tickets.

Therefore today they are expected to mimic humans when interacting with humans and be convincing. Having RPA technology takeover mundane human tasks such as password resets in customer care actually reduces error, labour costs and increases morale and productivity.

One area where this sort of automation is delivering higher value is in the auto-completion of standard order forms.

In particular it makes sense to have machines complete orders in procurement and ecommerce but there is also major utility in DevOPs. In operations, RPA is crucial when undertaking the mass automated configuration, updating and managing of disparate servers and the myriad of IoT components, which would have been infeasible manually. Hence, RPA is subsequently extremely useful in undertaking large scale, repetitive, manual work and it can be deployed as a strategic or commercial tool. Typically RPA is driven by whatever higher-level initiative there is to automate a task. For instance, if there is an initiative to reduce operational headcount in for example administrational duties – configuration and upgrading a multitude of network devices - then that is typically a trigger for an RPA project.

Implementing an RPA project is not always about saving money albeit it is often a key driver but it's not the only one. Securing the data quality and integrity of information that a company is storing and the information they collect, is a contemporary value driver. Similarly, the desire to increase customer satisfaction or manage customer expectations is another key initiative. Others look to implementing RPA as part of a general standardization initiative to assure that standards and compliance measures are applied equally across the domain.

In short, there are multiple objectives that can be targeted in an RPA project, but general observation is that there is always a strategic decision and a primary RPA initiative -- some of which are also done on a very tactical level, but the main objective is usually to remove tedious, repetitive, error-prone manual work.

Interestingly, software bots have also become frontline warriors in the ecommerce wars as they are being deployed to search competitor site for pricing. The ecommerce retail sector has become so competitive that a price differential of only 50c can be the difference in making or losing a sale.

Thus we are witnessing the intriguing bot war between two behemoths of retail Amazon and Wal-Mart.

As they battle it out to defend and counter-attack in equal measure, we get a glimpse into how demand shaping works in the modern supply chain. Bot-driven pricing has disrupted the retail industry since it became prevalent more than a decade ago. The huge advantage is in responsiveness as traditionally, brick-and-mortar stores changed prices no more than weekly because of the time and expense needed to swap labels by hand.

In the world of e-commerce, however, retailers update prices with ease, sometimes multiple times a day, helped by autonomous algorithms that consider amongst other factors, inventory levels, demand, sales forecasts and rivals' pricing data before automatically shaping demand by adjusting the prices to suit.

Robotics

Robotics spans a broad spectrum of technologies from software bots to autonomous vehicles to the heavy duty manufacturing behemoths. However, in the context of supply chain we will focus more narrowly on robot usage in warehousing, transport & logistics operations. Still, the diversity of robotics and their applications in large Distribution Centres is vast. This is due to Logistics being an early and enthusiastic adopter of automation technology through automated storage and retrieval systems, automated guided vehicles (AGVs), and manufacturing robotics. Nonetheless, robotics technology has experienced a monumental step-change in the last decade and robots are no longer fixed, dumb, difficult to program, blind and expensive. Instead, a 2016 pan-industry study, 51 percent of respondents said robotics is now a disruptive technology in the supply chain.

The automotive industry in particular has always been the biggest market for industrial robots, but suitable use cases for robots are expanding across many other light industries. In recent years, robots have been finding work in warehouses as the motivation to automate many warehouse processes has never been stronger. This has transpired due to the success of the ecommerce industry creating tens of thousands of new warehouse jobs. Therefore the desire to reduce labour costs and availability is the prime driver to deploying robots. Subsequently the high demand and sales volumes for robots has rapidly reduced prices.

In the supply chain robots can fulfil many tasks and here are some notable examples:

AGV/ASRS: Automatic guided vehicles (AGV) and automatic storage and retrieval (ASRS) applications have been around for many years in manufacturing and DCs.

 This type of DC with their high-rise, automated, narrow-aisle, lights-out areas, will be the future domain of automated guided vehicles.

Goods to Person: These robots help with order picking by taking the shelve to the human picker. Originally developed by KiVA (renamed Amazon robotics in 2015) the robot navigates the warehouse by scanning a grid on the floor containing hundreds of bar codes that provide an in-door GPS equivalent. By always knowing its relative position enables the robot to navigate and find then take the shelf to the proper location. There are currently 45,000 KiVA bots in Amazon DCs and in 2016 Amazon reportedly opened twenty-six fulfilment centres and had 361 DCs worldwide utilising KiVa bots.

Telepresence robots: These types of collaborative robots essentially allow someone to see, hear and communicate while moving around a remote area. Hence they have found a niche in conference halls were a remote delegate can conduct a tour and consult with presenters and fellow delegates as well as with salespeople and demonstrators as the robot navigates the exhibits in the hall. These robots are essentially a mobile computer screen, fitted with high density cameras and VoIP software, attached to a mobile remotely controlled chassis.

Other use cases are in retail where JDA is piloting a humanoid robot to access the complete inventory information and can take payment and schedule delivery. It is again in essence a tablet that speaks and interacts with customers. It can take vague descriptions of needs from a customer and then lead them to a good solution.

Follow-me robots: This application requires a robot that moves alongside a person or people in the picking operation in a warehouse. In this use case, the human picker will identify and picks the product and the robot delivers.

This is one example of a collaborative robot, or 'co-bot.' Locus robotics and Fetch robotics offer such mobile robots.

These type of collaborative robots have become pervasive as a result of the increase in ecommerce as these follow-me applications speeds up the picking operations. In essence, the cart follows the pickers, and when full, delivers to shipping. In the meanwhile another empty cart takes its place.

Manufacturing: Robotics started out in manufacturing and they are continuing to proliferate, with applications far too numerous to list. There are multiple companies in the game. iAm robotics makes autonomous picking robots that integrate with the WMS. Sensors allow it to detect and select items very accurately. Universal Robots (UR) makes easy-to-program co-bots. Clearpath has robots that are designed to move heavy pallets.

In addition inexpensive and easy to program robots are emerging rapidly. Baxter-2012 and Sawyer-2015 from Rethink Robotics are inexpensive and easy to program. A non-technical person can program these robots by moving the robot's arm to mimic the action they want the robot to perform. Moreover, cobots can be safely used beside humans and are easily reconfigured to perform any repetitive operation. Other new applications are grocery and meal deliveries in Europe and mobile security robots to patrol the grounds of a facility. One company is using AGVs to take inventory in a DC and even on store floors.

A futuristic distribution center may have to accommodate everything from narrow-aisle, high-rise ASR systems to goods-to-person (KiVA-type) systems and collaborative robots.

Given their falling cost and ease of implementation, robots will be used in many ways in the supply chains of the future. Many believe that robotic applications in the supply chain are at an inflection point and are about to grow exponentially.

Collaborative order picking: Collaborative order picking is another area where robots work in close proximity and in cooperation with humans. Robots can identify and pick and place specific components from a conveyor belt to fulfill orders.

Robot consumer deliveries: A number of experiments are taking place to use AGVs to deliver packages to consumer homes. In one example, a truck goes to a parking lot, and deploys AGVs to deliver the last mile. Some of the experts interviewed believe that robot delivery will greatly exceed drone delivery in the quest to find new fast ways to deliver to consumers.

Additive Manufacturing/3-D Printing

3-D printing has been viable for many years but has only come to the fore in the last decade or so. The process in principle works when an object is scanned and then represented in digital form. The printer then applies material in layers in an additive manner, building the product layer upon layer.

 Garter estimates that global shipments of 3-D printers will approach 7 million units by 2020 and that is an increase from 450,000 units in 2016.

3-D is used today in many companies for rapid prototyping but its applications within supply chains are varied. Some believe that service parts are the next big application. Nonetheless, 3-D printing technology continues to advance and current applications generally have some of the following characteristics: low volume, complex geometries for assembly, the need for fast consumer response, a need for customization.

Some specific applications include:

Running shoes: Nike, Adidas, and New Balance are experimenting with printing soles custom made for the user. The customer runs on a treadmill, and the custom insole is printed in the back room.

Dental crowns: In the past, when a patient needed a crown, the dentist took a mold impression and the customer came back a week later. With 3-D printing, the crown is made on the spot.

Rapid prototyping: for new parts or products.

Customized body parts: (e.g. knees, hips) Stryker has a 3-D printing innovation center and is investing heavily in a 3-D manufacturing operation in Ireland.

Promotion customization: items can be customized for individuals and used in sales/marketing promotions, from trinkets to chocolate treats.

Repair parts: In December of 2014, NASA sent a digital file to the space station for a much-needed wrench that was subsequently made with a 3-D printer. This type of application is also finding favour in Oil & Gas environments such as offshore rigs.

Low volume/High value components: Ge Aeronautics recently used 3-D printing to manufacture fuel nozzles for jet engines.

Metal additive manufacturing: in late 2016, Ge acquired a controlling stake in Concept Laser, a German company specializing in metal additive manufacturing. Metal 3-D printing has applications in the aerospace, medical, dental, automotive, and jewelry industries.

Experimentation: experiments are underway in hundreds of companies. For example, TNT Germany has established a number of 3-D printing stations around Germany to investigate how to utilize this technology. SAP is partnering with a number of companies, especially UPS, in developing distributed manufacturing capability to bring scalable 3-D printing applications to industry.

Some applications of 3-D printing that are expected to be widely implemented in the future are:

Print in route: Amazon has a patent for a mobile 3-D printer the idea is to avoid holding large inventory instead print a customer's order in route.

Repair parts: repair parts will be carried in digital form and chain professionals predict metal parts and other materials will be printed as needed. This will avoid a huge amount of very slow-moving inventory that is literally held for decades in many companies today.

Higher volume customized manufacturing: A swarm of 3-D robotic printing spiders comes to mind. Multiple robots will work together to build an object maybe even hundreds of them will someday build a car.

Mass personalization: Discussed for decades, mass customization to the specific needs of a consumer will become a reality.

Supply chain disintermediation: the elimination of certain parts of the supply chain will become feasible in some industries. Some component suppliers will disappear. Supply chains of the future will look very different as final manufacturing sites will be located much closer to the consumer.

Regional manufacturing: this technology will support regional manufacturing and the return to local manufacturing. A transition will take place from make-to-stock in low cost locations to make–on-demand close to the final customer.

4-D printing: this very futuristic concept is the ability for a 3-D object to transform with the addition of stimuli, such as water, light, and/or electricity.

For example, a flat item could be printed and shipped then the addition of a stimulus would cause the item to transform into its final shape. Some experts argue this will lead to future advancements in the use of active origami, where flat sheets automatically fold into a complicated 3D component. There have been some experimental examples of this where scientists have been able to demonstrate light weight material supporting exponentially more weight in its active origami state than it could support in its natural state.

3-D printing promises incredible benefits if it can be adopted widely these benefits fall into the following categories:

- Faster customer service: this technology should provide faster response to demand with fewer out-of-stocks.
- More customized product: 3-D printing may be the ultimate answer to the ubiquitous problem suffered by almost all companies, namely too many SKUs. This technology could create a utopian supply chain world of nearly infinite SKUs at no additional cost.
- Lower inventory: it will be possible to store 3-D files rather than the actual inventory. Smaller inventories also translate into less need for warehousing.

- Less transportation: it will be possible to compress network lows and disintermediate some parts of the supply chain.
- Lower cost product: 3-D printing offers the promise of product redesigns using drastically fewer component parts and fewer suppliers. it could, for example, eliminate the hefty investment required for expensive dies and moulds.

Driverless Trucks

Driverless vehicles became feasible over a decade ago and have continued to make major advances since. In mid-October 2015, it was reported that Mercedes-Benz introduced a production driverless truck. The driverless systems use short and longer-range radar and a camera for detecting lanes and markings. In one application, the driver simply presses a blue button, engages the highway pilot, and sits back and relaxes.

The National highway traffic Safety Administration has defined several levels of driverless vehicles:

- Level 0 is where the driver is fully and actively engaged in driving the vehicle (i.e. does everything)
- Levels 1-2: the vehicle can sometimes assist the driver in conducting or actually take over some functions (e.g. steering, acceleration).
- Level 3: the vehicle can conduct some functions pertaining to driving and monitor the driving environment, but the driver must be present and ready to resume full control when prompted by the vehicle.
- Level 4: the vehicle is fully autonomous with limitations. It is similar to Level 3, with the exception that the driver does not need to take back control from the automated system. There are limitations with respect to the environments and conditions under which the automated system can be engaged.

- Level 5: the vehicle is fully autonomous under all conditions, even extreme conditions. remarkable applications have proven the feasibility of driverless technology.

Some recent developments include:

Actual deliveries: An Uber-Otto/Anheuser Busch beer delivery occurred on October 16, 2016, from the Ft. Collins brewery to Colorado Springs, a 120-mile journey. For the majority of the trip, the driver left his seat and observed from the sleeper cabin. Uber bought Otto in mid-2016 for $680 million.

The uo system involves a $30,000 retrofit, including several light detection and ranging (LiDAr) units and a high precision camera above the windshield. In fact it offers true Level 4 autonomy. Drivers become like harbor pilots, who just bring the ship into port.

State regulations: A rapidly increasing number of states allow self-driving vehicles under some conditions. Nevada was the first in 2011. California, Michigan, Florida, North Dakota, Tennessee, Utah, Washington DC, and Arizona have followed recently. Pennsylvania, Ohio, and Michigan have agreed to work together as part of a Smart belt Coalition dedicated to initiatives involving driverless vehicles.

Many companies are in the game: Amazon has been granted a patent for a roadway management system capable of communicating with autonomous vehicles for driving assistance.

TomTom, a leading provider of navigation products, acquired an autonomous driverless German startup company Autonomous.

Tesla, Gm, Fiat-Chrysler, and many others are spending billions on developing driverless vehicles. In the Mercedes-Benz Future Truck 2025 project, once a truck reaches 50 mph on the highway, the driver activates an autopilot. Cruise automation bought by Gm can outfit a truck for driverless operation. Apple and Google are also developing the technology, some in partnership with automotive manufacturers. Fedex is partnering with several companies and experimenting with ways to link trucks into caravan groups or platoons.

- Global experiments: Driverless truck experiments are underway in several parts of the world. For example, a truck platooning system, in which groups of two to three smart trucks travel together communicating wirelessly, was introduced in Rotterdam in April 2016. In another example in the UK, autonomous vehicles by Nissan are being tested on the streets of London. The Nissan autonomous model is targeted for release in 2020.
- Driverless in DCs: Automated guided vehicles and forklifts in factories and DCs no longer have to follow fixed paths instead they can adapt to barriers that dynamically come into their path.

Driverless trucks may be a lot closer to reality than people think. Legal issues and government regulations will be the main barriers. Driverless trucks will first appear on the interstates with local drivers doing the first mile and last mile pickups. Local pickup and delivery steps are the most visionary aspect of driverless trucking. Platooning should go live within two to three years on some stretches of road, involving an active driver in the lead truck, followed by other trucks without drivers.

Technology will greatly outpace adoption as the forecasts for widespread implementation vary widely (e.g. from five to twenty-five years) but few doubt its viability. Indeed within the industry many are confident that driver-in-the-cab implementations will be widespread by 2020.

In the meantime, driverless technology is advancing rapidly. Reports are that Toyota and Nissan expect to have autonomous vehicles by 2020, and Tesla is planning for autonomous driving by 2023. Uber projects a significant driverless fleet by 2030.

The benefits of driverless trucks are obvious, and those benefits will drive the adoption at a rate faster than many think. Some of the most notable benefits include:

Productivity: there will likely be a return on investment even before fully autonomous trucks hit the highway. Once drivers can relax on the road in a Stage 4-5 environment, the hours of Service (hoS) regulations are expected to be relaxed. A driver can be resting and moving at the same time. With hoS regulations today, trucks are only 45 percent utilized, since drivers can drive only eleven of twenty-four hours. It will be interesting to see if future regulations address increased autonomous driving by making a distinction between total hoS and active hoS.

Fuel savings: the Department of transportation estimates that several trucks drafting via driverless convoys will save up to 7-10 percent of fuel. A test by Auburn University showed a fuel savings of 5-10 percent.

Safety: the legal cost of a crash can be astronomical, to say nothing of the human cost. Ninety-four percent of auto crashes are due to human error and result in more than 30,000 deaths annually. Insurance rates should come down over time as driverless trucks will be safer.

Driver shortage: there are 3.5 million truck drivers in the US to date. However, the American trucking Association estimates the driver shortage to be more than 50,000 drivers today and triple by 2024.

Faster customer delivery and lower inventory levels: if there is less time in transit due to a relaxation of the hoS rules, inventory will fall for a couple of reasons. One, there will be smaller amount of inventory actually in transit. Two, there will also be less need for safety stock as cycle times shrink.

More efficient flow of goods: Driverless trucks will impact network designs, and the number and location of DCs. Faster delivery times made possible by always-moving trucks would mean fewer DCs needed to provide the same level of customer service.

The technology is far ahead of regulatory environment and social acceptance so there are a number of barriers that must be overcome for driverless trucks to become widespread. Some of those barriers include:

Infrastructure: Appropriate infrastructure upgrades may be needed, such as signage, improved highway-to-vehicle communications systems, and more efficient refueling.

Reliability and safety: Cyber security, reliability, and maintenance will all be significant issues to address as this technology expands.

Cost: Although the cost of retrofitting existing vehicles with autonomous capabilities is slowly decreasing, such an endeavor is still expensive. There is still an unknown with respect to insurance despite the fact that experts believe driverless trucks will be safer.

Social acceptance: this will take some getting used to. Some report that being in a driverless vehicle or driving next to one is very unsettling. A single accident could send the public of the deep end. It is not difficult to envision a 'lose-lose' situation in which a driverless truck, which will likely rely on rules-based technology, faces a moral dilemma such as when the brakes on a truck fail on a downhill slope. If it veers to the right, it will go of a cliff. If it veers to the left, it will strike an on-coming car. If it stays in its lane, it will strike a slow moving car in front of it.

Regulatory environment: how fast will the regulatory environment allow for driverless trucks? The Department of transportation released the Federal Automated Vehicles Policy, a policy for self-driving vehicles, in September 20, 2016 and the policy includes detailed assessment guidelines for the design, testing, and deployment of these vehicles.

Technology: the technology needs to advance. Today trucks do very well at holding their lane and accelerating and decelerating smoothly. The technology to do more is advancing rapidly but the issues of phases will be hold the lane, move from lane to lane, move from exit to exit, and travel from dock to dock.

Some examples of challenges are wide turns that violate a lane, the absence of markings in a trailer yard, or bad weather conditions.

Wireless Communications

At the end of 2017, the wireless industry finally came up with the first official 5G standard. This was an important milestone because up until then several companies were working to their own definition of what 5G should be. Nonetheless, even with an industry standard it doesn't mean that all 5G will work the same.

The G in the name 5G stands for generation of wireless technology. While most generations have technically been defined by their data transmission speeds, each has also been marked by a break in encoding methods, or "air interfaces," which make it incompatible with the previous generation.

So for instance 1G was the old analogue cellular network. Its successor was the digital 2G technologies, such as CDMA, GSM, and TDMA, which were almost exclusively voice technologies that only supported data in small quantities. The transition to data networks started with the later 3G technologies, such as EVDO, HSPA, and UMTS, which data throughput and speeds from 200kbps to a few megabits per second. The first smartphones in the late 2000's accelerated the take up of 3G, and for the first time data became a priority for network operators as it usurped voice. Data usage soared and consumers rushed to embrace 3G mobile data service, which prior to then had been a pretty much stagnant service. The mass adoption of mobile data from 2010 onwards quickly delivered data enhanced 4G technologies, such as WiMAX and LTE, which were IP orientated and optimised for data and voice traffic was almost now simply an after thought. The consumer markets and the technology sectors however demanded increased bandwidth that was faster, more responsive and ha greater capacity so the next leap forward was to 5G. The initial projection for 5G is that it will scale up to hundreds of megabits and even gigabit-level speeds. Indeed, a technology claiming to be 5G must support three key features: greater bandwidth, lower latency, and the ability to connect a lot more devices at a cell concurrently as this is vital for IoT sensors and smart devices. The actual 5G radio system, known as 5G-NR, won't be compatible with 4G. But all 5G devices will initially need to ride on top of 4G because they will have to make initial connections before trading up to 5G where it's available. Initially this wil provide little benefit for low end performance constrained IoT devices but this does mean that the 4G will also continue to improve with time. For example, the Qualcomm X20 modem will support 4G speeds up to 2Gbps. Nonetheless, the advantages of 5G will be realised eventually in massive capacity and low latency, well beyond the levels 4G technologies can achieve.

How 5G Works

Similar to other cellular networks the 5G network will use a system of radio transmitter/recievers sites that divide their territory into sectors (cells) and send encoded data through radio waves to provide coverage to subscribers within the sector. Each tower site must be connected to a network backbone, whether through a wired or wireless backhaul connection.

5G networks will use a type of encoding called OFDM, which is similar to the encoding that 4G LTE uses. The air interface will be designed for much lower latency and greater flexibility than LTE, though.

The standard will work all the way from low frequencies to high, but it gets the most benefit over 4G at higher frequencies. 5G may also transmit data over the unlicensed frequencies currently used for Wi-Fi, without conflicting with existing Wi-Fi networks. However the desire for greater capacity and responsiveness - lower latency – means that 5G network architecture will likely consist of thousands of micro and pico sites rather than large cell coverage via towers typical in 3G networks.

  The nature of the frequencies used requires smaller cell sizes, but it is also required to increase network capacity as the more individual cells, the more data the network can ultimately support.

Hence, 5G networks need to be much smarter than previous systems, as the performance goal is to have far higher speeds available, and far higher capacity per sector, at far lower latency than 4G. The standards bodies involved are targeting circa 20Gbps speeds and less than 1ms latency, at which point all those IoT devices and futuristic innovation we have been hearing about will actually begin to happen.

AT&T has proclaimed that it will be first with mobile 5G when it launches a network in 12 cities by the end of this year. While it hasn't given details, it looks like it will be "millimeter wave" 5G, which requires dense networks of pico-cells that don't reach very far (say, about 1000 feet each), but deliver extremely high speeds.

AT&T's rollout could be slowed by a lack of 5G phones available before 2019, though. Qualcomm has said that 5G phones will be available in 2019, but not before then. AT&T said in early February that it would launch not with phones, but with a "puck" that we assume to be a mobile hotspot.

Similarly, Verizon is starting out with a fixed 5G home internet service launching in three to five cities in mid 2018. Presumably, this will offer gigabit internet to compete with local cable companies.

T-Mobile is taking yet another approach. The company is building a nationwide 5G network on the 600MHz band starting in 2019, with full national coverage by 2020. The low-band network will be supplemented by millimeter wave in large cities, which is the sort of 5G AT&T and Verizon are building out.

The speed of a wireless network is tied to how much spectrum you can use for it. Because T-Mobile is only using an average of 31MHz of spectrum at 600MHz as opposed to the hundreds of MHz that millimeter wave networks will use, its low-band 5G network will be a little bit faster than 4G, but not multiple gigabits fast.

It will still have the low latency and many connections aspects of 5G, making it usable for gaming, self-driving cars, and smart cities, for instance.

 In cities, the millimetre-wave network will be super-fast but the signal will be easily blocked by buildings, walls, trees or any obstruction that prevents a clear line of view.

How will 5G affect the Supply Chain?

The next mobile network generation, 5G, will enable new possibilities for manufacturing, supply chain and consumers by transforming many aspects of society and the way we do business. For one thing 5G will finally deliver on the promises of the Internet of Things (IoT). The IoT promise of connecting people and devices through the Internet will also connect almost everything we own.

But today's mobile network technology is not ready to fully handle these devices yet. However, this is an evolution and the first IoT solutions are being rolled-out on today's mobile networks.

Nonetheless, the IoT remains critically dependent on network devices that are more energy efficient, more reliable and use a mobile network with a much higher device density.

This is where 5G plays a crucial role. For to enable a future with thousands of interconnected objects - in the home, workplace and on the road – we need a new mobile technology able to handle all this connectivity and data.

Narrowband IoT (NB-IoT) is the first step in this direction and 5G IoT solutions will give further improvements. Narrowband IoT (NB-IoT) is a new technology using the existing 4G network. NB-IoT is energy efficient with high security and long range. However to fully leverage the possibilities of technologies such as autonomous trucks and dromes there will need to be a seismic shift towards the future 5G solutions.

For example 5G's huge improvements in capacity for device density, transfer speeds and in reducing latency, along with a 90% reduction in power consumption, are just some of the ambitions for 5G.

Furthermore in just a few years, the price of 5G-connected sensors will be so low, and the availability so high, that everything will be connected without worrying about cost or the loss of the sensors.

The low power consumption of the IoT devices also enables a long lifetime without the need for replacements. Being able to attach microscopic sensors to everything so it is labelled, tracked and recorded automatically will revolutionize transportation. Indeed it should be then end of losing cargo, misplacing containers and losses due to manual inefficiency and labour. Furthermore, the always-on technology used for tracking will create a framework for transparent and optimised supply chains that will deliver savings in both time and cost.

For example, today a parcel or container usually changes hands during transportation and temporary or permanent storage, thus posing a problem of responsibility, ownership and insurance in the supply chain. However, by installing 5G-connected sensors to every single item, either on the inside or outside of packaging, the stakeholders in the supply chain can, at any given time, see the item's location, temperature, humidity, g-forces, velocity and much more.

Having the capability to monitor and share data automatically with all parties involved, without the need for manual checkpoints, would give peace of mind to both businesses and customers alike. It could also speed up production, streamline complex logistical processes, and help cut costs drastically. And if incidents were to happen, contingency plans can be drawn up sooner giving better time for mitigation.

Technologies related to Supply Chain 4.0 Competencies

Now that we know the technology and the advanced strategies of how the supply chain may evolve we need to understand how it will relate to several key competencies such as Planning and Execution, Sourcing & Procurement, Warehousing, Transportation & Logistics as well as Post Sales Logistics.

Supply Chain 4.0 is having a profound effect in all of these functional areas through leveraging digitization via smart processes and new technologies. The following chapters will investigate the role technology plays in each functional domain.

Chapter 19 - Supply Chain 4.0 in Planning and Execution

Machine Learning is playing a key role in how Supply Chain 4.0 is revolutionizing the way planning and execution is performed. Indeed AI and Machine learning is already transforming supply chain planning by removing traditional roles. For example, the way planners work has been radically changed due to the ability for supply chains to sense demand and respond by shaping the demand in an autonomous manner. This facility has encouraged some organizations to shift from functional planning based on forecasting towards a network centric plan built around demand sensing and shaping. These network planners are developing "what-if scenarios" built upon cloud computing platforms and concurrent optimization tools, to drive autonomous self-correcting supply chains using "if this do that" style logic.

How this manifests itself is through faster decision making and hence a shift from the legacy approaches of mid-term forecasting operations to planning with more real-time optimization. This real-time functionality is being driven by AI and machine learning fueled by structured, unstructured and real time streaming of operational and process data.

Catalysts for faster and better decision making

Consequently, the result is much faster decision cycles, which optimizes and bridges the traditional gaps between planning and execution.

Furthermore, AI and Machine Learning provide for more that better informed and faster decision making as they also provide a means of distilling information without human bias.

Hence AI, when applied to a human-type job, can help us get rid of inherent human bias and avoid missing patterns of correlation.

There are so many possible combinations of machine learning, which can be applied across functional planning areas that typically introduce ambiguity. If we consider demand planning for example then unsupervised machine learning can identify a cluster of SKU's that have stable demand, but more volatility in quality. On the other hand, supervised machine learning can allow us to use external indicators to create a forecast for a product. In addition, deep learning facilitates for even more features, which can create a more powerful forecast.

The importance of features in ML is that it is an attribute that the algorithm will use as criteria. For example, if you are building a model for predicting a product price for example a mobile phone, some features might be screen size & type, OS Type & version, memory size, No of cameras and capability, case color, etc. The more features that are fed to the algorithm, then the higher the chance of the prediction model returning an accurate estimate. However, too many features can over-fit the model reducing its effectiveness – this is called overfitting. Therefore, planners need to find the features that are relevant to the question they are seeking to answer and are in alignment with the business. This means that the features are valuable to the company and indeed companies are beginning to compete on the design of their algorithms and the inherent feature sets. Hence, companies are reluctant to reveal their features – sharing only the normalized values. And here is where we are seeing a barrier to entry for most companies as they are still using traditional systems to manage their planning. Enterprise planning systems such as SAP or Oracle can integrate with machine learning but it requires custom work, it is not off the shelf. However, there are several open source algorithms available that can be implemented and then routed back to the legacy systems so there is no need to replace the current systems. However, despite this reliance on legacy systems for forecasting some companies are using machine learning use cases to add value and automate many processes within their business. For example:

- Root cause analytics – this is used to answer questions such as; why did we run out of stock; why did we miss a delivery date? This effort starts with a lot of data engineering and descriptive analytics.
- Anomaly detection in supply chain – stock-outs, bad data, etc.
- Forecasting – not just of future demand, but also end of life and new product introduction
- Supply planning – replacing some of the more mundane tasks & planner intuition
- Data cleaning – there are tools that do this now driving autonomic master data management
- Production planning – using sensor information to feed back to your planning processes; think dynamic replenishment
- Codification of customer intelligence – building in knowledge of promo phasing, buying patterns, etc. instead of human knowledge transfer challenged by attrition
- Improving Demand Planning. The power of machine learning in demand planning is the combination of (1) more algorithms to test your data against your performance, and more importantly (2) recognizing the set of features that drives sales in your business.

The real benefits though of implementing ML is revealed when we understand how the performance of machine learning or deep learning algorithms in forecasting compares to the status quo forecast from the incumbent advanced planning solution. More than 75% of the time, a machine learning algorithm delivers a better forecast. This is down to the customized feature sets deployed in ML, which are not feasible in statistical systems and new algorithms. It is important to note, however, that machine learning solutions should complement traditional advanced planning solution and not replace them. Other areas of Operations and Planning where Industry 4.0 technology is leveraged for performance and efficiency are:

- Sensor Analytics in Supply & Production Planning. The premise here is to ensure the yield is good and can catch any potential issues ahead of time through predictive maintenance. Predictive analytics allows engineers to collect data from affordable sensors and understand machine status and predict failure.
- Inventory Management. The purpose here is to use machine learning techniques to better understand variability through the supply chain, and to predict stockout's at DC or store level.
- Automating Root Cause Analysis. RCA takes many disparate data sources and aggregates them to determine a root cause, which also eliminates the human bias. Root cause analytics has applications in many areas of operations – order processing, warehouse operations, customer delivery, and vendor management, amongst others.
- Segmentation - Unsupervised learning is useful when there is a lot of data and you are trying to find correlations or meaningful patterns. The power of machine learning is to be able to segment or cluster data points using dozens of features.

From all those potential use case it can be seen that machine learning promotes efficiency through process automation in the repetitive, manual and transactional tasks within planning. In addition there is also the benefit of a reduction of human error and bias. Hence, by freeing up employees that are involved in non-value adding activities this will allow them to be redeployed in more strategic problem solving and analytical work. Moreover, algorithms enable planners to make better decisions.

Chapter 20 - Supply Chain 4.0 in Procurement

Digital procurement or Procurement 4.0 as it is now knows embraces the disruptive IoT technologies such as AI, advanced analytics and Machine Learning, that enable Strategic Sourcing (S2C) to be predictive, Transactional Procurement (P2P) to be automated, and Supplier Risk Management (SRM) to become proactive.

The relevance for Supply Chain Management is that procurement practitioners i.e. those concerned with sourcing goods and services, selecting suppliers, and securing the best value and prices for their organizations are typically concerned with the Strategic Sourcing or Source to Contract (S2C) business. In this case, they are predominantly concerned with:

- Categorizing and managing spend in real time, leveraging machine learning
- Predicting demand using artificial intelligence
- Knowing landed cost for any commodity for all alternate countries of origin
- Predicting future sources of supply
- Acting on timely alerts from all negotiated agreements (e.g., indexed pricing, penalties, renewals) through smart contracts

In the digital age, the business of S2C has become more transparent and predictive, where the metrics of supply bases, prices, and costs are all visible. This enables suppliers/buyers to reach transparent agreements due to the visibility of the transaction. This visibility allows partners in the Transactional Procurement or Procure to Pay (P2P) space - those that enable operations to process transactions, and ensure goods and services are delivered and rendered - to operating in a trading ecosystem in which it is possible to:

- Automatically sense material demand and requisition replenishment deliveries from suppliers

- Eliminate repetitive processing through robotic process automation
- Trigger payments utilizing real-time signals of material delivery
- Execute automated secure payments
- Exchange goods through validated and trusted decentralized ledgers

Transactions, which are considered as being, amongst others, the processing of purchase orders, requisitioning goods and services, validating reception of materials, or the paying of invoices. Will in the P2P digital world become automated, routine and hence require minimal human intervention.

Indeed those participating in Supplier Relationship Management (SRM) will tend to develop strategies aimed at increasing the value of supplier relationships and importantly in identifying risks so they are in a domain in which focuses are on:

- Monitoring and evaluating potential supplier risks in real-time through the aggregation and visualization of third-party data feeds
- Conducting checks and balances by verifying via supplier visits from their own office utilizing augmented reality
- Enhance supplier audits through crowd-sourcing i.e. social media sentiments

Where SRM becomes proactive, as a risk mitigation strategy is when it becomes pre-emptive, allowing managers to focus on continuously optimizing operations and processes, as opposed to conducting reactive damage control.

In order to leveraging valuable data from the S2C, we need to know and have P2P, and SRM processes, advanced analytics, increased computing power, as well as improved visualization technologies. Ultimately, digital procurement provides better evidence-based options for decision making and improves the accuracy of strategic decisions.

The fact is that organizations are deploying several tactics when deploying the core procurement technologies. These strategic approaches often aim at platforms that are a hybrid of spend analytics, contract management, and eProcurement, amongst several others. These core analytical systems have typically been developed by departments requiring justification for their capital spending and system integration work. In contrast, today, Software as a Service (SaaS) models, do not need significant Capital (Capex) or Operational (Opex) expenditure but the preparation of data for these systems, requires a high level of skill and manpower.

Many companies which have delved into the machine learning ideal and followed the digital potential, solutions and capabilities have entered the maturing phase. On the other hand emerging companies that have not already embraced the competitive digital advantage are typically not sure on their objectives.

Technologies that support Procurement

Cognitive computing and artificial intelligence:

Modern Machine Learning technology leverages the art of pattern recognition. It also demands iterative machine learning algorithms to consume vast quantities of operational and marketing data. AI can categorize unstructured spend, cost, contract, and supplier data to deliver new insights and opportunities. But it must be fed true data and have a clear criteria.

Intelligent content extraction: Optical Character Recognition (OCR) is a source of clean data that learning algorithms are able to read. In addition we have unstructured documents such as video, text chats, photographs, social media sentiment or specification drawings, as well as Bills of Material. Furthermore they can extract data from all the noise pieces of data like pricing tables, payment terms, and termination clauses that would have taken days or weeks to assemble.

Predictive and advanced analytics:

By combining modeling, statistics, machine learning, and artificial intelligence with multiple third-party data sources enables a planner to predict the most probable scenarios for cost/price fluctuations, demand, supplier/country risks, etc. and enable proactive decision making.

Visualization: Data is raw and to transform that into understandable, executive-friendly, dashboard and visual formats that can simplify decision making. It requires software that can organize information and deliver fresh operational insights and informed recommendations.

Collaboration networks: This factor requires operational platforms that share data generated by both buyers and suppliers with visibility into all elements of their joint value chains. The premise is that suppliers and Buyers can access customer demand information and then; measure, analyze, and manage supplier performance; uncover joint process improvement opportunities; and identify, monitor, and escalate supplier risks.

Crowd Sourcing: This is a modern approach to demand analysis as the capture of large and diverse inputs (e.g., data, user sentiment) and usually leveraging mobile technology, organizations, social media, text and chat can determine trends and events impacting supply chains and supplier performance. By harvesting social media for consumer sentiment a supply chain can gain invaluable information.

3D printing: Additive manufacturing, or 3D printing technology as it relates to procurement, can quickly make a physical object from a digital model by producing a proof of concept model. Hence it is currently used mostly for rapid prototyping of goods but the technology has the potential to eventually eliminate some kinds of stocking activities for low-volume items, replacing them with on-demand production. Rapid prototyping will become an integral part of the strategic sourcing process for direct materials.

Robotics: As it relates to procurement, robotics can play a major role. Robotics Process Automation deploys software that recognizes and learns patterns and can perform rule-based tasks. This process is used to automate multiple repetitive manual tasks (e.g., some P2P tasks), driving efficiency and reducing errors and risks in execution. Hence bots are used in order taking and fulfilment.

Four additional emerging solutions are expected to impact procurement in the future and procurement leaders should be educating themselves and preparing for adoption are:

Blockchain: This distributed ledger data structure uses a trusted peer-to-peer network to create digital transaction ledgers which can verify and validate transactions in the P2P process (or any other supply chain process) and then be used to trigger automated payment.

Sensors and wearables: These are devices that trough embedded computer power can detect, capture, and record physical data. These devices can note the movement of goods and inventory levels for reordering, and enable audit tracking during site visits.

Cyber tracking: Real-time tracking of online or physical activity can be used to provide proactive monitoring of supplier behaviour and performance. When combined with third-party data, the technology can deliver trends and predictions on supplier (or supply chain) risks.

Virtual reality and spatial analytics: Detecting events or changes of status using video, location data, or pattern analysis, and conducting supplier visits or audits can empower procurement professionals to do more with less.

 As a stand-alone deployment, each of the solutions mentioned above brings additional value to procurement. However, organizations that combine multiple technologies and solutions could see the value of their deployments grow exponentially. Given the pace of change, procurement leaders should take every opportunity to expose their organizations to these disruptive technologies and to consider their applicability within their own organizations.

Connecting Physical and Digital Worlds

Digital procurement solutions are allowing for many more physical and digital inputs to be connected, driving better decision making and improving efficiency, and ultimately producing results in the form of:

- Improved insights and strategies, leading to accelerated cost leadership
- Enhanced process excellence, leading to greater organizational efficiency and effectiveness
- Better assurance of supply and improved risk mitigation

Improved Inputs

Many digital solutions are designed around providing access to previously unavailable data, or bringing order to massive (but unstructured) data sets. Examples include:

- *Mountains of text files in hard-copy Word or PDF form:* An intelligent content extraction solution enabled by machine learning will convert static documents such as contracts, standards and specifications, into digital data points for quick access, review and action.
- *Multiple and disparate sources of spend information*: Procurement practitioners require a single and constantly refreshed source of supplier spend that handles all types of structured and unstructured data as input.
- *Demand, delivery, and consumption of raw materials*: All these changes can be captured through sensors that digitize the analogue flow, status and transaction of materials.
- *Third-party information;* External data is collected and fed into automated solutions that utilize artificial intelligence to layer this

third-party data on to in-house data to support better sourcing and supplier strategies. Some examples of third party data are; supplier data, commodity trends, weather, traffic, social media, local media, duties and tariffs, country risk, and socio-political risk.

Improved decision making and efficiency

The use of external third party data to supplement and enrich in-house spend data in digital procurement solutions is driving more complex analysis, better supplier strategies, and more efficient operations. Some examples include:

- Advanced analytics models that use large volumes of manufacturing and procurement data to generate cost-takeout and design improvement insights through visualization technology.
- Predictive analytics models that calculate total landed cost differences across products, country viability, country risk, and future-state forecasts by category and country.
- Cyber tracking and collaboration network capabilities which access real-time, relevant data across ecosystems and link physical events of the supply chain to information and action. These solutions help control, measure, and quickly respond to supplier or supply chain events.
- Blockchain solutions that can verify and validate transactions in the P2P process and can trigger automated payments.
- Robotics process automation solutions that deploy macro-like software and replicate tasks like processing information, interacting with ERP systems, and sending emails.

Digital analytical solutions help procurement generate new insights and strategies to surface new sources of value, increased efficiency and greater effectiveness in achieving process excellence. Furthermore, digital analytics will deliver assurance of supply and successful risk mitigation.

Digital procurement and legacy systems

With so many digital procurement solutions coming online, many procurement leaders struggle to determine their strategy in light of other legacy investments they have already made.

Regardless of the current state, core, emerging and maturing capabilities will continue to work together for the foreseeable future. The good news is that many of the maturing and emerging solutions "meet you where you are" in terms of data and existing systems. A digital procurement strategy should take into account the current level of core technology maturity such as:

- Companies with minimalist investments in core technologies can find value in maturing solutions that eliminate the need to make certain core technology investments – the leapfrog approach.

- Organizations that have a moderate level of existing investments often can use targeted investments to plug gaps and drive even more value from these legacy investments by augmenting the existing technology.

- Organizations that have made substantial investments in core technologies can utilize emerging and maturing technologies to accelerate value capture and differentiate their teams.

It is worth remembering that many of these maturing and emerging technologies are not time- and resource-intensive capital investments, and payback is often measured in weeks, not months or years. In light of this, organizations should start small, act fast, and think big.

Chapter 21 - Supply Chain 4.0: Intralogistics

The introduction and proliferation of omnichannels sales and support has tasked the business with supporting the fulfilment across a growing number of diverse and distribution channels. Previously, a warehouse or DC was simply a storage facility for goods as it made its way through the supply chain however the modern-day facility must be agile and capable enough to support brick-and-mortar, e-commerce, B2B, home deliveries and parcel shipments—to name just a few. Hence, warehouses and distribution centres (DCs) are increasingly looked upon as strategic business assets rather than cost centres.

Achieving this transformation is non-trivial as it requires advanced technology to offset issues like high labour costs while also streamlining the process. While most companies are investigating ways to accomplish this change, many are still using antiquated processes such as spreadsheets to manage inventory and track product movement within the four walls of the warehouse.

The majority of companies are still using basic warehousing techniques and even the larger shippers are lagging behind but they are at least trying to get better in areas like automation, robotics, virtual reality, voice and radio frequency identification, in an effort to get to the 'next level' with their warehousing. For those seeking to improve their warehousing processes the good news is that software and equipment vendors are producing the technology they require. From complete supply chain solutions to advanced inventory tracking systems the options are available to produce more efficient smarter facilities.

As a result warehouse management is rapidly evolving, along some common tracks.

1.) Software that adapts and personalizes easily

Similar to their end customer's expectations of quick, personalized service, logistics professionals also share an expectation that their warehouse management systems (WMS) will be configurable and flexible with regards customization. As a result software vendors are developing systems that can accommodate and address their customers' specific needs and pain points.

For example, more logistics operations are asking for WMS that can be built out rapidly and put in place without having to go back to the vendor for specialist configuration and additional customization of workflows and processes. Through these bespoke builds, logistics managers can train their own people a lot faster than they'd be able to with a more standard WMS offering.

2.) Warehouse Control Systems (WCS)

The synergy between warehouse control systems (WCS) and WMS is growing especially where more automation is being introduced into warehouses and Distribution Centres. Traditionally, WCS provided the interface for machinery such as the carousels, sorters, conveyors, while WMS managed processes, people, and activities. Hence WCS managed the material handling systems while WMS handled the material production processes such as inventory, shipments and orders.

However, with the advent of more automation and autonomous systems companies are upgrading their WCS so are looking to leverage their investments. One way to achieve this is to have the WCS undertake warehouse management functionality. Merging the two systems is desirable on many technical and business levels and as WCS systems become more capable in this field the trend is likely to continue and the borders between WCS and WMS will blur.

3.) Autonomous mobile robots on the warehouse floor

Wärtsilä and DHL have completed a successful pilot where the companies tested Fetch Robotics to investigate possibilities to utilize the latest technology innovations in the daily operations of the warehouse. The robots are designed to work alongside employees, and to relieve them from physically strenuous tasks.

Through modern technology logistics is on the cusp of some very radical changes to the warehouse largely to automated robots. While warehouses and DCs have been equipped with robots and automation for some time it has typically been "bolted to the floor" type automation which was expensive to design, build, and install—and complicated to reconfigure. A major constraint was they were difficult to redeploy and had to be reprogrammed and retrofitted by expert programmers and engineers. Today, modern robots are mostly autonomous and easy to reconfigure and redeploy by non-technical employees.

4.) Robots that coordinate with the workforce

To be effective on the warehouse floor the robots have been designed to be more intelligent and universal in their applications and with safety in mind so that they are compatible with a human workforce.

For example, Fetch Robotics has successfully introduced robots that work in collaboration with humans in a picker role. The company sees the optimization of robotics in conjunction with pickers as a good way to streamline warehousing processes without adding additional labour as it just requires getting the robotics coordinated with the workforce.

5.) Advanced planning capabilities

Warehouse and logistics managers are often very good at reactive troubleshooting and expediting, but not as diligent or competent at proactive planning. However, the growth of e-commerce and omni-channel are pushing managers to rethink the way they approach the warehouse process.

High-volume e-commerce requires warehouse execution systems [WES] to apply more sophisticated logic to how they manage their work. Ideally this would be through optimization and machine learning techniques. These are viable ways to proactively plan in even the most challenging distribution environment. Indeed more companies are striving to move away from "after the fact" reporting to "advanced planning", which allows shippers to effectively look ahead in planning their operational processes. This is sometimes referred to in transportation as being comparable to shifting the focus from the rear view mirror to the windscreen.

Smart logistics: logistics 4.0

Modern-day logistics has undergone radical change and is almost unrecognisable from the legacy one-dimensional storage and distribution processes and systems of the past. This is due to the introduction of smart technologies, which have facilitated a step up in the interaction of machines and processes. Machine to machine communication is not something new but it has evolved through the introduction of Industry 4.0 and the industrial internet of things into the central nervous system of the modern factory. However to leverage the maximum benefits of the smart technologies they ideally should be introduced throughout the supply chain. Consequently, these smart technologies are increasingly finding their way out with the factory and into the area of transport and logistics and this is revolutionizing industry. These 'smart' technologies are intelligent systems which are capable of controlling processes autonomously i.e. without any human interaction. Their introduction is the foundation of Industry 4.0 and the concept of the Smart Factory.

Chapter 22 - Smart Factory

The intelligent factory of the future

In conjunction with various manufacturers and academic institutions, the German Research Centre for Artificial Intelligence (DFKI) developed a conceptual model of an intelligent factory of the future – the Smart Factory. At its core is advanced M2M communications which allows independent autonomous production modules to communicate with each other without any human interaction.

The smart factory model is based on three key elements:

- An intelligent, communicating product
- A networked information system
- An assisting operator of the system

In this context an intelligent product is one that is permanently aware and kept informed about its current status and stores production data such as the process order and material required with the help of integrated sensors (e.g. RFID or Bluetooth) and is thus able to influence its own production. The role of the networked information systems is to enable real time bi-directional communication between the intelligent products and other production modules. The network comprises cyber physical systems (CPS) that enable and monitor the individual work steps. In this system, the CPS control production but a human operator is informed about the production process with details of the assembly process and the necessary work flow.

As a result the usual distinction between production planning and production management no longer applies in the Smart Factory. Due to the networked infrastructure and the integrated approach the machines share information and forecasts on the production process among each other and interestingly with the product so can collaboratively determine the work flow. This means that all related data required by the material flow, such as the machine utilisation, storage capacity and other use of resources also flows into the process and is taken into consideration when an action plan is created. The information has to flow between the machines in real time so that it can have an immediate and interactive effect on ongoing production.

This is where data logistics plays an especially important role, because it is responsible for ensuring that all data – current as well as forecast – is available swiftly and in full, and is forwarded with no time delay whatsoever. Therefore the concept underlying the Smart Factory, the integrated, order-oriented production approach, extends to the entire value chain from the raw material to the finished industrial product. As a result this extension of the Smart Factory model requires cross-company interaction and collaboration that guarantees sharing of information through the supply chain.

Nonetheless, introducing Industry 4.0 throughout the supply and value chain is technically challenging. Not only is there a prerequisite to share a huge flow of data, which will necessitate an extensive reorganization and merging of OT and IT infrastructure. This will inevitably lead to an expansion of the communication and data security networks if the vision of an integrated value chain is to be realised. And there lies one of the obstacles, how to guarantee comprehensive data security. For not only is it necessary to ensure that data is available to authorized users, it is also mandatory to ensure confidentiality and integrity of the shared data. The mitigation of threat from the loss, compromise or release of confidential data through unauthorized access or from potential intruders is paramount. Consequently, data logistics experts are faced with the real word dilemma of collaboration through data sharing with partners and enforcing strict data security and confidentiality. This necessitates that IT security practitioners develop and implement wide-ranging security concepts and standards across the supply chain.

Linking data and transport logistics

As Industry 4.0 comes into vogue, transport logistics is coming to the fore. The advancement in this discipline entails the integration of the key elements in the transport chain such as flexible route planning, vehicle and shipping capacity, forecasts of the traffic situation, notifications of traffic congestion, inclement weather or geopolitical news are some examples. Nonetheless, although many of these elements are already in common practice the introduction of intelligent, self-driving vehicles will be a catalyst for major disruption. Autonomous trucks based on the Internet of Things and AI will introduce completely new dimensions and create even more avenues for automated and flexible logistics solutions. This is an area of compatability between data and transport logistics. Data logistics provides the information which is the fuel used to optimize the transport logistics. The more extensively information on capacity, weather, traffic, and vehicles is shared, the more efficiently the transport logistics are managed. In the e-commerce era where smaller batches are being transported the production and distribution sides are virtually dependent on the efficiency and flexibility of the transport logistics. The premise of Industry 4.0 can only become reality if the supply chain can guarantee that raw materials, products, and finished articles are ready for shipping and are in the right place at the right time.

Smart transport systems in the warehouse

Industry 4.0 is the catalyst for the introduction of smart transport intralogistics through "cellular transport systems" in the warehouse. This operation involves swarms of autonomous vehicles operating on the warehouse premises. These vehicles can sense their surroundings and navigate their environment using laser scanners, infrared sensors, and RFID chips. Further, they can do this autonomously with no central control system or human interaction as these devices allocate incoming transport orders among themselves. They also set rules governing the right of way, and share data on the position of each vehicle in the warehouse. Since each vehicle processes its own information the entire control system is distributed. Thus, if disruptions should occur, then the onus is on the vehicle swarm to rectify the problem.

Autonomous transport robots

Inspired by the "Smart Factory" model two companies have developed a solution for optimizing their customers' internal production logistics. Dynamic retrieval solutions from Kardex Remstar and a robotic transport system from Servus Intralogistics, form the basic elements of the technical solution. In essence the systems store parts required in the assembly area in Kardex Remstar's vertical storage lifts, vertical carousels, or box storage system. At the time of retrieval the Servus transport system automatically picks up the parts from the warehouse and transports them to the assembly area with the help of autonomous transport robots running on tracks. Simultaneously, the devices automatically receive information about the necessary work steps and take care of all further steps independently. Accordingly, the Servus system requires no central control system, because the transport robots communicate directly with other transport robots and workstations via infrared and thus react to their immediate environment. The Servus transport system has proven to be particularly flexible, because the track route can be freely configured in the production hall and optimally adapted to existing building structures. As such, the track can be installed anywhere – from the floor to the ceiling – in the warehouse and production halls.

Swarm intelligence from the Fraunhofer Institute

Another style of box storage and transport system has been designed by the Fraunhofer Institute for Material Flow and Logistics which goes by the name of Multishuttle. This system demonstrates an approach that is essentially similar but extends the functionality. The concept is that a storage system should not only be measured in terms of storage but also in terms of efficiency and performance in retrieval measured by the speed at which the boxes arrive at their destination. At the Fraunhofer IML specialists worked on the premise that the conveying and use of storage systems for mini load carriers will continue to increase in comparison to pallet conveying and storage systems. The rational behind this is that ecommerce is driving smaller consignments and advances in inventory management has resulted reduce stock levels in industry and commerce.

 Fraunhofer's design was based upon the development of a transport system with cost-effective, track-guided vehicles. These should also be able to perform storage and retrieval tasks in the warehouse independently so that they can handle the entire transport process from the warehouse to the workstation without having to transfer the goods at any point. This idea led to the development of the so-called Multishuttle, which works in a similar way to the Servus transport vehicle. However, the engineers soon discovered the limitations of this solution: the inflexible track system. As a result, they set to work on an advanced version of the Multishuttle, which would be able to navigate around the warehouse with no tracks. That is how the institute came to work in conjunction with the company Dematic to develop the MultiShuttle Move, which is compatible with the conventional track system, but is also equipped with a floor-based chassis and an intelligent navigation system. The vehicle has front- and rear-mounted laser scanners which help it to find its way when working on the floor while also serving as a safety feature. With the help of integrated locating technology it can move completely freely in the room and react dynamically to changes without any guidance or other fixed markings. This reduces the fixed conveying technology to a minimum while guaranteeing maximum flexibility.

With an intelligent system and interlinked vehicles that perform all transport tasks, for instance from a high-bay storage system to the workstations where the goods are processed or picked. Then the agile helpers are not guided on their journeys by warehouse management software, but instead manage their coordination independently among themselves without any kind of central control system. Since this kind of storage logistics demands a great deal from the little helpers, any kind of software responsible for the complex task of guiding this swarm of robots would also be overwhelmed. As a result, however, they are able to move around freely on the floor and on track sections within the high-bay storage area.

The vehicles communicate with one another and control themselves using the principle of swarm intelligence. This is made possible by the use of newly developed sensor technology equipped with functions such as radio location, and distance and navigation instrumentation. Such technology helps the individual shuttles to select the shortest and most direct route to their destination at all times and determine among themselves which shuttles will handle particular orders and the best route to take, thereby guaranteeing maximum throughput and thus efficiency in the warehouse.

Collisions are also prevented by the integrated sensor concept, which automatically stops the vehicles if there is an imminent threat of a collision with another device or a person. Otherwise, there are fixed rules governing the right of way in the warehouse, just like in road traffic.

If extra resources are needed, the performance of the transport system can be flexibly adapted by increasing the number of vehicles. There is no need to invest in fixed systems.

Chapter 23 - Transportation & Logistics

The supply chain discipline of trucking logistics at one time consisted of simply tracking the locations of delivery vehicles on route. This process was concerned with where the vehicles were at any given time relative to their schedule and service level agreements (SLA). Some pioneers of technology even allowed their customers to track their shipment via a web portal. Latterly, the visible tracking of a shipments progress via GPS - whether that is by sea, land or air – also allowed management to see if they were meeting their ETAs.

Since the advent of commercial GPS and ubiquitous internet access the technology and the customer's expectations of service have changed but the pervasive attitude to transport logistics remains locked to location tracking. The reality is that transport logistics is today about far more than just location and shipment tracking.

Trucking Logistic Route

Transport logistic technology is about planing the best route for reaching a destination as clients need goods delivered to specific locations on time. Hence, this will require software solutions for monitoring and adjusting the routing by simplifying the process of figuring out the optimal route for getting from source to destination. To achieve this, AI and Machine Learning are often utilised and the algorithms take into account several factors. The foundation of any route planning exercise is the ability to read a map in order to plan a route. However, it is not as simple as just selecting the shortest distance or fastest route because when choosing which roads to take, a variety of factors are taken into consideration. One is the speed limit for different roads, which can have a huge impact on how long it takes to reach a certain place. However, congestion must also be considered as a heavily congested motorway could well be much slower than an alternative road albeit with a lesser speed limit. Weather can also have an influence so modern logistics software monitors forecasts for areas along the planned route, making recommendations to avoid potential problems. The algorithms can work continuously monitoring progress and variations in traffic congestion, weather and road closures in real time and can send notifications or adjust the routing along the way. For example, the software could notify drivers to take a minor road instead of a major route so as to skirt around a serious traffic accident and road closure.

Having software that can reliably forecast and plan best routes is an essential part of transport logistics. After all traffic congestion, bad weather and road construction are typical factors that can turn a typically short run into a journey that for truckers is a tremendous waste of resources such as time and money.

Fuel costs are another concern for every transport organization, no matter how big or small and it is the job of logistics to improve efficiency by planning routes that avoid unnecessary travails along the route and that means using less fuel.

Estimated Time of Arrival

Technology delivered via transport logistics software, makes it possible to provide an accurate ETA. With technology transport companies can now calculate how long under forecasted conditions it will take to get from one the Distribution centre to the destination. Moreover as the software continuously monitors the progress customers can receive an automated message when there's a delay, supplying them with the new ETA. Forecasting and planning algorithms may also use historical data to create possible fall-back scenarios such as making contingency plans so drivers always have a 'Plan B' to fall back on if the worst were to happen.

Another benefit of continuous tracking and monitoring of vehicles is in the case of a breakdown. The control centre will be notified immediately when a breakdowns occurs. The transport logistics technology will speed things up by getting a service vehicle to a stricken vehicle faster, and ultimately reducing the downtime.

Driver Performance

When Michelin Solutions launched their Tires-as-a-service back in 2013 they were pioneers of a new business model enabled by IoT embedded sensors and big data analytics. By embedding smart components such as RFID, pressure, temperature and tilt sensors and accelerometers into their commercial tires Michelin Solutions were able to provide their product as a service. By collecting the data produced by each tire allowed Michelin to provide customers with important analytical data about the vehicle. One such key metric was that of driver performance as the sensors in the tires relayed back to Michelin how the vehicle was being driven. The solution enabled companies to accurately set and monitor KPIs so they could assess each driver based on a score determined by numerous factors, which affect not only on-time deliveries but also safety on the road. Most companies now have similar solutions which allow transport managers to select which factors to track, such as speeding, driving harsh or frequency of breaks, producing a customized report which reflects the values of the organization. Management can also track improvements in these scores over time. This isn't just anther spy in the cab it is a way to use technology to improve efficiency and increase profitability.

Other Benefits of Trucking Logistics

Other efficiencies can be leveraged with modern truck logistics technology. A potential area for improvement is in assisting Dispatchers in recognising the reason for a late delivery in real time. Another area is in multi-period planning where machine learning algorithms can create optimal schedules for customers that require multiple deliveries in a certain period of time. Over time, the software can learn by analysing performance trends and make accurate forecast recommendations to avoid seasonal or perennial problems.

Less than Truck Load Transportation (LTL)

In Transportation logistics the products are conveyed by a number of different modes of transport: air, rail, water, and truck. In the US, the movement of goods by truck offers shippers infinite flexibility due at a relatively low cost. Truck transportation can move large items faster than rail as the shipment is not dependent on the railroad's timetable. Truck transportation can also be cost effective if there are sufficient products to transport to a single destination that will take up a trucks capacity. However in the era of e-commerce there is usually many products being delivered to multiple destinations so a different style of transportation is required.

Therefore, general freight carriers in the US offer two types of service; Full Truckload (FTL) service or Less Than Truckload (LTL).

While the FTL carrier moves full containers or trucks of one product from one customer, the LTL carrier moves goods from many different customers on one truck. The LTL carrier offers customers a more cost-effective method of shipping goods than the FTL operator.

How LTL Works

A LTL freight operator has within a local area a number of vehicles which collect shipments from their customers. The relevance is that after finishing their daily collection, the delivery vehicles take the shipments to a terminal where they are unloaded. Each shipment is tracked, weighed and rated which enables customer bills to be processed. Each individual shipment is therefore loaded onto an outbound vehicle, which ensures that outbound shipments are trucked to appropriate regional terminals, where they are unloaded. The shipments are then received and sorted then placed on local vehicles for delivery. Hence, every individual shipment, which is common with e-commerce, will be handled multiple times from the source until it reaches its destination.

Advantages of LTL Carriers

The advantage of using an LTL carrier is obviously the cost. This is because the price of sending a shipment using an LTL rather than an FTL carrier is significantly lower. The LTL carrier competes with parcel carriers, who generally will not accept shipments of more than 70 to 100 pounds in weight. Nonetheless, the competition in the LTL market usually results in LTL carriers offering lower rates per pound than parcel carriers.

To understand the difference, LTL carriers generally utilize van trailers which are anything from commercial vans, pick-ups, or covered or enclosed trailers. There are even a few refrigerated LTL carriers who utilize temperature controlled trailers and IoT sensor technology. Sometimes carriers will use trailers that they can haul in tandem and LTL carriers will not accept shipments that are too large too fit onto a single trailer. The carriers will have strategically placed terminals where they are able to consolidate all their locally collected freight, which will then be placed with other freight that is bound for the same area.

How do LTL Shipping Rates Work?

To fully leverage the cost benefits of LTL shipping it is important that businesses shipping products or their third party logistic party are outsourced to a provider. This is necessary because there needs to be a relationship with a carrier in order to analyse historical freight shipping data. This is required as part of a freight analysis, which will be used to get the best rates. By conducting freight analysis this will yield a more productive negotiation and create a win/win scenario, which ultimately will deliver the shipper the most competitive rates that saves the most amount of money on their LTL shipping costs.

One additional overhead that should not be overlooked in contemplating the costs of LTL shipping is fuel surcharges. These additional charges are the surcharges associated with the conveyance of a shipment and are added on top of transportation costs. With rising e-commerce business and fuel costs using LTL shipping becomes more beneficial. Smaller and more widely distributed consignments mean that a company may only need a fraction of the trailer space and so they can ship their product cheaper by going LTL instead of using a full truck load carrier.

The main factors that play into LTL shipping rates are:

- Distance
- Weight
- Classification of Freight
- Accessorials

Chapter 24 - Post Sales\Service Chain

We have already seen how digital transformation has massive appeal and utility for most businesses because of the efficiencies, agility, savings and revenue gains it enables by fundamentally changing enterprise-wide functions, and no more so than in the supply chain. In fact, 80 percent of companies believe supply chain digitization will deliver great competitive advantage and 77 percent have instituted some sort a digitization initiative and according to Gartner 85 percent of executives expect their companies to be a digital business by 2020.

Furthermore, in the post-sale, or service, supply chain, the benefits of digital transformation are vast and will revolutionise the business. Traditionally, the post-sales or service supply chain was one of the least-automated aspects of business. Paradoxically, it was also one of the most complex and fragmented, and most in need of automation. Its core functions such as Customer Care and Parts Management through to Field Service and Product Returns/Repair—are highly interdependent. Yet, they typically operate as manually-driven silo, which creates intelligence gaps, major delays, high costs and unnecessary customer dissatisfaction. For example, the typical service supply chain is extremely reactive by nature as there is only limited or no visibility across functional silos into existing and potential issues. However, when fully digitized, the post-sale supply chain transforms into a proactive, transparent, end-to-end operation. As a result a digital transformation eliminates many of the inherent inefficiencies and breakage points, and delivers cost savings and major improvements in customer experience. Unsurprisingly the new disruptive technologies play a major part in a successful digital transformation process. After all the driving force behind digital transformation is the collecting, sharing, processing, and analyzing of data through increased visibility but it should not be just about technology. For within a successful digital transformation the supply chain methodologies, customer experience and corporate culture are equally important components. Hence, to achieve a truly digital post-sale supply chain, there has to be a holistic approach.

Key Technology Components

The IIoT is a critical enabler of digital business transformation as it is the catalyst for the convergence of the physical and digital worlds. Using data harvested from connected products in the field provides new insights for streamlining operations and enhancing triage, service events, repair and spare parts inventory. Hence, when developing an IoT strategy for the post sales supply chain, bear in mind:

• **Customer buy-in:** The days of gathering data from consumer products without their express permission are gone. Now due to privacy regulations customers have to be willing participants, they need to know firstly, that their data is being collected, then secondly for what purpose. Therefore, it is imperative to clearly explain to the consumer why allowing the collection and processing of their data will benefit them. This requires that the company develop a closed-loop process so that both parties can clearly see the benefits of the sharing of data.

• **Data overload:** The IoT generates massive volumes of machine data, which if not controlled will overwhelm the network infrastructure and slow everything down. In addition, collecting data should not be the goal there must be a specific purpose in mind as it can also overwhelm the capacity of the analytical engines. Therefore, to prevent this from happening, selectively collect data for a clear analytical purpose and use IoT technology that sites the analytical engines logic closer to the network edge i.e. where the sensors are located. This will enable data to be captured and analysed in real-time or at least to minimize latency. By speeding up the transfer of data and refining the data streams to only what is relevant will prove to be more effective than collecting and storing vast quantities of unspecified data in the cloud.

• **Bidirectional transfer:** The boom in connected products, those with IoT capabilities, has not been totally driven by companies harvesting data. In many cases companies have made their products smart so that they had remote transfer capabilities. Hence it is important to plan how to build a digital path back to the product. For instance, it is very attractive for manufacturers to push firmware upgrades remotely to a product. Similarly, they might wish to send control signals to the product to reset the sensor, alleviating the requirement for a return of the product or for a service technician to visit.

Data Processing and Manipulation

With IoT and edge consolidation enabling engineers to remotely access and selectively identifies machine data to capture, the focus changes to how to analyse the data. The approach here should not be which hardware and systems to use but instead on the specific purpose – what do you hope to achieve. The data scientists will need to know from the subject matter experts what questions to ask of the data that aligns with the overall business plans. Since data is collected at various levels and types and from many different systems (IoT, ERP, Social Media sentiment, etc.), it is necessary for the data experts to cleanse and map data to derive a baseline system of record. Assuming all that has been achieved and the data is global, the data scientists and security practitioners will also need to be well-versed in international data requirements and regulations. This will require making sure the data resides in the right place and is secure as well as in compliance with regional or international requirements for particular industries.

Cloud Services

Cloud services are now deemed to be essential for large scale digital transformation. Primarily, cloud makes it much easier to manage partner ecosystems, which are critical in multi-partner supply chains. Furthermore, cloud enables businesses to continually and quickly innovate, with minimal Capex. Having cloud-based resources at the ready whenever they need them, makes it possible to rapidly test and prototype new post-sale supply chain models, such as propensity to return, and to get quick validation. To this end it is quick to spin-up virtual machines to handle new projects and provide parallel data processing, and just as easily to scale down when prototyping is complete. Amazon Web Services, Microsoft Azure or Google Cloud Platforms are the major vendors, which provide robust and highly scalable infrastructure for compute, memory and storage but also importantly provide cloud services that enable country-specific data compliance requirements.

Automation

Digital transformation drives efficiencies through automation at different stages of the post-sale supply chain. For instance, it's used to accelerate data ingestion, trigger the running of algorithms that predict outcomes that drive better informed decision making.

Automation also replaces manual task that are tedious, dangerous, or repetitive tasks that slow processes and are prone to human error. For example, software called Robotic Process Automation uses business logic to accomplish routine tasks that an agent might otherwise perform, such as processing standard forms in customer service. Machine Enablement is a variation of this type of automation as it makes it possible for robotic handling of exceptions. Here, the robot software watches and learns from the agent's actions which effectively teach the robot what to do with non-routine tasks. It's similar to cognitive learning for physical collaborative robots. When an agent enters data that varies from the typical process, the robot views it as a new pattern and labels it as such, so that in the future it knows what actions to perform when faced with certain exceptions.

Post-Sale Control Tower

Control towers provide end-to-end, cohesive visibility which has been lacking in the silo post-sale supply chain. The right control tower will understand how the various supply chain functions integrate and flow, the attributes of the value chain and the nuances that make it work. This deep understanding of the supply chain provided by the real-time, deep visibility across and within functional areas realises actionable insights that deliver high-impact results. Furthermore an overarching control tower that provides visibility and control across the supply chain is also a precursor for deploying deep machine learning as it becomes more prevalent and feasible in the next few years.

Analytics

The bedrock of digital transformation is analytics, as the data that is collected and stored has no value until it can be transformed into information. The ideal approach to analytics is to concentrate on the entire supply chain, encompassing all its specialised functions and attributes as a single holistic analytical model. The holistic approach realises the greatest business impact, but to do so requires the business to automate analytics on all the operations and process data across the entire post-sale supply chain. An important aspect of analytics is that it changes the perspective from cost of transactions to business value of transactions. For example, when contemplating how to recover high-value parts faster, reduce inventory, or speed customer delivery. The algorithms can find casual-effect or anticipate and predict events, such as who will return products in a timely manner, or who will activate products on their own or will need technical assistance, who is likely/unlikely to churn, and how to avoid issues from happening in the first place. Another type of algorithm can provide segmentation or clustering of correlated features within vast data sets. This type of clustering algorithm is the bases for developing differentiated services for categories of end-customers. These tailored operations and processes can deliver significantly improved outcomes and drive high levels of customer experience.

New Supply Chain Models

Legacy service supply chain models may not work as well in a digital business. They could dilute the impact of the digital transformation. Therefore it will be wise to evaluate whether the models currently in place need to be altered or enhanced. For example, change may be required in the following scenarios:

Service Parts Inventory Forecasting

Spare parts inventory planning has traditionally been a 'review-and-stock' endeavour. The failing in this approach is that being a time-series method it doesn't account for volatility in demand link directly to failures of parts in the field. As a result, the forecasts are often inaccurate and this leads to overstocking, which is expensive for business, and under-stocking, which hurts customers. However, another approach is to use real-time IoT demand driven data to predict machine failures, and incorporating that data into the inventory modeling. This method has been known to reduce spare parts inventory stock by up to 10%.

Transportation Management for Parts Dispatch

In the post sales supply chain when products inevitably fail, the onus is on vendors to ship the spare and service parts to the customer.

According to general contract or business practice, parts are typically sent via costly Next Flight Out, Same Day or Two-Day transport. This is an expensive and unsatisfactory approach for vendors and a significant downtime for the customer. However, there is another approach that entails predictive analysis and algorithms that instead of waiting for failures to happen, can predict why and when a part is likely to fail. Effectively pre-warned, the vendor can immediately ship the part and inform the customer of the pending problem. By proactively shipping a replacement either directly to the customer or to a distribution centre close by, the part can be shipped via a slower, less-expensive means. Not only will this reduce transportation and process management costs substantially, it will reduce product downtime and, as a result, increase customer satisfaction.

Customer Experience

Digital business advancements over the last decade have had a significant impact on end-customers expectations. Managing customer expectations requires ensuring the customer's experience is a positive one. Therefore planning the digital-enhanced customer experience in terms of front-end processes, omnichannels communications and service channels that facilitate the type of interactions the customer favours is now a necessity. The variety of communication channels available to the customer is important as have just a phone service is no longer sufficient. Instead customers prefer email, text or social media as ways to interact so bear this in mind, for example, five out of six millennials prefer using social media to connect with vendors.

Indeed social media has become a vital source of distilling customer sentiment regards products. Importantly, social media is also a fine gauge of how customers view the post sales supply chain. If they feel they're not treated fairly and arbitrarily, they will not be slow in voicing their sentiment and sharing it with others over the internet. This can lead to an escalation of public complaints, brand dilution, and churn. These types of problems can be largely avoided by analyzing and segmenting customers, based upon social media sentiment analysis. By using data-driven customer insights to create experiences customers want it is easier to provide the services and interactions they expect. However, it appears generations differ in their preferences and expectations and this is where segmentation analytics can be effective. By customizing processes and scripts dependent on the category of customer for example, specifically for each of generation x, y or millennials, then customer interactions can be tailored in ways that meet individual customers preferences and expectations ensuring an improved customer experience.

Culture

For digital supply chain transformation to succeed, requires that the analogue systems – and humans - realigned to the new practices and methodologies. Otherwise, digital systems will be deployed but employees will still use the old procedures and processes such as spreadsheets. They will be unlikely to accept the new technology and it will consequently fail to improve on the status quo. In order to improve performance by the orders-of-magnitude that digital transformation promises requires a company culture focused upon digital technology brought about through training and involvement.

For example, IoT-based intelligence, analytics and automation may make some employees suspicious of its pervasiveness and fear for their jobs. Therefore, it has to be demonstrated that technology will not only help resolve routine customer problems, but free employees to take on more complex but meaningful tasks. Thus, instead of keeping to a well-defined script in first line support, employees may take on customers whose problems aren't so straightforward in a second or third line role.

Ultimately, organizations can't transform to digital unless people do. Therefore employees must be well-trained on the latest technologies so that the impacts of going digital aren't diluted by people who aren't proficient with it.

The Role of Outsourcing

The issue of employee acceptance of new technology and work practices leads many organisations to seriously consider outsourcing portions of digital supply chain transformation in order to accelerate the transition. If that is the desired route then the post-sale control tower is a good place to start. It's the overarching system that provides visibility and control over how the supply chain interacts with and solves customer problems. Because the service supply chain is so nuanced and complex, outsourcing it to post-sale supply chain experts may accelerate the digital transition. Gartner believes supply chain outsourcing will help companies transition to digital business while they concentrate on dealing with the inherent complexities of the digital supply chain. They predict an increase in the number of pure "brand companies" over the next four to five years. These are companies that have reduced the supply chain functions and processes handled internally, and expanded the use of outsourcing across the supply chain. Consequently, Gartner believe that even more complex ecosystems will develop, requiring robust orchestration capabilities and real-time data and visibility platforms. Hence, in the near future end-to-end supply chain visibility and data security, in conjunction with trust and transparency, will be extremely critical factors to success in the digital era.

In summary the age of the digital supply chain has arrived and although it might seem overwhelming, the potential is vast. By deploying core technical components and implement them in a systematic, intelligent way, organisations of any size can quickly begin to see substantial benefits and realise greater efficiencies, savings, customer experience improvements and competitive advantage.

Chapter 25 - Value Chain 4.0 and the future

Supply Chain 4.0, realises the concept of supply-chain management in the context of Industry 4.0. In doing so it leverages technical innovations — the Internet of Things, robotics, advanced analytics, and wireless communications, amongst others — to accelerate performance, add value and increase customer satisfaction.

Currently many industrial transformation initiatives focus on ad hoc initiatives and no-regret projects hence the value created is often limited and oriented towards productivity gains and cost savings through automation, whereas the major value sits in the higher digital transformational goals within the entire supply chain. This is simply because Industry 4.0 covers the full supply chain and strives towards value creation in an iterative, incremental and strategic way.

Indeed the value created in Industry 4.0 is likely to manifest primarily in efficiency gains such as in product quality, innovation and in operational agility. Whereas, the top line impacts and savings are likely to appear in Time-to-Market, Improved Service, and in reduced manufacturing and supply chain costs, respectively. There is also value created through increase in revenue and new revenue generating models but currently these are very much secondary sources of value. This is not a new phenomenon and as Industry 4.0 revolve more about 'business assets' that don't appear on the balance sheet such as actionable data, partnerships and ecosystems of value, innovation capacity, customers, agility, trust and security, modularity and transparency ... amongst many others, that is perhaps not surprising.

Nonetheless, what is indisputable is that through Industry 4.0 the value created from increased supply chain agility, flexibility, quality, and efficiency have been obtained while reducing cost. As a result the traditional supply chain has undergone significant change over the last decade or so on the journey to digitalization.

What was once a purely operational logistics function that focused on ensuring supply of production lines and delivery to customers has become a core business function. As a result the focus of the supply-chain management function has shifted to advanced planning processes, such as analytical demand planning or integrated sales and operations planning (S&OP).These strategic planning functions have become established business processes while often the operational logistics parts have been outsourced to third-party logistics providers.

Nonetheless, the purpose of the supply-chain function is still to ensure the free flow of materials, information and operations albeit nowadays through well-integrated functions, from suppliers through to customers. Ultimately, decisions on cost, inventory, and customer service are made from an end-to-end perspective rather than by each functional silo and this is the result of digitalization. However, digitization requires companies to radically rethink the way they design their supply chain. Organisations today must consider their supply chains in the terms of globalization and booming e-commerce, which has resulted in heightened customer expectations: recent trends indicate growing customer service expectations combined with much more smaller, distributed but detailed customer orders.

Similarly there is a definite trend toward further mass individualization and customization of products and this is accelerating growth and driving continual changes in the SKU portfolio. This online-enabled transparency combined with easy online access to a multitude of options regarding where to shop and what to buy drives the competition between supply chains.

To take advantage and build upon these trends, adapt to ever changing requirements, and enable a wide range of new technologies, supply chains need to become much faster and much more precise.

Vision of the future value chain

The digitization of the supply chain enables companies to address the new requirements of customer experience as well as support supply side and intra-supply chain demand via efficiency improvement. Digitization leads to the concept of a Supply Chain 4.0, which becomes a major source of value:

Responsive:

The booming e-commerce trend in retail is driving supply chain reorganisations as a vast increase in small individual customer orders requires an efficiency drive in intra-supply chain logistics to cope. The new approaches to product distribution, enhances value as it can reduce the delivery time to a few hours. Advanced forecasting, via predictive analytics of internal data (e.g., demand) and external data (e.g., market trends, weather, school vacation, and construction indices), combined with machine-status data for spare-parts demand, provide a precise forecast of customer demand. What once were monthly forecasts instead become weekly—and, for the very fastest-moving products, hourly.

In the future, "predictive shipping," for which Amazon holds several patents is where products are pre-emptively shipped before the customer even places an order. Predictive analytics working on customer shopping trends can predict customer behaviour with high accuracy and determine the high probability of a customer order. Based upon this forecast the products can be shipped to a distribution centre close to the customer. A confirmed customer order is later matched with a shipment that is already in the logistics network, and the shipment is rerouted to the exact customer destination saving a lot of time.

Incredibly there is the potential that a more flexible approach is obtainable. This is where Supply Chain 4.0's, real-time planning allows companies to respond flexibly to changes in demand or supply, minimizing planning cycles and frozen periods. In this scenario planning becomes a continuous process that is able to react dynamically to changing requirements or constraints (e.g., real-time production-capacity feedback from machines). In this scenario even after products are sent, agile delivery processes lets customers reroute shipments to the most convenient destination.

Innovative business models accelerate the supply-chain organization's flexibility. Rather than maintaining resources and capabilities in-house, companies can extend their capabilities to buy or make individual supply-chain functions as a service on a by-usage basis. By doing so service providers' provide greater specialization, which creates economies of scale and scope, increasing the potential for attractive outsourcing opportunities. This leads to an "Uberization" or "Crowd-Sourcing" of services such as having freelance drivers provide a less than truck load transport delivery over the last-mile, which will significantly increase agility in distribution networks as well as reduce costs. Crowd-sourcing of last mile delivery may see accelerated direct-to-consumer opportunities for manufacturers in what once was an under utilised facility.

Become more granular:

With customers looking for more individualization in the products they buy, companies must respond to this demand at a much more granular level. Smart manufacturing with its lots sizes of 1 as well as techniques such as last minute customization, and sophisticated scheduling practices provide the necessary flexibility in production. But the delays still remain in the distribution networks.

Innovative distribution concepts, including assemble in transit or drone delivery, will allow companies to manage the last mile more efficiently for single-piece, high-value, and even packages containing several products thereby fulfilling customers' customization needs while delivering their orders even faster than is possible today with mass-market, standard products.

Supply Chain Accuracy:

A major characteristic of supply chain 4.0 is its visibility and that enables accuracy. It is this real-time, end-to-end transparency throughout the supply chain, which enables next-generation performance management systems to work. The visible span of information enables planners to obtain precise operational data from granular processed data, such as the exact position of trucks in the network or to synthesize top-level key performance indicators, such as capacity level indicators at each stage of the production process. The catalyst for this end-to-end transparency is a 'single source of truth' which is accurate data distributed throughout the supply chain. This allows suppliers, service providers, planners and others in a "supply chain cloud" to share a common accurate set of real-time information. This ensures that all stakeholders in the supply chain steer and decide based on the same accurate facts.

Furthermore, regardless of the type of digital performance-management systems being used, whether they are spreadsheet models for warehousing, transport, or procurement, the systems will still have to automatically adjust targets that can no longer be achieved. Thus, in supply chain 4.0 we are seeing performance-management systems based upon advanced adaptive, predictive and prescriptive algorithms that "learn" to automatically identify risks or exceptions. Furthermore, these advanced machine learning systems will adjust and change supply-chain variables or apply controls to mitigate threats. These capabilities enable an automatic performance-management control tower to handle a broad spectrum of exceptions even disruptive, unplanned events without engaging human interaction.

This advancement in autonomous performance management realises the potential of the continuous-improvement cycle. Ultimately, gains in this field will push the supply chains to unprecedented levels of efficiency.

Efficiency: Automation provides efficiency at the performance management level but supply-chain efficiency as a whole is determined by the automation of both physical tasks and digital planning. In fact Robots and automated machines can handle the material flow and the repetitive tasks that are commonly automated throughout the warehouse. Indeed, the product handling processes from receiving/unloading, to placing in storage bays, to picking, packing, and shipping is now automated. Furthermore, these autonomous transport vehicles transport the products within the network efficiently and safely without any human intervention.

To capitalise on the benefits and to optimize autonomous truck utilization and increase transport flexibility, participating companies within the supply chain are sharing capacity through cross-company transport optimization. Therefore, the network itself is continuously optimized to ensure the high degree of transparency required to drive efficiency at every stage of the dynamic planning process.

Include the Customer: By adding the customer into the Value Chain we can finally realise the promise of Industry 4.0 and the digital supply network. As it is today Industry 4.0 can solve many key challenges faced by manufacturers such as cyclical demand, market volatility, pricing pressure and the need for quick-turn innovation.

It delivers value through using technology to automate, integrate and optimize manufacturing processes, which improves cycle times, product quality and efficiencies across all the supply chain operations.

But as challenging and formidable as it is optimizing processes within the manufacturing plant is only the first stage of industry 4.0.

The real potential value of Industry 4.0 is only realized fully when the customer is added into the value chain.

The first step in integrating customers into the value chain is by making products with embedded sensors. Intelligent products are delivered through The Internet of Things, which provides companies with the means to collect post-sales information on the products usage and performance throughout its life-cycle. By collecting and analysing this working-life data for their products enables companies to quickly remediate faults, improve service and enhance the products through remote firmware upgrades or in future product development. This provides real value, through integrating the "Voice of the Machine" into the decision-making process.

Nonetheless, to really synthesize value we need to bring not just the product but the customer into the value chain by including them into the decision-making process. Therefore it is not just product life-cycle data that needs to be collected but consumer information.

Furthermore, this is a practice which customers seem more willing to accept, if they see the mutual value. A study entitled, "What is the future of data sharing?" found that 75% of the millennials surveyed were willing to share personal, sensitive information with a company or brand they trusted.

Provided customers are clearly informed of the why, what, where, when and how and are required to explicitly opt-in to the transparent data-sharing partnership by taking an affirmative action there should be no ethical or privacy issues.

By collecting data on how customers use their products or services, manufacturers can begin incorporating the "Voice of the Customer" into nearly every aspect of the product value chain.

Analysing customer usage data gives designers and planners a more thorough understanding of the customer experience. Having a deep understanding of how the customer uses the product is invaluable to vendors.

With this knowledge they can identify and remediate issues and proactively address end-user concerns. Manufactures can also use customer information to identify trends, changing needs and usage, to respond quickly with customer-centric solutions.

However, bringing the customer into the value chain means more than efficiently manufacturing customized products. Customer insights can be used to develop new business models and operational processes for even greater value. Below are three benefits achievable when including customer data in decision making:

- Greater Customer Retention and reduced churn – Industry 4.0 involves using machine, process and consumer data and technology to improve operations. This will result in shorter cycle times, better quality and real-time customer communication. Companies that deliver on their promises generate goodwill and trust within their customers, thereby increasing customer retention and loyalty. This can help fortify a business against existing competition and potential new market entries. For example, a pharmaceutical manufacturer could integrate its plant production data with a customer's store PoS and inventory system, providing the customer with a vendor held inventory service, automatic stock replenishment, real-time updates on delivery dates, automated document creation and online payment.

Manufacturers can also use intelligent products to gather helpful customer usage data such as rates of wear and tear, when and how often products are used and even when products need to be refilled or replaced. This information can be used to develop new and better products that deliver meaningful value to customers.

Customers' input also can be added at the development stage of new products as part of a company's innovation team. By including the end-user perspective into the specification gathering process helps identify not only new features, but also related services. For example, Michelin Tires, offers am as-a-service program, which uses sensors embedded within the tires to determine mileage, usage and wear and tear. Michelin collects the customer data and bills according to usage but by harvesting valuable real-world usage data allows it to make valuable incremental improvements to it tires.

In the future, products will become platforms for creating value throughout the value chain. Companies from different industries will work together in Smart Supply Chains to complete offers focused on meeting customers' demands according to their unique specifications. When customers are brought into the value chain it opens up worlds of opportunity in mass individualisation which no one company can be the single provider. Instead, it will take an integrated Supply Chain 4.0 ecosystem to fulfill their requirements.

Sense not Respond

Today's supply chains do not sense they respond at best. They typically still do batch processing of historical data rather than streaming live data so are largely out of step with markets. In spite of this situation, supply chain leaders boast about being customer-centric, yet in many cases they cannot see and/or use their customer data.

The vision for Supply Chain 4.0 enables the use of digital technology to realise greater value in demand-driven networks. It improves the interoperability between and among smart value networks.

In supply Chain 4.0 the impact is from outside-in, from the customer's customer to the supplier's supplier, and the demand signals would be real-time and bidirectional, with a focus on sensing, shaping and minimizing waste.

Unfortunately today, despite a focus on Industry 4.0 projects, continuous improvement programs, and functional process design, supply chain leaders are unable to drive improvement in both demand sensing/shaping and reducing waste. Indeed although corporate investment is still focused on in-ward looking ERP systems there are future spending tagged by some innovative companies that understand the potential of new forms of advanced analytics. We are very early in our journey to Industry 4.0 with only a precious few organisations having well defined digital supply chains that extend the concepts to building a digital, demand driven, outside-in value network(s). Technical and business innovation driven by Supply Chain 4.0 requires a radical reimaging of the supply chain but it is happening albeit slowly. By leveraging, Industry 4.0 technologies and advanced algorithms tomorrow's companies will be able to enhance demand forecasting and be able to react quickly to sense and shape demand.

Increasing operational efficiency by leveraging Supply Chain 4.0

Undoubtedly, Supply Chain 4.0 will eventually affect all areas of supply-chain management in the creation of value. This is evident in the way that the main elements of Supply Chain 4.0 maps to six main value drivers. Ultimately, the improvements enable a step change in service, cost, capital, and agility.

Six main value drivers

1) Demand Planning

The exercise of supply-chain planning benefits from the automation of advanced data analytics. As a result a few major consumer-goods players are already using predictive analytics in demand planning. They utilise these complex algorithms to analyse hundreds to thousands of internal and external demand-influencing variables (e.g., weather, trends from social networks, social media sentiment, as well as real-time Point of Sales data). By utilising a machine-learning approach the planners can model complex relationships to derive an accurate demand plan. Because of this improvement in analytical forecasting errors often fall by 30 to 50 percent.

Consequently, there is no longer the clearly defined boundary between demand and supply planning. Hence, instead of for example depending on an inventory safety stock, each replenishment-planning exercise reconsiders the expected demand probability distribution as one fluid continuous planning exercise. Consequently, the implicit safety stocks are variable so differ with every reorder. By minimizing inventory levels prices can then be dynamically adapted to optimize profit.

2) Increased Physical flow

Logistic efficiency and accuracy has advanced through better connectivity, advanced analytics, additive manufacturing, and advanced automation. In doing so they usurped legacy warehousing and inventory-management strategies. Driven along by a seemingly endless stream of technological innovations, logistics realises small but significant improvements such as through easy-to-use human-computer interfaces for example, augmented reality glasses that relay location-based instructions to workers, guiding the picking process. Advanced robotics and exoskeletons are also having equally dramatic effects on human productivity in warehouses.

Similarly, advances in autonomous vehicles are delivering significant operating-cost reductions in transportation and product handling, while at the same time reducing lead times and environmental costs. Autonomous vehicle systems are linking warehouses to manufacturing loading points and these enable entire processes to be carried out with only minimal manual intervention. In addition, as production facilities start to rely more on 3-D printing, the role of the warehouse may change fundamentally.

3) Enhanced Performance management

Performance management has also changed beyond all expectation, and several supply chains are making detailed, continually updated, easily customizable dashboards available throughout their organizations. Dashboards are no longer developed using spreadsheets or data from diverse databases instead they are generated using data from the 'Single Source of Truth'. As a result, performance management is now a fully integrated operational process rather than a retrospective exercise on a monthly or quarterly basis.

Geared to real-time exception handling and continuous improvement by using data-mining and machine-learning techniques, performance-management systems perform root cause analysis on exceptions by comparing them with a predefined set of underlying indicators. The performance management system automatically triggers remediation controls, such as activating a replenishment order or changing deliver times or adjusting other parameter settings.

4) Precise Order Management

The process of Order management is optimised by integrating the ordering process with the available-to-promise (ATP) process to deliver a no-touch order processing.

This tight integration with the real-time replanning system allows the replenishment of stock to over-ride all constraints.

In addition it also enables order-date confirmations through real-time rebuilding of the production schedule. This results in reduced costs via increased automation as well as improved reliability which is realised by granular feedback, providing consistent and reliable response and better customer experience.

5) Increased Collaboration

The highest level of integration is collaboration and the supply-chain 4.0 cloud provides for the highest levels of collaboration. The cloud is a shared platform providing a shared logistics infrastructure, where partners can decide to tackle supply-chain tasks collaboratively. By forming non-competitive relationships, partners save administrative costs and benefit from one another's knowledge and experience.

For example some leading enterprises have already found that collaboration allows for much higher performance and much lower inventories. These results are achieved through an exchange of reliable planning data. Collaboration is also partially responsible for the minimisation of lead times, providing the ability to react fast to disruptions anywhere within the supply chain.

6) Advanced Supply-Chain Strategy

A mixture of globalisation and ecommerce is driving the need for further individualization and customization in the market, Hence to succeed in the internet-era supply chain requires the ability to cluster or micro-segment the market. Consequently, there is a need for a dynamic, analytical approach which allows for the clustering of end-customer data points related to demand and product features.

Clustering end-consumer demand by preference and features determines demand. By understanding the market's appetite for specific tailored products provides optimal value for the customer. In addition understanding demand minimizes costs and inventory in the supply chain.

Impact of Supply Chain 4.0

Adopting new technologies together with eliminating non-value cost increases the operational effectiveness of supply chains. The potential impact of Supply Chain 4.0 suggest improvements of up to 30 percent lower operational costs, 75 percent fewer lost sales, and a decrease in inventories of up to 75 percent. At the same time, the agility of the supply chains should increase significantly. Nonetheless, the huge upsurge in ecommerce has resulted in unprecedented returns of products so this also must be taken into consideration.

However, numerous studies and quantitative calculations deem that three performance indicators are highly correlated;

1. An improved inventory profile - will lead to improved service level and lower cost

2. Supply-chain service/lost sales - Poor customer service is the driver for returns and is either due to misrepresentation of the product and/or unrealistic promises leading to inflated customer expectation; a wrong inventory profile; and/or an unreliable delivery of parts or poor post-service. Consequently, due to poor post-sale service customers will decide to switch to another brand. This is true for both B2C and B2B environments.

3. The damage caused by poor post-sales management will not just be in immediate lost sales but also in poor future sales if the products are not deemed fit for purpose, available to buy or unreliable. Fortunately, this risk decreases considerably when the post-sales supply chain significantly improves interactions with the customer in the post-sales/service processes.

Supply-chain cost

It is believed that supply chain cost, driven by transportation, warehouse, and the setup of the overall network, can be realistically reduced by up to 30 percent. In fact, roughly 50 percent of this cost reduction can be achieved through deploying advanced analytics to calculate the clean-sheet costs (bottom-up calculation of the "true" costs of the service) of transport and warehousing and by optimizing the network.

The goal should always be to have minimal touch points and minimal kilometres driven while still meeting the required service level of the customer. In combination with smart automation and productivity improvement in warehousing, onboard units in transportation, etc., these efforts can achieve the savings potential. The remaining 15 percent cost reduction can be reached by leveraging approaches of dynamic routing, Uberization of transport, use of autonomous vehicles, and—where possible—3-D printing.

Automating Supply-chain planning:

The planning tasks such as demand planning, preparation of S&OP process, aggregated production planning, and supply planning are often time intensive and conducted mainly manually. With advanced system support, 80 to 90 percent of all planning tasks can be automated and still ensure better quality compared with tasks conducted manually.

The S&OP process will move to a weekly rhythm, and the decision process will be built on scenarios that can be updated in real time.

This combination of accuracy, granularity, and speed has implications for the other elements, such as service, supply-chain costs, and inventory. Automating systems will allow them to learn to run the processes and apply countermeasures on a 24/7 basis an also be able to detect the rare exception where an escalation for human interaction is required.

Inventory: If we consider the legacy supply chain the inventory is used mainly to decouple demand and supply as it is a buffer for volatility in demand and variability in supply. Implementing new planning and predictive algorithms will reduce the dependency and uncertainty thus making holding large amounts of safety stock unnecessary. Of course supply is affected by other important variables which effect inventory levels such as the replenishment lead time: with more production of lot size 1 and fast changeovers driven by Industry 4.0, the lead time will be reduced significantly. Also, we must consider that transport time will reduce the required inventory as manufacturing will be closer to the consumer. Overall therefore the inventory reduction of 50 to 80 percent can be realistically realised.

Transformation to a digital supply chain

A successful transformation into a digital supply chain will require three key enablers:

1) A definition of the purpose when defining the digital supply chain, a catalyst which understands the reduction of the current operation's non-value cost - waste.

2) A comprehensive understanding of digitization, which needs to be built; typically it requires the targeted recruiting of specialist subject matter experts.

3) The final catalyst is the deployment of a model aligned to an existing business model but enhanced by the creation of an innovative, collaborative environment with a start-up culture.

To understand this business model requires a pragmatic approach that develops and provides a level of organizational freedom, flexibility and agility. This model is in addition to an IT system, which will enable rapid cycles of development, testing, and implementation of solutions and deliver a collaborative ecosystem.

Indeed, a common supply chain technology platform will deliver a fast realization of projected promise and cumulative gains. Also, to derive operational feedback with suitability and impact, and to steer next development cycles towards early success. The evolution of Supply Chain 4.0 requires innovation within the organization, which is — fast, flexible, and efficient – that is the future.

Printed in Poland
by Amazon Fulfillment
Poland Sp. z o.o., Wrocław

65618968R00188